D0147229

TWAYNE'S WORLD AUTHORS SERIES
A Survey of the World's Literature

Sylvia E. Bowman, Indiana University

GENERAL EDITOR

THE NETHERLANDS

Egbert Krispyn, University of Georgia

EDITOR

François Hemsterhuis

TWAS 277

François Hemsterhuis

By HEINZ MOENKEMEYER

University of Pennsylvania

TWAYNE PUBLISHERS

A DIVISION OF G. K. HALL & CO., BOSTON

Copyright © 1975 by G. K. Hall & Co.
All Rights Reserved

Library of Congress Cataloging in Publication Data

Moenkemeyer, Heinz.
  François Hemsterhuis.

  (Twayne's world authors series, TWAS 277)
  Bibliography: p.
  1. Hemsterhuis, Franciscus, 1721-1790.
B4027.M63   199'.492   74-13651
ISBN 0-8057-2419-2

MANUFACTURED IN THE UNITED STATES OF AMERICA

Contents

About the Author

Heinz Moenkemeyer, born in Hamburg, Germany, studied philosophy, German and English philology and literature at the University of Hamburg. He received his M.A. and Ph.D. in Germanics from the University of Pennsylvania. A book, based on his dissertation, entitled *Erscheinungsformen der Sorge bei Goethe*, came out in the *Beiträge zur deutschen Philologie* (Giessen, 1954). He has published in German and American scholarly publications a number of articles on several works by Goethe (including *Faust*), on Klinger, Zacharias Werner, Heine, Immermann, an article comparing Werner's *Der 24. Februar* with Camus' *Le Malentendu*, and one dealing with the first Swedish book on Schiller by the romanticist Lorenzo Hammarsköld. A lecture on Heidegger was printed in *Existentialist Thinkers and Thought* (ed. by Frederick Patka).

Dr. Moenkemeyer is Professor of German Literature at the University of Pennsylvania, where he has also been teaching courses on European Enlightenment and Romanticism.

Preface

François Hemsterhuis, born in Holland in the eighteenth century, considered himself an ancient Greek "by birth," wrote all his published works in French, and gained fame mainly in Germany. He was known through his writings to such authors of European renown as Diderot, Lessing, Kant, and Goethe. Besides Spinoza, he is the only Dutch philosopher who played a significant role in German *Geistesgeschichte*. These facts as well as the place he occupies in the history of esthetics and as a thinker marking a transition from Enlightenment to subsequent modes of thought warrant an inclusion of Hemsterhuis in a series dealing with Netherlandic writers who found an echo in other countries.

In the English-speaking world, however, the philosopher has remained almost unknown. We know of no translations or studies of Hemsterhuis' works in the English language. The present book is therefore meant to be an introduction for English-speaking readers, and concentrates on the philosopher's published works. As far as letters and manuscripts are concerned, we rely entirely on the publications of scholars who had access to them.

Grateful acknowledgment is made to Professor Georges May and to the Yale University Press for permission to quote from Diderot's comments in their edition of the *Lettre sur l'homme*.

I am very grateful to Dr. Leendert Brummel (The Hague) and Professor Erich Trunz (Kiel) for their kind interest and valuable bibliographical references. I owe a special debt of gratitude to my colleagues and friends Professor André von Gronicka (University of Pennsylvania), for his sincere interest and encouragement, and Professor Egbert Krispyn (University of Georgia), whose invaluable editorial help and advice is deeply appreciated.

HEINZ MOENKEMEYER

Philadelphia

Chronology

1721   François Hemsterhuis born December 27 in Franeker.

1747   Matriculates at the University of Leiden.

1755   Accepts a position as clerk in the State Council of the Netherlands at The Hague.

1762   *Lettre sur une pierre antique . . .* privately printed.

1769   Promoted to First Secretary in the State Council. Publication of *Lettre sur la sculpture.*

1770   *Lettre sur les désirs.*

1772   *Lettre sur l' homme et ses rapports.*

1773   Writes a eulogy on François Fagel entitled *Description philosophique du caractère de feu M. F. Fagel.* Meets Princess Gallitzin for the first time.

1778   *Sophyle ou de la philosophie.*

1779   In May, he travels with the Princess to Münster (Germany), where they meet Baron Franz von Fürstenberg. After their second journey in August, she stays on to live in Münster. Publication of *Aristée ou de la divinité.*

1780   Visits the Princess in May, is pensioned in November.

1781   During another sojourn in Germany, meets the philosopher Friedrich Heinrich Jacobi.

1782   A collection of Hemsterhuis' writings appears in an unauthorized German translation.

1785   Tours Germany with the Princess, meeting Goethe, Herder, and Wieland in Weimar.

1787   *Alexis ou de l'âge d' or* published simultaneously with Jacobi's authorized translation, *Alexis oder von dem goldenen Weltalter.*

1788   Visits the Princess for the last time.

1789   German translation of the *Lettre de Dioclès à Diotime sur l' athéisme* (written 1787) published in Jacobi's second edition of his *Über die Lehre des Spinoza.*

1790   Hemsterhuis dies July 7 at The Hague.

CHAPTER 1

Hemsterhuis' Life and Personality

I Youth and Years of Study (1721—55)

F RANÇOIS Hemsterhuis was born on December 27, 1721, in Franeker, a small Frisian town, known at that time mainly for its university. Although baptized as Franciscus, he signed himself François.[1] He belonged to a Frisian family in which there had been doctors for a couple of generations, but which rose to European fame only with François' father Tiberius (1685—1766), the outstanding figure in the revival of Greek studies in Holland at the beginning of the eighteenth century, and founder of what has been called the "Schola Hemsterhuisiana" in the history of Greek philology.[2] Although François did not become a philologist, he inherited from his father a deep and lasting interest in classical learning, especially in all aspects of Greek culture.

Little is known about the first nineteen years François spent in Franeker. Referring to this time in later years, he mentions the instruction he received from his father, who used his considerable collection of coins to teach history and art. He imparted to François an insatiable desire for knowledge, resulting in a universal breadth of interests. Young Hemsterhuis received a thorough training in Latin, Greek, and French. He acquired subsequently a knowledge of English and Italian. Only late in his life did he begin reading German. Subjects of early instruction were history, mathematics, philosophy, drawing, and music. The practice of music he gave up too soon, as he wrote later.[3] But for mathematics, especially geometry, he retained a lifelong fondness and esteem. In this discipline, which he called the "queen of sciences," he saw the basis for a truly liberal education and the organon of philosophy. While still in Franeker, where he was probably enrolled at the university, Hemsterhuis began the study of optics and astronomy.

In 1740, when Tiberius Hemsterhuis became professor of Dutch history and Greek at the University of Leiden, François and his younger brother, Tiberius, who died a few years later (1748), moved also to Leiden, where François officially matriculated at the university in 1747. At this institution, François seems to have concentrated on the study of the sciences. Although engaged for a while in zoological research, his more enduring interest lay in the field of optics. His friendships with L. C. Valckenaer, who later dedicated his edition of Theocritus to him, with David Ruhnkenius, likewise a philologist, who introduced François perhaps to the study of Plato, and with Petrus Camper, a student of medicine, who subsequently gained wide fame through his work in anatomy, testify to the diversity of Hemsterhuis' interests.

II   *Professional Career and First Publications (1755–73)*

After leaving the university, Hemsterhuis joined for some years the corps of military engineers. In connection with this position he traveled perhaps to Germany and France. His life took a decisive turn in 1755, when he was considered for a professorship at Franeker. He did not obtain this position, but was offered, and accepted, employment as a clerk in the State Council of the Netherlands at The Hague.[4] The decision to take this post, for which, to be sure, his course of studies had not specifically prepared him, determined the external course of his life for many years to come. His office allowed him, who never married, to live free from financial cares. He never bothered to obtain an academic degree. Modest, sympathetic to the lot of the lower classes, and lacking worldly ambition, he was content with his position, which allowed him to lead a life divided between his duties in the Council, the pursuit of his private studies, and the cultivation of friendship, which was to play such an important role in his life and thought. Eventually promoted to the rank of First Secretary, in 1769, he remained in office until 1780, when, after twenty-five years of service, it was suggested that he give up his position, with the understanding that he would retain his salary and title, as well as all rights connected with it. On November 9, 1780, he was formally relieved of his duties. But even after that he remained in contact with the Council and was called upon for special assignments.

Hemsterhuis' position at the State Council carried with it a good salary and prestige, but was no sinecure. The Council, which met six times a week, dealt with matters relating to the budget, the defense of the country, and even with foreign policy. Hemsterhuis had access to classified information, a fact which shows that his position was an important one. He fulfilled his duties conscientiously, even though they were not always to his taste. When he joined the Council it had lost some of its former significance, since the Netherlands were no longer a great European power. He served his country when, beset by external and internal difficulties, it was steering a sometimes precarious course among England, France, and Austria. His sympathies were with a group of Anglophiles, such as Henric Fagel and Willem Bentinck. With respect to the interior affairs of his country he espoused a moderate standpoint, siding in general with the *Stadhouder* against the Francophile Patriots' Party, though critical of Willem V in many particulars.

In connection with his office, Hemsterhuis developed a strong interest in politics and political science. He writes that actual experience has shed light on what he had read in Aristotle, Grotius, Montesquieu (Dec. 11, 1780; III, 101). Meyboom published excerpts from his letters to Princess Gallitzin (III, 93 ff.), which show his concern with political questions: he comments on England's undignified politics in her American colonies, France's maladministration, and on the desirability of reducing standing armies. Witnessing the beginnings of the French Revolution, he applauds the downfall of despotism, but doubts that it will usher in a new, rational order. Although a freedom-loving republican, Hemsterhuis evinces sympathies for enlightened absolutism. Nevertheless, he believes that the principle of perfectibility will ultimately prevail and that the evils engendered by present society can be remedied by modifying it.[5] Such hope for the future of mankind, with eschatological undertones, is also expressed in *Alexis*. Of greatest concern to Hemsterhuis is, of course, the fate of the Netherlands. He mourns over the pitiable state of the once illustrious and powerful Republic, observes the lack of a common national goal, and deplores the absence of greatness in the Dutch people, tempted by the pursuit of an affluent life into inaction. As an individual, Hemsterhuis writes with amused detachment about the state of the nation, as a Hollander with genuine solicitude (III, 100; letter of

Oct. 26, 1780). A similar wavering between aloofness and *engagement* can be noticed in his views about patriotism, as Marie Muller has shown in her commentary on a letter written to the Princess on May 2, 1785.[6]

In many letters addressed to the Princess or to Baron Franz von Fürstenberg, Hemsterhuis used from 1782 on a code to convey messages relating to political events, contemporaries, or personal matters. While Brummel had deciphered the code, but did not publish his findings, Waltraud Loos has recently furnished a key to the cryptogram.[7] A future publication of Hemsterhuis' letters should shed considerably more light on his concern with political events.[8]

Hemsterhuis knew and corresponded with many people. But most of his contacts were based on his universal scholarly or scientific interests. In this connection we may mention Lamettrie, d'Alembert, Grimm, d'Holbach, Raynal, who planned an edition of Hemsterhuis' writings, and above all Diderot. The latter met the philosopher in person while visiting the Gallitzins in 1773 and 1774. At that time they did not find much interest in each other. Diderot was much more impressed by the Princess.[9] Hemsterhuis wrote later, in 1784, that Diderot, whose writings he admired, disappointed him as a person.[10] They kept up contacts, however, and the *philosophe* received a copy of the *Lettre sur l'homme*, to which he wrote a running critical commentary in the form of marginal notes.[11]

During Hemsterhuis' first years at The Hague, a close friendship, matched only by his later attachment to Princess Gallitzin, developed between him and François Fagel (1740–1773). Their relation was inspired by a pedagogic *eros*, and beyond that by a true affinity of minds. Even many years later, in 1786, Hemsterhuis told the Princess of his love for this man.[12] He wrote for him, who had asked for a "petit cours de philosophie," the *Lettre sur l'homme et ses rapports* (1772), and published after his friend's early death the *Description philosophique du caractère de feu M. F. Fagel* (1773).

Hemsterhuis, who needed a stimulus to crystallize his thoughts and to commit them to writing, had dedicated his first three works to Theodoor de Smeth, an Amsterdam banker, who was interested in antique gems. The first publication, the *Lettre sur une pierre antique du cabinet de M. Theodore de Smeth . . .* , was written in

1762, and privately printed by de Smeth. Hemsterhuis made use of
the epistolary form also in his next two publications, the *Lettre sur
la sculpture . . .* (written 1765, printed 1769), and the *Lettre sur les
désirs (1770)*, a sequel to the preceding work. While the first letter
to de Smeth was an occasional piece of writing, of interest only to
antiquarians or collectors, the *Lettre sur la sculpture* contained,
besides a much discussed definition of the beautiful, a survey of the
history of sculpture. Elaborating on some ideas in this work,
Hemsterhuis proceeded to a consideration of man and his place in
the universe in the *Lettre sur les désirs* and the *Lettre sur l'homme*.

Hemsterhuis made his literary debut as a learned connoisseur of
antique intaglios, in which he had become interested when he was
still a boy. Tiberius Hemsterhuis owned a rather large cabinet of
coins and gems, a considerable part of which had belonged to his
father-in-law. François took over and enlarged his father's
collection, but concentrated on intaglios, following an esthetic
rather than antiquarian interest. He was no passionate collector,
however, and eventually gave his collection to Princess Gallitzin. It
was subsequently lent to Goethe for several years, finally sold by
Princess Gallitzin's daughter to King Willem I and incorporated
into the Royal Coin Cabinet at The Hague.[13] Through his
collection, which attracted even the attention of Catherine the
Great of Russia, Hemsterhuis gained European fame as an expert in
gems. The *Stadhouder* Willem V entrusted to him the care of his
cabinet of antiques as well as the instruction of his sons in the
history of art.

Largely influenced by his interest in coins and gems,
Hemsterhuis' own artistic production was limited mainly to a
classicistic *Kleinkunst*, although he voiced in theory an admiration
for the grand and sublime. Having practiced drawing since
childhood, he later also took up modeling. He adorned a number of
his writings with vignettes, executed in a classicistic style, drew
profiles of some of his friends, planned the tombstone for J. G.
Hamann, which is still extant, and designed coins commemorating
patriotic occasions or persons.

While the *Lettre sur une pierre antique* was printed by de Smeth,
Hemsterhuis had the *Lettre sur la sculpture,* after some years of
hesitation, so typical of him, published by the Amsterdam book
dealer Marc Michel Rey, known as publisher of some works by

Rousseau and Diderot. Apparently dissatisfied, the author took the edition and distribution of most of his subsequent publications into his own hands. The printing was done by Ch. W. Dumas, printer, editor, and secret agent of the United States, to whom the philosopher referred as "l'Américain."[14] Despite the fact that Hemsterhuis' writings appeared anonymously and were distributed only among a small group of friends or acquaintances, his fame spread slowly but steadily, due to his many contacts with scholars, scientists, or persons of high rank.

III   First Years of Friendship with Princess Gallitzin (1773—79)

The person who gave a decisive turn to his externally uneventful existence was Princess Gallitzin,[15] born in 1748 as the daughter of the Prussian field marshal Samuel von Schmettau and named Adelheid Amalia. Brought up in high society, she became dissatisfied with its way of life when she was still a young girl and turned to a serious interest in philosophy, which was stimulated by reading De l'Esprit, a treatise by the French materialist Helvétius. In 1768, while staying in Aachen, she met Prince Dmitri Golitsyn, whom she married the same year. The Prince, who knew Voltaire and Diderot personally, patronized scientists and writers, among them Helvétius, whose De l'Homme he published in 1772 at his own expense. It soon became apparent that his outlook on life, determined by Voltaire, the Encyclopedists, and French materialists, could not satisfy Amalia, who had hoped for guidance in the solution of metaphysical perplexities engendered by reading Helvétius. Her husband was unable to fulfill her expectations of a marriage based on a communion of souls and a desire for mutual perfection. After the Princess had given birth to a daughter (Marianne, or "Mimi") in 1769 and a son (Dmitri, or "Mitri") in the following year, she began to withdraw from society life to devote herself to the education of her children.

Although Hemsterhuis and Amalia agree that their friendship began in 1775,[16] we know that Diderot had already met the philosopher at the Gallitzins' two years before. Hemsterhuis was at first mainly a guest of the Prince, to whom he gave a copy of his Lettre sur l'homme; after the Princess had shown interest in this work, she also received a copy. By 1775 Hemsterhuis had lost his friends Fagel and Bentinck. He felt lonely and frustrated in his work. At the same time Amalia needed support for her educational plans. She had just read Plato and conceived "une passion violente pour Socrate."[17] Now she met a man who admired Plato, who saw in Socrates, whose birthday he celebrated annually, the great example to follow. Vastly superior in learning and formal education, Hemsterhuis became her teacher, under whose guidance she studied Greek, Euclid, Plato's *Symposium,* and her mentor's writings. They met for discussions and started a correspondence, an invaluable source for our knowledge of both of them, their interests and activities. Hemsterhuis sent her, often undoubtedly upon request, epistles dealing with certain scientific or philosophical problems which grew into small treatises or outlines of such. While his letters are elegant and polished in style, following the French tradition of epistolary writing, her correspondence is less artful, more spontaneous.

The Princess and her mentor became very soon close friends. They dropped formalities, calling each other "Diotima" or "Socrates," respectively. Their relation was based on a sublimated Platonic *eros* rather than on sexual desire. It is noteworthy that nobody ever uttered suspicions about the nature of their association. Friendship between the sexes was valued highly in certain intellectual circles during the second half of the eighteenth century, and existed often besides marriage.[18] Whereas the latter was considered a merely societal institution, one regarded the former as a truly altruistic bond, rendered sacred by God and nature. This view was shared by Diotima, who placed friendship above marriage except for the paramount obligations to her children.[19] Hemsterhuis wrote to her that he had for a long time looked with disdain at so-called love, but Meyboom expressed misgivings as to whether friendship had not turned to love, adducing the fact that Hemsterhuis kept a lock of Diotima's hair, and anxiously tried to preserve some of her footprints to kiss them (III, 177f.). Their friendship was certainly not free from expressions of erotic exaltation. Agreeing that the sensual element was not to be repressed but even added charm and a new dimension to their friendship,[20] they strove for its sublimation in accordance with their ideal of mutual perfection. It is apparent that their relation was love, prone to jealousy and exalation, but Platonic, and with it subject to the irritability, tension, and frustration of sublimated eroticsm.

One of the reasons for which the Princess became attracted to Hemsterhuis' writings was the emphasis on man's perfectibility and his duty to perfect himself. But this philosophical ideal assumed in her the character of an obsession and became a matter of relentless pursuit. She carried the Socratic-Hemsterhuisian maxim "Know thyself" to the point of pitiless self-scrutiny, of which her friend stopped short. The Princess showed a somewhat masculine strength of mind and character, which contrasted with the philosopher's lack of energetic resolution and self-admitted "inertia." This becomes apparent in the stubborn determination with which she pursued her educational plans, whereas Hemsterhuis shied away from the full commitment and support that she had expected of him and he had promised.

Around 1775—76, the Princess, to whom life with her husband and in high society had become an ever heavier burden, moved into the countryside to devote herself as much as possible to her children. She rented a house, which she named "Niet'huis," to indicate that she was "not at home," except for a very few persons especially invited there. But even this place did not seem secluded enough to the Princess, who soon conceived a plan to move to a country house at Lavigny, near Geneva, in order to devote all her time to her educational plans. There seems to have been an agreement, almost a "contract" between her and Hemsterhuis concerning these plans. While the Prince, always *bonhomme*, perhaps even glad to be rid of her, agreed to her Lavigny plan, Hemsterhuis hedged on promises apparently made, took to all kinds of subterfuges, and finally said he would not go. He was not ready to exchange the stimulating atmosphere at The Hague for life in a Swiss village. In addition, he held an honored public office, allowing him much freedom, which he feared he might lose if he entered the binding arrangements planned by Diotima that mixed business with the vicissitudes of a by no means unruffled friendship. While we can hardly blame him for rejecting the Lavigny plan, there remains the fact that he lacked frankness in his dealings with the Princess, whose friendship he did not want to lose. She seems to have thought of breaking with him, but finally decided to continue their relation on new terms. Mutual freedom was to be restored by scrapping the "contract" Hemsterhuis had refused to honor.[21] Finally, Lavigny was sold in May, 1781.

But even apart from this, their friendship went through many small crises. The Princess, who had not found fulfillment in her marriage, had formed a high ideal of friendship as an aid to mutual self-perfection. But she was soon struck by the discrepancy between her ideal and an all-too-human reality. High-strung and nervous as she was, she suffered intensely from her disappointment in Hemsterhuis as a person, who lacked the Socratic serenity of his writings. Realizing a distressing discordance between the ethereal, sublime spirit and its embodiment in an incongruous earthly existence, she urged him to live according to the precepts of "sacred philosophy."[22] As he admitted himself, he was excessively jealous in love, and suspicious in friendship, a disposition for which he was repeatedly chided by Diotima. Being over-sensitive, he became easily offended and then resorted to insults or moody, hypochondriac sulking. There are some desperate letters by Diotima in which she complains to him about the torments she suffers from the insulting insinuations uttered by her "pitiless" friend, who shows equanimity, kindheartedness, magnanimity in his relations with strangers but only cruelty to her.[23] Again and again, Diotima emphasized the fact that their friendship was jeopardized by Hemsterhuis' inveterate penchant for introspection as well as by his too vivid imagination. Hemsterhuis, who said of himself that he was born a Greek and hater of tyrants, detesting all kinds of enslavement (III, 205), prized freedom above all. Behind this love for freedom, however, lurked a fear to get deeply involved, an egotistic desire to keep life on an even keel, free from disturbances. There were no overwhelming passions in his life, no crises or conflicts that threatened the fundaments of his very existence. To live a sober, serene life of wisdom was not only suggested by his natural disposition, but became also, a conscious ideal,[24] almost a pose of Hemsterhuis, the "humanist," whom Diotima criticized for his lack of genuineness and simplicity. Although Hemsterhuis evinced throughout his life a great need as well as desire for friendship, he remained strangely reticent even toward his close friends. Incapable of complete devotion and openness, he retained a stance of detachment. His penchant for introspection prevented him from ever being entirely natural and from indulging in jovial conviviality. Since he had an inclination to avoid energetic, irrevocable decisions, he never assumed the risks and re-

sponsibilities of marriage. Friendship, which he praised as
"Céleste Amitié," was mainly confined to the intellectual sphere,
thus no substitute for the close bond of marriage. Unwilling either
to live as a recluse or to commit himself wholeheartedly, he
remained lonely in spite of his many friendships and found peace of
mind only in philosophy.

Princess Gallitzin noticed that Hemsterhuis' mind was stronger
than his character, that there existed a discrepancy between the all-
too-human person and the philosopher. The harmony, the peace of
mind that he sought and extolled in philosophy was not attained in
his own life. He was not the beautiful, sublime soul that Meyboom
found expressed in his writings (III, 216), but rather, as Poritzky
observes,[25] a problematic character given to hypochondria,
endowed with a fantasy that made him suspect the motives even of
his closest friend, Diotima. While she suffered acutely from her
friend's indecision and lack of frankness, he cannot bear all the
blame. It seems that she had a tendency to be domineering at times
and tried to use him for her own purposes.

As was pointed out above, Hemsterhuis assumed at the beginning
of their friendship a tutorial role toward the Princess, who was eager
to make up deficiencies in her desultory education. Very soon,
however, she outgrew the status of a passive pupil to become a sort
of "symphilosopher." Introduced to his thought by reading the
Lettre sur les désirs, she felt immediately drawn toward his
philosophy. Their letters contain references to "notre philosophie"
or "notre psychologie." While it is characteristic of her that she put
more emphasis on the active function of the "organe moral" than
Hemsterhuis,[26] she contributed otherwise relatively little to the
contents of his writings. But she had a decisive influence on their
form. Whereas the earlier works, though entitled "Letters," had
been dissertations, often dealing with a great number of questions
in a somewhat diffuse manner, especially noticeable in the *Lettre
sur l'homme*, Hemsterhuis began now to write dialogues, each of
which treated a definite problem. His writings gained in vividness,
clarity, and grace of style. There was an increased enthusiasm for
moral beauty and self-perfection, manifesting a certain "rejuvenation" on the part of the philosopher under Diotima's influence.

Concerning *Aristée* Diotima made annotations and suggestions which the philosopher used when this dialogue was printed. In a letter to Diotima he pointed out that *Aristée, Sophyle,* and other works would hardly have been finished if they had not been discussed and read over and over again.[27] The two dialogues just mentioned were composed between 1776 and 1779; besides, a good deal of *Simon* was completed in August, 1779, when the Princess moved to Münster. We owe it to her, who constantly urged Hemsterhuis to overcome his inertia, that these dialogues were completed in a relatively short time. *Sophyle ou de la philosophie* and *Aristée ou de la divinité* came out in Paris in 1778 and 1779 respectively, whereas the French text of *Simon ou des facultés de l'âme* was not published until after the writer's death.

Summing up the first years of their friendship, we find that in spite of the many obstacles and shortcomings their relation proved to be a lasting one, mainly because both decided that the all-too-human realities should not interfere with the ideal essence of their friendship. The aging philosopher gained in the Princess a disciple and friend, even a "symphilosopher," genuinely interested in his thought and work. She fulfilled his longing for a love based on sublimated *eros,* which aims at a fusion of "homogeneous souls." Diotima found in him an understanding and depth that her husband lacked. She embraced enthusiastically the teachings of her Socrates who freed her from doubts engendered by the study of atheistic materialism, a doctrine thoroughly uncongenial to her, and became increasingly aware of her intellectual and moral powers. Both were united in a concern for self-perfection and a humanistic *cultura animi.* They shared an awareness of spiritual values which for Diotima constituted the first step toward her rejoining of the Catholic Church.

IV   *Later Years (1779—90)*

Their friendship took a decisive turn when Diotima decided to move to Münster to pursue her educational aims with the aid of Franz von Fürstenberg, minister of the diocese of Münster from 1762 to 1780, and Vicar General since 1770. Interested in furthering education at all levels, he published in 1776 a memorandum on teaching in schools, which he sent late in 1778 to Hemsterhuis, whom he had met earlier in the year while on a diplomatic mission to The Hague. Diotima took great interest in this document, translated it into French, and planned to add to it her own ideas on preschool education. A correspondence with Fürstenberg ensued, and in May, 1779, she and her friend visited him in Münster. They went there for the second time in August, accompanied now by Diotima's children. While Hemsterhuis returned to The Hague after a few weeks, she stayed on in Münster, which thenceforth became her permanent abode.

From then on Diotima and Socrates corresponded regularly, the latter writing about twice a week, the former less frequently, her letters being more hastily and carelessly composed, but as lengthy as those of her friend. Correspondence meant less for the Princess, who embarked on a life of fresh activity in her new environment, than for Hemsterhuis, who felt lonely, expressed an acute sense of loss, and gave in to an "extrême inertie" and the sweet grief of melancholy over a past of which he now recalled only the moments of happiness.[28] Diotima agreed that the two years at Niet'huis had been the happiest of her life, but thought their separation was good, and that their friendship would be less beset by difficulties. As we have seen, however, reasons for friction remained, especially in connection with the Lavigny plan.

The Princess widened her sphere of activities and met a number of interesting men, among whom Fürstenberg soon took the place Hemsterhuis had previously occupied in Diotima's life. She eventually became the center of the "Münster circle,"[29] a group of devout Catholics, with which F. H. Jacobi and J. G. Hamann were also loosely connected, both in very different ways staunch defenders of "Faith" against atheistic Enlightenment or freethinking rationalism. Diotima transferred her enthusiasm for Plato and Hemsterhuis to the circle around Fürstenberg, and contributed largely to the growing recognition of her Socrates in Germany.

Soon after Diotima had settled in Münster, Hemsterhuis met Mme. Perrenot, known as the author of some volumes of mediocre poetry. His relation to her remained somewhat superficial, confined to a certain amusing *galanterie*. There were friendships with other ladies, but they were of little consequence for Hemsterhuis, in whose life Diotima retained a unique position. No other friend furthered his work as much as Diotima.

Even after the Princess had settled in Münster, the friends saw each other occasionally. She revisited Holland, and Hemsterhuis made several journeys to Münster (1780, 1781, 1785, 1788). When he visited her in May, 1780, there were disputes about the Lavigny plan and he became ill. After having been pensioned in November, 1780, he had more time to travel, and visited Münster again the following spring, when he met Jacobi in Düsseldorf.

Of great importance, as Trunz has recently emphasized,[30] was a journey Hemsterhuis undertook with the Princess and Fürstenberg in the autumn of 1785. They went to Weimar where they met Goethe, Herder, the Duke, Wieland, and Charlotte von Stein, to mention the most notable persons. On the trip that followed, Hemsterhuis, who had seen the art collections in Düsseldorf and Kassel, took great interest in collections at Gotha, Leipzig, and, above all, Dresden. After the travelers returned to Weimar, they went with Goethe to Erfurt to meet Hemsterhuis' fervid admirer Karl Theodor von Dalberg, who became known later through his political activities during the Napoleonic Wars.

In Weimar there were discussions with Goethe and Herder on Spinoza, called forth by Jacobi's controversial book *Über die Lehre des Spinoza* (1785),[31] but the differences of opinion did not interfere with mutual esteem and friendly feelings. The day after the visitors departed, Goethe sent a letter to Jacobi, in which he praised Diotima as a "sublime soul" ("herrliche Seele"), whose presence had a beneficial effect on everyone, and referred to Hemsterhuis as always "communicative and obliging" ("mittheilend und gefällig"), although apparently not in good health.[32] Herder's wife, who admired Diotima's strong character, commented on Hemsterhuis' wide range of knowledge, and characterized him as a delicate, old-maidish bachelor, who won everybody's affection ("ein so zarter, jungfräulich alter Jüngling"). For Herder himself the most interesting of the visitors was the philosopher, whom he described as an old, refined republican, a man who had gathered everything that is beautiful in the arts and sciences, a vessel containing exquisite wine.[33]

At the end of November, 1785, Hemsterhuis returned from Münster to The Hague. About a month later, he gave a rather long account of his trip to Germany in a letter to C. Ploos van Amstel (III, 76 ff.), who was interested in antique art and instrumental in spreading Hemsterhuis' ideas.[34] The letter, written in the Dutch language and published in 1791 by its recipient, comments mainly on the towns and art collections visited in Germany. Turning to other matters, Hemsterhuis writes that during the journey he became acquainted with all kinds of educational and cultural institutions, as well as with the most illustrious minds of Germany, a country of great promise, intellectually and politically, if circumstances would continue to be favorable.

The last time he visited Diotima was in 1788. He arrived on the day that Hamann, who at that time was staying in Münster, died. The Princess, deeply shaken by this death, found it difficult for a while to bear the humanistic pose of her Socrates, which contrasted so sharply with Hamann's Christian meekness. This was a passing mood, however; Diotima realized soon how much her Socrates still meant to her. When he became seriously ill, she cared for him with great devotion, and as he left in the beginning of September, she felt she would not see him again.

Brummel emphasizes that we owe it mainly to the Princess that Hemsterhuis made in his later years an effort to present a number of his ideas in a publishable form.[35] Diotima's continued interest in his projects, as well as a growing awareness of the resonance his oeuvre found among the German intelligentsia, encouraged Hemsterhuis to go on with his work. He was full of plans for new treatises on the most diverse subjects. But after Diotima moved to Münster he worked less regularly and more slowly, so that only a few works, the fruits of long meditation, were actually finished.

A considerable part of *Simon*, a dialogue dealing with the faculties of the soul and with pedagogical questions, had been written before Diotima's departure for Münster. As early as November, 1780, Hemsterhuis had communicated in two letters to Diotima (III, 86—91) some ideas concerning a future golden age that were to become the substance of his next dialogue, *Alexis ou de l'âge d'or*, a part of which he sent to Münster in April, 1782. Around this time (1781—82) the Princess was occupied with translating *Sophyle* and *Aristée* into German. In 1782, however, there appeared an anonymous German translation of all of Hemsterhuis' published writings,[36] containing even the hitherto unpublished *Simon* in a rendering based on an earlier "unauthorized" manuscript. Diotima, understandably angry and disappointed, decided to go ahead with the translation of *Alexis* and an "improved" version of *Simon*. The latter was to be entrusted to A. M. Sprickmann, then a member of the "Münster circle." Jacobi agreed to translate *Alexis*. While the translation of *Simon*, as far as we could ascertain, never appeared in print, Jacobi's German version of *Alexis* and the French original were finally published in 1787.

Out of dissatisfaction with the sad plight of his country, Hemsterhuis had conceived a plan to write a political treatise on the Netherlands, dealing with this theme from a philosophical viewpoint. While he mentioned this project to Diotima as early as January, 1780, the actual writing of the essay, known as *Réflexions sur la République des Provinces-Unies* (see note 8), was not begun until 1781.[37] In spite of Diotima's and Fürstenberg's great interest, the work remained a fragment, since there were other projects that kept the philosopher busy. The Princess, who considered for a while the possibility of a military career for her son, had asked Hemsterhuis to write something concerning "l'esprit militaire." He started to work on a dialogue called *Alexis II ou du militaire*, parts of which Diotima received in February and May, 1783. Another stimulus came to him in connection with her serious concern for the religious life of her children. Her reading of the Bible, as well as living in a circle of high-minded, devout Catholics, confronted Diotima with the necessity of a decision regarding her own religious commitment. In a letter of January 21, 1783,[38] Hemsterhuis indicated that he planned to write a treatise on religion for his Diotima. Later in the year, referring to the religious indifference of her son, about which she had complained, he wrote that he would like to investigate this phenomenon in a "Traité de la Religion". A few weeks later (November 7), Diotima sent a letter in which she expressed her qualms concerning revelation, an afterlife, and original sin. She asked her friend to present arguments against faith in Christ's miracles, emphasizing that she could marshal reasons enough in their favor. She appealed to him to help her in a crisis. Characteristically, however, there was no straightforward answer to this appeal. Her Socrates referred to his still unwritten "Traité."

In March, 1784, the Princess fell seriously ill. Mental strain had contributed to her illness, which coincided with a spiritual crisis. After her recovery, which she attributed to Divine grace, she was on the way that finally, in 1786, led to her reunion with the Catholic

Church, in which she had been raised. This preoccupation with her own religious life led to a lessened concern with the work of her Socrates, who in turn felt less inclined to carry out his projects. Once Diotima had solved her religious perplexities, however, she returned with new vigor to her broad cultural interests. Hemsterhuis, who read German only with difficulty and was rather unaware of intellectual currents in Germany, was kept *au courant* by her on developments in German philosophy and literature, especially on the disputes centering on Jacobi's book on Spinoza. She and Hemsterhuis agreed tacitly on a *modus vivendi* based on tolerance and mutual respect. But there is no doubt that the unredeemed neopagan, who disdained the Bible and had often mocked Christian revelation,[39] was no longer her spiritual guide: Christ had taken the place of Socrates, the humanistic ideal of self-reliance gave way to self-humiliation before God and Christ. In her diary Diotima compared Hamann's "childlike sublime simplicity" ("kindlich erhabene Einfalt") with Hemsterhuis' humanistic pose, to the latter's disadvantage. After Hamann had died on the day of Hemsterhuis' arrival in Münster, the Princess recorded that for several days she could not stomach the "high-flown Graecism" ("hochtrabenden Gräcismus") of her Socrates; that Hamann had taught her more about "inner dignity" than the philosopher in all his—incidentally beautiful—writings.[40] Although Hemsterhuis was no longer close to her innermost concerns, she retained gratitude, sympathy, even admiration for him. But her admiration bore now an esthetic character. She did not discuss her "conversion" with him. When he fell ill, she tried to console him with his own philosophical arguments. There remained, as the Princess wrote to him on May 10, 1787, a common concern with and striving for perfection.[41] Even if each of them used the word in a different context now, they still shared the endeavor to approximate infinite perfection in an asymptotic process.

Hemsterhuis' promise to write on the subject of religion was finally fulfilled when he sent a letter to Diotima on September 7, 1787, consisting partly of a short treatise on atheism. Jacobi came to know of this essay and published a German translation of it in the second edition of his book on Spinoza (1789). The French text appeared in 1792 in Jansen's edition of Hemsterhuis' works as *Lettre de Dioclès à Diotime sur l'athéisme*. With this treatise, it seems, Hemsterhuis had concluded his life's work. In his correspondence he speaks of *Alexis II* and the *Réflexions sur la République des Provinces-Unies*, ponders over changes in the former, and thinks of finishing the latter for some young friends. He regrets that *Simon* has remained unpublished. Stimulated perhaps by Jacobi, he began to work at a "Lettre sur le fatalisme," which is also mentioned by the Princess, in a letter of November 1791, as an item bequeathed to her by her friend (III, 223).

During Hemsterhuis' later years there occurred, as we have seen, important changes in his personal relations. But otherwise he continued his life as a keen observer of human affairs, an avid reader whose interests ranged over a wide field of most diverse subjects, and as a writer wont to set down the results of his observations or meditations in letters, essays, or treatises. Fame had come to him, as a result of Diotima's efforts to make him known in Germany. At The Hague as well as during his journey through parts of Germany he had met a number of German princes, some of them interested in or even acquainted with his works. He received many visitors, among them Karl August, Duke of Weimar, whom he had seen before in 1785.

Hemsterhuis' last two years were overshadowed by illness and suffering. Visitors became too burdensome for him. He complained that he had to confine himself to reading, since meditation was too strenuous. In 1788, while visiting Diotima, he fell seriously ill. On September 12, he wrote to his "Daphne": "I am returning from a faraway place. I had a close look at the famous gates to the nether world."[42] Suffering greatly, he thought of suicide as an escape from unbearable pain, but rejected this way out as well as the impassibility of the Stoics (III, 202 f.). He wanted to die like Socrates; no thought of death should influence his remaining days. During the last year of his life, correspondence became a painful burden to the inveterate epistolographer. Hemsterhuis made a will, sent his letters and papers to Diotima, asked her to take care of his works, and expressed a wish that she should edit them together with parts of their correspondence. The last letter he sent her bore the date of June 18, 1790. On the seventh of July he died.

CHAPTER 2

General Character of Hemsterhuis' Writings and Thought

I T was only late in life that Hemsterhuis began to publish. All his printed works were written in French to attain a wider circulation of his ideas. His slender oeuvre consists of "letters," dialogues, and small treatises, popular with many eighteenth century thinkers. He did not expound his philosophy in a comprehensive, systematic work. In a letter written in 1777 to Diotima, Hemsterhuis criticizes the fabricators of systems for aiming at a childish glory. Years later, he expresses his indifference toward Spinozism and other philosophical "-isms," confessing that Socrates and Newton are his only "heroes."[1] The rejection of a system, however, does not imply unsystematic, aphoristic thinking. Aristotle's exactness, Socrates' *bon sens*, "la poésie de Platon" guided the author in his work, as the preface to *Aristée* suggests (II, 7). The convincing *philosophie géométrique* of Socrates, Aristotle, and Newton must be distinguished from the fictions of the Sophists and Descartes.[2] Like Socrates, Diotima's friend wants to teach to philosophize, to stimulate philosophical reflection rather than expound a doctrine.

An almost pedantic care for style and content contributed to slowing down his productivity. While on the one hand he referred with a pose of modesty to his writings as bagatelles, to his ideas as "mes petites idées," "jargon," or "galimatias," he expressed on the other hand satisfaction that his works had come to the attention of the Queen of England and Frederick the Great.[3] Behind his apparent modesty there dwelt a certain pride to write only for the select few who would understand him.

All of Hemsterhuis' writings, mostly addressed to friends, to de Smeth, Fagel, and above all to Diotima, arose from concrete situations, like young Fagel's death or the wish of friends to be enlightened about certain subjects. The philosopher wrote with a purpose that can be called "pedagogic" in the Socratic sense of the word.

While there is much speculation in the works of the "Batavian Plato," speculative, theoretical truth interests him mainly in its moral, practical aspects. Hemsterhuis, in whose philosophy the notion of an *organe moral* occupies a central position, is essentially a moralist. On May 4, 1776, he writes to Diotima that he aims at a philosophy of "general usefulness" that applies Newton's method of investigation to the moral world[4] and thereby will remedy the ills of present society. Imbued with an enlightened sympathy for mankind, Hemsterhuis makes man the primary concern of his philosophy, which addresses itself, as he believes, to all men and considers all human faculties. Their perfection and harmonious interplay within a rounded personality is the ideal he advocates in most of his writings. Although aware of human insufficiencies, he strongly believes in man's essential perfectibility. Hemsterhuis wants to stimulate the human desire for perfection. Insight into his *rapports* with the universe will lead man to improve them and issue in happiness and wisdom, the two goals Hemsterhuis strives to attain through philosophy. Wisdom entails liberation from all kinds of prevailing prejudices, especially from the dogmatic assertions of theologians and materialist *philosophes.*

While Diotima's friend had a deep concern for man's *rapports* with the Supreme Being, the Creator of the universe, and devoted his philosophical writings to a refutation of atheism, he was not a Christian. Meyboom and Galland, who regretted this fact, pointed out that Hemsterhuis spoke privately of the Bible and Christianity, which he thought would not survive another century, in derisive or disparaging terms.[5] Somewhat more cautiously, the philosopher criticized in his writings the Christian Middle Ages as semi-barbarous, a commonplace in his time. Far from being irreligious, as Goethe recognized when he found in Hemsterhuis writings an inclination toward religion tinged by Platonism,[6] Diotima's friend embraced a religion of the philosophers, a kind of panentheism as we shall see. In his humanistic religiosity, concerned only with man's relations and duties toward the infinitely remote Supreme Being, there is no place for salvation or grace bestowed by God on man.

All his writings evince, as we shall see, a highly refined sense for spiritual and moral values, a sense for which Hemsterhuis coined the term "moral organ" *(organe moral)*. His esthetic sensibility was not confined to the appreciation or theory of arts, but also found expression in artistic production, in drawing and designing. While the philosopher did not publish any poetry, drama, or fiction, he showed a deep understanding for all these forms of "poetry" in the wider sense *(Dichtung)*. His late dialogues display at times an imaginative detail and an inspired language that prompted some critics to praise them as "poems." We have mentioned Hemsterhuis' interest in the sciences, a topic that would deserve a detailed study based on a thorough knowledge of his correspondence. He investigated fresh water polyps, the eyes of insects,[7] and worked on the improvement of binoculars and telescopes in order to enlarge man's cognitive faculties. A list of the philosopher's writings bequeathed to the Princess includes a letter containing a small but "complete" treatise on optics (III, 223), a field Hemsterhuis cultivated especially for its close connection with his theory of knowledge, as Waltraud Loos has recently pointed out.[8] *Alexis* and the notes to this dialogue, which advances a hypothesis concerning the origin of the moon, show a thorough acquaintance with then current astronomical theories. Hemsterhuis wrote two small treatises on infinite divisibility and the incommensurable respectively, dealing with these problems in a nonmathematical fashion from a philosophical standpoint. While he made no original contribution to mathematics, he emphasized in a letter to Diotima of September 24, 1779, its educational value, not for the information this science conveys but rather as a method that teaches reasoning by steps, inspires a desire for seeking truth, and establishes connections between truths.[9]

Hemsterhuis, who maintained that mathematics alone attains to perfect knowledge (I, 156), shows in most of his writings a predilection for what he calls the "geometric method," whose character and scope has recently been discussed by Hammacher.[10] Already in the *Lettre sur la sculpture* he aims at a sort of formula for beauty. Step by step reasoning, the use of algebraic symbols, and a penchant for taking illustrations from elementary algebra or geometry are features that prompted Madame de Staël to speak of Hemsterhuis' "langage mathématicien."[11] The "geometrical method," however, does not involve the use of mathematical operations, nor do the symbols designate magnitudes that can be exactly measured. While Hemsterhuis' quasi-mathematical method of argumentation strikes us often as pedantic and lacks the precision and evidence he admired in Newtonian physics, his conviction that the method of the exact sciences could and should be applied to the study of man determines one important aspect of many of his writings. We say one aspect because he became more and more convinced that basic truths are intuitively grasped rather than arrived at through ratiocination.

Despite his predilection for the "geometric method," Hemsterhuis did not always achieve clearness, cogency, or coherence, partly because he did not define his terms clearly— e.g., *idée* means idea, perception, thought and its object, *sensation* stands for feeling, perception, awareness — and partly because he lacked the power of synthetizing his thoughts in a coherent, comprehensive fashion. Instead, we have a number of smaller writings of limited scope, which are linked by the recurrence of relatively few basic ideas. The main line of argument is often interrupted by side issues. Hemsterhuis' turn to dialogue in his later productions brought with it more vividness in the presentation of his thoughts, but did not enhance clarity and conciseness in argumentation.

Attention to imaginative detail, inspired enthusiastic passages as well as the use of compositional devices, of narrative, allegory, and myth are artistic features of the dialogues that have led many critics to speak of Hemsterhuis as a poet-philosopher. The literary value of his dialogues, with their presentation of modern, Hemsterhuisian thought in an antique setting, has been a matter of dispute. While Heinse saw in them only a bookish imitation of Plato, an estimate shared by Poritzky, the Schlegel brothers praised his "Socratic poems" and Trunz has recently voiced the opinion that *Simon* is one of the outstanding works of European classicism in the eighteenth century.[12] Indeed, all of the dialogues must be considered in this context instead of measuring them against Plato's unique achievement. Only then one will arrive at a fair estimate of the esthetic sensibilities and compositional skill evinced in the best dialogues, in which their author proves to be not only a thinker but also a writer.

Too much emphasis has been placed on the so-called eclectic character of Hemsterhuis' philosophy. It combined, to be sure, such heterogeneous elements as the Socratian and Newtonian methods of inquiry, the Platonic tradition, and a variety of modern currents of thought. However, too often "influences" have been asserted without actual proof. The fact that Hemsterhuis, well-read as he was, adopted thoughts from very different thinkers does not make his philosophy anemic and completely derivative, as Poritzky maintained.[13] That there cannot be any question of his indulging in an indiscriminate eclecticism has recently been shown by Hammacher, who indicates by the title of his book, *Unmittelbarkeit und Kritik bei Hemsterhuis*, that he sees in "immediacy and critique," i.e., in the attempt to account for the immediate inner experience *(Erlebnis)* of life before the forum of critical reason, the central concern of Hemsterhuisian philosophy as well as its claim to relative originality. Realizing that cognitive acts are always part of a total *Erlebnis* involving also emotions and volitions, Hemsterhuis arrived at a new evaluation of the cognitive role of feeling, neglected by modern philosophy, which took its cue from scientific reasoning. Love of wisdom and the desire to know are essential but nontheoretical presuppositions of philosophical inquiry. Feeling *(sentir)* or felt conviction, far from being a mere psychological concomitant of cognition that must be disregarded by logical and scientific thinking, is the ultimate ground of evidence and certainty. Perfect conviction is given in the feeling of truth ("sentiment du vrai"; I, 86). Feeling or, as Hemsterhuis says in his later writings, intuition discloses truth and reality. Truth is grasped directly, without intercession of the intellect. Reality in all its fullness is only experienced in the immediacy of *Erlebnis* and inaccessible to ratiocination. Hemsterhuis' ideal of a knowledge gathered in one intuitive act can already be found in his definition of beauty in the *Lettre sur la sculpture*. Not content with merely asserting the certainty of feeling as ultimate basis of knowledge, Hemsterhuis endeavored to vindicate his newly won standpoint by critical reflection. His theory of the *organe moral* tries to account for the autonomy of a realm of spiritual experience that had either no place in scientific philosophy or was not recognized as autonomous. The figurative use of the term "organ" in a nonphysiological sense enabled the philosopher to ascribe to phenomena outside the grasp of usual sense-perception an evidence that is on a par with that of the so-called physical world. While some critics, notably Bulle and Brummel,[14] correctly emphasized the new *Lebensgefühl* expressed by the philosopher, they exaggerated the irrationalist tendencies and underestimated the critical intent of Hemsterhuisian philosophy as well as its close ties with Enlightenment. Like several other thinkers of the eighteenth century, above all Rousseau, Hemsterhuis criticized the then prevalent rationalism and the Enlightenment *philosophes*, turned his attention to the nonrational *Erlebnis* aspects of life, but remained essentially within the framework of rationalism and Pre-Kantian metaphysics. Thus, Hemsterhuis' thought marks a beginning and an end, a transition from rationalism with its scientifically oriented philosophy to a philosophy of the mind. Although the Dutch thinker influenced Herder and Jacobi, who also occupied an eccentric position, he did not enter the mainstream of German philosophy, which proceeded via Kant's transcendental criticism to the Post-Kantian systems of speculative metaphysics. But his thought, mainly assimilated as a ferment for further cogitation, found during the last three decades of the eighteenth century a considerable echo among German intellectuals.

CHAPTER 3

The Letter on Sculpture

I *The Argument*

HEMSTERHUIS started his literary career with two works devoted to the visual arts. The first of them, written in 1762, is a short description of a Greek gem belonging to the collection of the Amsterdam banker Theodoor de Smeth. The *Lettre sur une pierre antique du cabinet de M. Theodore de Smeth*, privately printed by de Smeth, is an occasional piece of writing, of interest only to connoisseurs or antiquarian experts. It contains no intimation of the breadth and depth of inquiry which becomes apparent in Hemsterhuis' next work. The *Lettre sur la sculpture* (henceforth referred to as Letter), completed for the most part in 1765 but not published until 1769, was written at the behest of de Smeth, who had asked Hemsterhuis to communicate his ideas on sculpture. In view of numerous agreements with Winckelmann's *Geschichte der Kunst des Altertums* (1764) it has often been argued that this work had a decisive influence on the Letter, especially on its historical part. It may well be that de Smeth made his request to Hemsterhuis after having heard, possibly through Diderot, of Winckelmann's book. A French translation did not appear until 1766, so that Hemsterhuis, whose command of German was insufficient, could not have had a detailed knowledge of Winckelmann's work when he wrote his Letter. Whether he made any changes between 1766 and 1769 must remain a matter of conjecture.

The Letter consists of two parts, one dealing with art in general, the other with sculpture. In the latter section we find a survey of the history of sculpture, followed by a discussion of the characteristics of this art. While it is true that the historical survey is only loosely connected with the other parts of the work, its very title indicates that Hemsterhuis did not claim to write a systematic treatise on esthetics. In a letter on sculpture he was free to discuss or clarify any aspects he chose of that art. Like Winckelmann and Lessing, he combined a rational reflection on esthetic principles with an empirical interest in the historical forms of art. It would have been more logical, however, if he had placed the historical survey at the end of the letter, following the discussion of art and sculpture in more systematic terms.

At the beginning of the Letter Hemsterhuis states his intention to investigate the principle and aim of sculpture as well as the perfection of which it is capable. In addition he wants to point out its historical and national modifications. To carry out his intentions he found that he had to begin with a discussion of the principles underlying all arts and then return to sculpture.

The aim of all arts, we read, is to imitate nature and, beyond that, to improve on it by producing effects rarely or never found in nature.[1] How the arts attain their goal of imitation and what it means to surpass nature must, then, be examined. Hemsterhuis indicates that he will limit his discussion mainly to the visual arts.

Visual objects are distinguished by shape or contour, by the distribution of light and shade, and also, but least, by color, which for Hemsterhuis, as for Winckelmann, is only an accessory quality. Sculpture alone renders the three-dimensional visual object in all its aspects or "profiles," while painting and drawing are more limited modes of imitation. Implied is a hierarchy of arts based on a concept of imitation that insists on extreme verisimilitude. Sculpture ranks highest because it represents all dimensions of physical objects. Such a ranking of the arts was also enunciated by Addison and James Harris.[2] As an example of a visual object Hemsterhuis adduces the cone. This illustration, taken from solid geometry, allows him to disregard color as an unessential feature and to concentrate on contour and the other characteristics of solid bodies mentioned above. Such abstraction, however, does hardly any justice to the principle of imitation as it was invoked by Hemsterhuis, since visual objects are characterized by color. The reason for neglecting this factor is, of course, to be found in the esthetic canon of classicism which discounted the role of color in sculpture. Furthermore, while it is justified to abstract from haptic qualities as long as one deals with "visual objects" in the narrow sense of the term, such an abstraction disregards an essential feature of sculpture. It seems that "visual objects" are defined in terms rather of solid geometry or geometrical drawing than of sensual or esthetic experience. The cone that serves as example of such objects may stimulate a sort of esthetic experience, but belongs per se hardly to the realm of art.

It is at this point of his discussion that Hemsterhuis enounces his much debated definition of the beautiful as that which evokes, or allows us to grasp, the greatest number of ideas in the shortest time.[3] He arrived at this formula by an empirical procedure, namely, by testing the reaction of spectators to a drawing of two vases differing in contour and ornaments. Hemsterhuis appended this drawing to the Letter. It was found that the vase whose shape and ornaments could be grasped in the shorter time was adjudged beautiful. Paying attention to the minimum of time alone, however, might lead to the absurd conclusion that one idea grasped in one instant would constitute perfect beauty. While Hemsterhuis adheres to the definition of beauty as unity in variety, he gives to this formula, widely current in the eighteenth century, an original turn by linking unity with the minimum of time in which a manifold can be grasped as a whole and by specifiying that the latter must represent a maximum of ideas. It has been pointed out that Montesquieu's *Essai sur le goût,* which appeared in 1757, contains adumbrations of Hemsterhuis' formula. Besides stating that an object must be simple enough to be grasped and at the same time varied enough to be perceived with pleasure, Montesquieu also suggests that the best writers are those who stimulate more ideas ("sensations") in a given time than other writers.[4] One readily sees that these casual observations lack the preciseness and methodical basis of Hemsterhuis' formula. They are, of course, also less dogmatic and pretentious.

Hemsterhuis adduces chords in music and sonnets or epigrams in poetry as examples that illustrate his definition of beauty. Artists realize that what we call grand, sublime, and in good taste are large wholes whose parts are composed in such a way that we can connect them easily and in the shortest time.[5]

On the subjective side the perception of the beautiful depends upon the ability of the perceiving subject to connect parts rapidly so that they form a whole. Such an ability requires training, which is lacking in children, as Hemsterhuis exemplifies by a child's drawing of a horse. Another subjective factor determining the rapidity with which a total is grasped as such is the "situation morale" (I, 23) of the subject vis-à-vis the object represented by the artist. An object is more easily perceived and evokes more ideas when it can be associated with a previous actual experience, for example, when a person who lived through a shipwreck is confronted with an artistic representation of such. The "situation morale" corresponds to Diderot's *rapports* as far as this term applies to the associations that accompany an impression and add to the esthetic experience.[6]

Although any true work of art evokes a maximum of ideas in a minimum of time, some artists tend to emphasize the former, others the latter, condition. Ease of contour facilitates a rapid perception. The expression of passion, emotion, or action added to the representation of beauty in repose increases the number of ideas evoked. In this connection Hemsterhuis speaks of the work of art as an optimum resulting from the observance of a conjoined maximum and minimum condition. The optimum is jeopardized by confused contours — of which an example is given in one of the drawings appended to the Letter — or by an incongruence existing between the whole and its parts. If, for example, one of the figures of the Laocoön group showed joy this would be completely out of tune with the predominant expression of pain. Hemsterhuis refers in these passages obviously to sculpture, whereas in other places his theses or observations are explicitly extended to other arts.

It has become clear, Hemsterhuis asserts, that art surpasses nature inasmuch as it realizes an "optimum" (I, 31) hardly ever found in nature.

If the mind needs time to grasp an ensemble, even more time is required to actually form such a whole out of its parts. All artistic production is bound to the law of succession. This means, according to Hemsterhuis, that the "splendor of idea" (I, 21) the artist had in mind at the moment when he conceived his work is diminished in the course of its execution. "The first distinct and well conceived idea of a genius or a man of great talents, whose mind is filled with the subject he wants to treat, is not only good but quite beyond [his power of] expression" (I, 26). Connoisseurs and men of genius alike, it is pointed out, hold first sketches in highest esteem because of the divine liveliness of the original conception. Moreover, and more important, the "poetic and reproductive" faculties are set in motion by sketches urging the mind to complete and round off their fragmentariness. With the expression "faculté poétique et reproductive" (I, 27) Hemsterhuis refers to the imagination, which for him, in accordance with the usage prevalent in his time, is still a mainly reproductive faculty. Poetry and rhetoric rely entirely on the imagination, since they use the arbitrary signs of words to evoke mental images of sensations or ideas; hence the expression "faculté poétique" for the imagination. Poetry and rhetoric, Hemsterhuis asserts, produce greater emotional effects than painting or sculpture, which are limited to relatively fixed "natural signs." The arts that use words as medium appeal to the free play of the imagination and have a greater evocative power. Even silence becomes eloquent. Further on in the Letter (I, 43), while speaking of the representation of the Devil by Milton and the Dutch poet Vondel, Hemsterhuis mentions another advantage the poets enjoy over sculptors or painters. The former can represent the enormous and gigantic, transcending all finite "natural signs," and can show it in action.

Hemsterhuis arrives here at a ranking of the arts that is different from the one based on the degree of imitation of visual objects. Poetry, not restricted to such objects, has a wider scope than the visual arts. These ideas are in line with discussions concerning the limits of painting by Shaftesbury, Dubos, Harris, Diderot, and Lessing.[7] In connection with Hemsterhuis' assertion that sketches are especially apt to evoke the activity of the imagination, Grucker referred to Lessing's *fruchtbarer Augenblick*,[8] the fruitful, pregnant moment the sculptor or painter has to choose in order to indicate action by avoiding an extreme of expression and thus leaving room for the play of the imagination. All that Hemsterhuis and Lessing share, however, is an emphasis on the role of the imagination, which they discuss in entirely different contexts.

As we have seen, Hemsterhuis maintains that the work of art achieves an optimum which could be produced in nature only by rarest chance (I, 14). This optimum, he claims, is not based on the essence of things, but is rather the effect of a rapport between things and our sense organs. He affirms: "If you change the things, the nature of our ideas of what is beautiful will remain the same; but if you change the nature of our organs or the way they are constructed, all our present ideas of beauty will soon become naught" (I, 31). The subjective factor in our perception of beauty is brought into relief by an observation which Hemsterhuis calls "humiliating" and which he adduces as proof for his assertion that beauty has no reality in itself (I, 31). It has been observed, he says, that if we look daily at two vases, the one beautiful, the other ugly, we notice first surfeit and then a blunting of distinctions. Through continued exercise we perceive the contours of the ugly vase more rapidly, which means, according to Hemsterhuis, that we adjudge it less ugly, or closer to beauty than before. While it is true that practice or habit facilitates perception, it is hardly correct to state, as Hemsterhuis does, that our perception of the beautiful vase encounters more and more obstacles, so that its beauty becomes diminished. Actually, the ease of perception should tend toward a maximum. The fact that habit facilitates but also blunts perception might have led Hemsterhuis to the conclusion that ease of perception is at most a necessary but by no means a sufficient reason for adjudging an object beautiful. Instead, he superimposed a spurious dogmatic interpretation on correctly observed facts to save his formula for the beautiful. As it is, he noticed the effects, positive or negative, that habit has on our awareness of beauty. Being a Platonist, he found this dependence upon habit somewhat "humiliating" (I, 31). The Platonic strain made him also remark that man seems to feel a repugnance to succession and duration. Such aversion leads to a desire for an intuitive knowledge that rises above temporality, a subject on which Hemsterhuis elaborated in his subsequent publication, the *Lettre sur les désirs*.

Agreeing with Hogarth and Burke that ease of comprehension — *finesse* and *facilité* of contour (I, 29) — make for beauty in the visual arts, the author of the Letter stresses the subjective element in our perception of beauty, although the characteristics just mentioned refer to a basis in the objects as well. This applies also to the concept of *rapports*, as Diderot realized;[9] he is probably responsible for Hemsterhuis' extensive use of the term.

Turning to sculpture specifically, Hemsterhuis repeats that it takes the first place among the visual arts. Bas-relief and painting, in this order, rank below sculpture. The latter, being the most

natural and perfect form of imitation of visual objects, is also older
than painting, which presupposes a practiced eye for contours and a
faculty of abstraction. Obviously, the term "painting" refers above
all to designing and drawing. In agreement with Condillac's *Traité
des sensations* (1754), Hemsterhuis claims that tactile sensations
were developed earlier than the perception of visual qualities. The
sense of touch, neglected in the earlier part of the Letter, is now
given due emphasis in the consideration of sculpture. The tactile
sensations were shown to be the very basis of this art in Herder's
essay *Plastik* (1778), written to correct Lessing's failure to furnish a
clear distinction of painting from sculpture in his *Laokoon* (1766).

The initial remarks on the nature of sculpture are followed by a
lengthy consideration of its history, from which Hemsterhuis
returns toward the end of the Letter to a discussion of sculpture as
an art: its specific characteristics, the limitations imposed by its
nature, and the choice of subjects most suitable. Sculpture, which
appeals to touch and sight alike, represents the solidity and outline
of objects. Hemsterhuis emphasizes that his remarks about the
limitations of this art will apply only to works executed in hard
materials, like marble or metal. Their hardness forces the sculptor to
limit himself to *one* figure or to a very few, rather simple figures.
Unity and simplicity are essential features of his art. His efforts
should be directed at achieving a work that can be grasped in a
minimum of time rather than at the representation of a maximum of
ideas. The sculptor should aim at facileness and excellence of
contours more than at a perfect, highly detailed expression of
actions or passions. It follows, then, that repose and grandeur are
most befitting in sculpture.[10] The artist must also bear in mind that
a sculpture can be looked at from all sides and that all profiles must
be equally pleasing from the distance as well as from nearby.

As to the subjects treated in sculpture, Hemsterhuis emphasizes
the following limitations: (1.) The subjects represented must
conform to the ideas of things as they are formed or stored by the
reproductive faculty of our mind. This means not only that
nonrepresentational art is excluded, as we should expect, but also
the advocation of a rather narrow standard of verisimilitude. (2.)
Sculpture, by dint of its durable materials, addresses itself to a
posterity far removed and must therefore speak the "language of
nature" (I, 45). For that reason, Hemsterhuis argues, subjects from

the Bible, especially those involving the "Supreme Being" *(ibid.)*, personifications of virtues and vices, as well as clothing belonging to a peculiar age or nation are not suitable for sculpture. These remarks imply a criticism of the art of the moderns and the conviction that Greek sculpture conforms to the "language of nature."

Unity and simplicity being of fundamental importance, the sculptor achieves highest perfection in the representation of *one* figure. The latter, according to Hemsterhuis, must be beautiful and graceful, shown in a natural stance, almost in repose; as many parts as possible should be visible at a glance; a little bit of clothing or drapery should satisfy the demands of decency; augment the number of ideas, and contrast with the rotundity of flesh. To enhance the effect of contrast, the artist may add a pedestal, part of a column, or a vase, whose regularity will show "the beautiful irregularity of the figure" in an advantageous light (I, 46). If a sculptor has chosen to represent a subject through a group of figures, its individual members should be different in sex, age, and proportions; the action depicted should be *one* and simple, with all the members of the group enforcing it. All profiles should show as many salient features as possible. With these demands Hemsterhuis gives concrete hints how to combine unity and variety in an optimal fashion. Horror and fear, if they are essential to the subject, should be tempered by the piquant beauty of one figure. Painters, whose compositions are large enough to allow for balancing factors, may sometimes use the loathsome to heighten the intended effect of horror. In sculpture, however, the loathsome would prevail unmitigated and should be avoided. Apart from this limitation, the sculptor may emulate the painter in depicting actions and emotions. But his main concern and his forte is to represent as great a variety of "profiles" as possible.

Applying the criteria outlined above, Hemsterhuis finds that there are hardly any perfect groups in sculpture. The Laocoön group, for example, tends too much toward the picturesque to be exemplary. It exhibits a tendency which became a characteristic feature of modern sculptors, that is, to cultivate the picturesque, while the Greeks inclined toward sculpture even in their paintings. August Wilhelm Schlegel adduces this remark at the very beginning of his widely renowned Lectures on Dramatic Art and Poetry (1809) to support his famous characterization of the spirit of ancient and modern art and poetry as *plastisch* (sculpturesque) or *pittoresk*, respectively.[11]

Much of what Hemsterhuis has to say about sculpture is, in keeping with prevailing tendencies within the esthetics of his age, prescriptive or normative rather than descriptive. Like Lessing and many others, he adopts a canon of beauty for the visual arts that excludes the ugly and loathsome.[12] He adheres to the neoclassicist demands of decency. The "beautiful irregularity" joined to regularity is a widespread formula in eighteenth century esthetics. Hemsterhuis' emphasis on repose and grandeur reminds us of Winckelmann. In contrast to the latter, who sees in *edle Einfalt und stille Grösse* ("noble simplicity and quiet grandeur") a characteristic feature of Greek morality which finds expression in art, the author of the Letter introduces repose as an artistic requirement for sculpture. Herein he agrees with Lessing, without giving detailed reasons, however, as the latter does. While both writers also agree that the expression of horror should be mitigated, Lessing enjoins that an extreme of any expression should be avoided, a demand he supports by lengthy arguments. Hemsterhuis, on the other hand, asserts without further elaboration that the expression of horror in one person should be balanced by another figure exhibiting beauty. Although Lessing's *Laokoon* and the *Lettre sur la sculpture* show agreements or similarities in certain points, the works are very different in intent and execution. The Letter contains, besides reflections on the nature and history of sculpture, a definition of beauty claiming validity for all arts. Lessing is concerned with delimiting poetry and the visual arts. He writes a learned treatise studded with footnotes and filled with polemics. Hemsterhuis chooses the casual form of an epistle. The assumption that he knew Lessing's *Laokoon*[13] must remain doubtful.

A portion of the Letter (I, 35–43) is devoted to a brief survey of the history of sculpture. Influenced most likely by Montesquieu's *De l'esprit des lois* (1748), Hemsterhuis wants to show the ruling spirit ("esprit") behind any of the various forms that sculpture assumed in the empires of the Middle East, in Egypt, Greece, among the Etruscans, Romans, "Goths," and in the centuries following the "renascence of arts" (I, 35). The idea that the art of a nation or an age manifests a specific *esprit* furnishes the thread connecting a large number of isolated items of antiquarian learning.

Like Winckelmann, Hemsterhuis is convinced that the Greeks created an art of their own, independent of the Egyptians, from whom they may have learned some skills without ever becoming copyists. In the small states of ancient Greece every individual was of importance. Since mathematics and the sciences were still rather undeveloped, the mind turned mainly upon itself and the human heart. This led to the flowering of the *sentiment moral,* which became the prevailing spirit of Greek art and science. Influenced perhaps by the English moralists or Diderot, Hemsterhuis introduces here the concept of moral sentiment, from which he will proceed in his later writings to a key idea of his thought, the *organe moral.* He shares Winckelmann's predilection for sculpture as the most characteristic manifestation of the Greek mind. Both authors point out the eminently human as well as humane quality of Greek art, whose characteristic feature is the pursuit of an ideal beauty ("beau idéal"; I, 38), and detect in the Greek ideal of beauty a manifestation of an ethos.

Hemsterhuis' views concerning medieval art evince a negative attitude toward the Middle Ages often so typical of the Enlightenment. Characteristically, he speaks of the art of the "Goths," insinuating that we deal with half-barbarian tribes. Like Winckelmann, Lessing, and Goethe, he judges medieval Christian art by standards taken from the sculpture of the Greeks, which for all these writers furnished a canon of artistic perfection. Connected with the bias in favor of classical or classicistic art is a neopaganism that criticizes Christianity for its otherworldliness, its lack of sense for the *beau idéal* of human perfection, and finds nothing but praise for the Greek pantheon. Greek art and religion alone represent "nature." The *Lettre sur la sculpture* is in line with an esthetic paganism that extends in Germany from Winckelmann into the twentieth century, and it is partly in the context of the "tyranny of Greece over Germany," to use E. M. Butler's striking phrase, that Hemsterhuis found interest and sympathy in Germany.[14]

The author of the Letter concludes his historical survey with a positive evaluation of Renaissance art. Michelangelo, above all, receives praise as the astounding genius, who would have been worthy of Periclean Athens. While the moderns achieved in their sculpture a power of expression equal to the one found in Greek statues, the latter excel in the treatment of contour. Hemsterhuis explains this by referring to the prevailing spirit of each age. Modern art is subject to the "esprit de symétrie" or "esprit géométrique" (I, 43), whereas the ruling *esprit* of the Greeks favored artistic expression.

Although, as Brummel has pointed out,[15] a direct influence of Winckelmann on Hemsterhuis cannot be proven, there are many ideas shared by both authors: the assertion that sculpture preceded painting, the characterization of the art of the despotic Oriental empires and of Etruscan sculpture. They also agree in their predominantly negative attitude toward Christian religious art, Winckelmann attacking Baroque artists, Hemsterhuis criticizing medieval art. The agreements do not prove much, since they concern rather widespread tenets, in part derived from Caylus as their common source. Besides, while the two authors never agree completely, they often differ widely. Hemsterhuis takes a standpoint between Caylus, who sees art moving from people to people, and Winckelmann, who regards it as an autochthonous growth in each nation. Concerning the Greeks, Hemsterhuis shares Winckelmann's views, toward which he shows by and large greater affinity than toward those of Caylus.[16] It has been noted that the Letter adduces examples from Greek sculpture which play also a prominent role in the German art historian's writings. To assume that these influenced Hemsterhuis' choice of examples is not cogent, however, since it may very well be that both writers were independently attracted by the artistic excellence of the same sculptures. Apart from the difference in the interpretation of the Laocoön group, the historian's detailed, enthusiastic descriptions of individual works of art cannot be compared with the brief references to them by the philosopher, who wants to illustrate some generalizations.

While the question of the relation of poetry to the visual arts was taken up again much later in *Simon*, two observations made in the Letter, — the tendency of the human mind to strive for a maximum of ideas in a minimum of time, and the blunting of our perception of beautiful objects by constant exposure to them — furnished the point of departure for Hemsterhuis' next publication, the *Lettre sur les désirs*. He turned with this work away from the special field of esthetics and the history of art to his proper concern: man and his place in the universe. The philosopher realized that his definition of beauty, a description of the subjective esthetic attitude rather than of the beautiful object, contained a principle that applies to man's mental life in general. The maximum-minimum formula became a leitmotiv of Hemsterhuis' thought. Implied in it was a transposition of the esthetic values into the realm of metaphysics, a conception of an infinitely perfect archetypal mind capable of grasping an infinite number of ideas in one instant. Man, to whom duration and succession are repugnant (I, 32), tries to overcome these limitations of a finite mind, whose knowledge depends upon the senses bound to space and time. Unable to achieve archetypal perfection, man must be content with grasping a relative maximum of ideas in a relative minimum of time.

Sketchy as it is, the Letter can hardly be compared with the many, often voluminous, systematic treatises on esthetics that appeared in print during the eighteenth century, and it occupies only a minor place in the history of esthetics. While Funder in his comprehensive study of the philosopher's views on art tends to overestimate their often merely conjectured indebtedness to English eighteenth century authors, he makes it clear that Hemsterhuis' contribution to esthetics involves no radical innovations. His sensitive and knowledgeable observations on the arts and the history of sculpture, original as they may be find a parallel in much more elaborate works by Lessing and Winckelmann. Hemsterhuis' definition of beauty, the most striking feature of the Letter, is but a variation of the unity in variety formula. Although the latter may still have some value and appear in different forms in contemporary esthetics, Hemsterhuis' views are today only of historical interest, mainly because they attracted the attention of Goethe and other prominent German writers.

II *Reception of the Letter*

The Letter found a wider echo than any of Hemsterhuis' other writings. It was above all, of course, the definition of the beautiful that aroused interest and ensured the philosopher a place in the history of esthetic doctrine.

Unfortunately, we do not know how Lessing reacted to the Letter, the only work by Hemsterhuis he was familiar with when he met Jacobi in 1780.[17] Moses Mendelssohn, known through his own contributions to esthetics, wrote in 1776 a very brief account of the Letter.[18] While agreeing that beauty consists ("Schönheit . . . besteht") in a maximum of ideas perceived in a minimum of time, he insists that the maximum must be correctly understood: not only extensively as quantity of ideas ("Begriffe") but also intensively, involving the greatest possible clarity, effectiveness, etc., of ideas. The minimum applies to time as well as the minimal effort to grasp the object of esthetic contemplation. Applying algebraic operations, the critic tries to show that beauty cannot be said to be directly proportional to the quantity of ideas and inversely proportional to time ($B = \frac{Q}{T}$). It would be more correct to say that beauty is proportional to the quantity of ideas in a given time. We do not see much value in Mendelssohn's algebraic proof, since the quotients for $\frac{Q}{T}$ could also be compared, as Hemsterhuis suggested, if T were a variable. The difficulty presented by Hemsterhuis' formula lies in the fact that the maximum of beauty is tacitly related to an archetypal intellect perceiving an infinite number of ideas in an instant, where the measured time interval becomes zero. The formula $B = \frac{Q}{T}$ would involve in that case operations not allowed in algebra. The whole argument is today no longer convincing, but was in keeping with the widespread tendency in the eighteenth century to apply quantitative methods to the theory of beauty,[19] a penchant that Mendelssohn detected also in Hemsterhuis' "formula." Being thoroughly familiar with Lessing's *Laokoon*, the critic was especially interested in the distinction between sculpture and painting made by Hemsterhuis, with whom he essentially agreed.

Christian Garve, a German *Popularphilosoph*, wrote some comments on the Letter that were incorporated as footnotes to the text by Jansen and afterwards by Meyboom. Concerning the definition of the beautiful, Garve emphasizes that beauty depends also upon the character of the ideas and their *rapports*, above all on proportion (I, 18 f.). Indicative of the reputation Hemsterhuis enjoyed then in Germany is the fact that one year after his death and the publication of Kant's *Kritik der Urteilskraft* (Critique of Judgment) Christian Gotthilf Herrmann published a booklet containing, as its title indicates, a comparison of Kant's definition of beauty with that of Hemsterhuis, and objections to the latter.[20] Herrmann has high praise for the Dutch philosopher, who can very well stand comparison with Kant. Both thinkers emphasize the mental activity that goes into esthetic experience. Dividing in a dubious procedure Hemsterhuis' definition of beauty into two parts, the critic asserts that shortness of time does not measure beauty, but only the ease with which ideas are perceived. Since Herrmann considers here only the minimum condition, he cannot see that Hemsterhuis' formula for beauty implies unity in variety, and maintains wrongly that according to the author of the Letter the simplest object would cause the greatest pleasure. The separate treatment of the maximum condition misleads Herrmann into imputing to Hemsterhuis the assertion that the greater quantity of ideas distinguishes a beautiful from an ugly object. Weightier, however, is Herrmann's objection that Hemsterhuis speaks of ideas without further qualification, whereas Kant refers explicity to "esthetic ideas." The author of the Letter should have spoken of the content and not merely the quantity of ideas. He has dealt only with the effect and the external, formal aspect of beauty, without explaining its nature.

A much larger public became acquainted with Hemsterhuis' definition of beauty through Jean Paul, the then very popular German novelist, presented to the English-speaking world by Carlyle. The Hemsterhuisian formula is discussed in the *Vorschule der Ästhetik* (1804), an introduction to esthetics.[21] Jean Paul raises incidentally the question of how ideas can be measured by time when actually the former furnish a measure for the latter. Much more important to Jean Paul is the following objection: since soritical arguments in logic and mathematics present also a great number of ideas in the shortest time, a distinctive criterion for beauty ought to be found.

Neither August Wilhelm Schlegel nor Goethe dwelt on the difficulties presented by Hemsterhuis' formula when they referred to the philosopher's esthetics. In the first part of his Lectures on Belles-Lettres and Art, held in Berlin in 1801—02, Schlegel points out that according to Winckelmann and Hemsterhuis sculpture is older than painting. Both agree also that the ancient sculptors aimed at moderation in expression. Hemsterhuis' observation on the prevalence of the sculpturesque in ancient and of the picturesque in modern art is cited already in these early Lectures, where Schlegel mentions also the application of the theory of aphelia and perihelia,

expounded in the *Lettre sur l'homme*, to the history of arts.[22] While
the Berlin Lectures remained unpublished until 1884, a wider
public read of Hemsterhuis' views on ancient and modern art in
Schlegel's Lectures on Dramatic Art and Poetry of 1809. More than
a decade later Goethe referred in his *Campagne in Frankreich*
(published 1822) to Hemsterhuis' definition of beauty. According to
it, the poet writes, we experience beauty and that which pleases us
in it whenever we can grasp or perceive with ease a maximum of
ideas in *one* moment. We notice here a significant change in
wording. As Goethe points out, he had to "translate" the
philosopher's views into his own idiom to assimilate them, and
therefore offers the following interpretation: we perceive beauty
whenever we become intuitively aware of a living form, obeying its
own laws, in its highest activity and perfection; this *Anschauung*
stimulates a maximum degree of activity and the urge to reproduce
the living form. Though Goethe seems to pay more attention to the
creative artist, he believes that what he says agrees substantially
with Hemsterhuis' views. The poet also refers in the same passage
to the *Lettre sur les désirs*, commenting on the philosopher's
observation that habitual exposure to a work of art often diminishes
our enjoyment. Goethe maintains, however, that our joy and
admiration will forever increase provided the object is worthy of the
initial enthusiasm.[23]

Only a few years after the publication of the *Campagne*, a prize-
winning treatise on Hemsterhuis' esthetics written by J. H. N.
Defooz in answer to a question proposed by the Academy of Liège
appeared in the Annals of that institution.[24] While Goethe wrote
about Hemsterhuis and his ideas out of a personal concern for a
man he had met, Defooz' Latin dissertation was motivated by a
purely academic and historical interest, evinced already in
Herrmann's book. According to Defooz, Hemsterhuis failed to
distinguish the beautiful from the merely pleasing and considered
only the external "shadow of beauty," the subjective factor in
esthetic experience. Although the philosopher erred in not defining
what kind of ideas constitute the beautiful, he is praised by the
author, obviously impressed by Kant, for having emphasized the
activity of the mind and the role of *Anschauung* ("contemplatio")
in esthetic experience. Defooz assigned to the author of the Letter a
position between Kant and the empiricism of Montesquieu.

After the publication of Defooz' dissertation, Hemsterhuis' views were mainly discussed in surveys of the history of esthetics. These are mentioned here because they were mostly intended to reach a wider public and attest to a continuing interest in the philosopher. The most detailed account was given by Robert Zimmermann, who pointed out that the philosopher assumed a basic discrepancy between man's desire for fusion with the suprasensual One and the limitation by his senses; between an intellect able to grasp an infinite number of ideas in one instant and the human mind. Beauty, a substitute for that which is denied to man, is a relatively optimal compromise to achieve unity in variety in accordance with man's sensual nature, destined to enjoy rather than to know. Wavering between Platonism and sensualism, Hemsterhuis did not dare assert unequivocally the priority of an internal sense ("innerer Sinn") endowed with direct intuition ("unmittelbare, intellektuale Anschauung"). Max Schasler, whose History of Esthetics appeared in 1872, fourteen years after Zimmermann's book on the same subject, did not contribute essentially new viewpoints. He mentioned, like Zimmermann, the "internal sense," which subsequently turned up in the brief references to Hemsterhuis in the surveys of the history of esthetics by Knight, Croce, and by Gilbert and Kuhn, the latter and Croce indicating their indebtedness to Zimmermann or Schasler. Independent of the two last-mentioned authors, K. H. von Stein discussed Hemsterhuis' definition of beauty as the final stage of the unity in variety formula.[25]

We do not include in our survey of the reception accorded to the Letter discussions of Hemsterhuis' esthetics given by van de Weyer and Meyboom in their Hemsterhuis editions, or by Grucker, Bulle, Boulan, Brummel, and Hammacher in their books specifically concerned with the philosopher's works and ideas. A consideration of these authors would rather belong to a history of Hemsterhuis scholarship.

CHAPTER 4

On the Nature of Human Desire

THE *Lettre sur les désirs,* which deals with the nature of human desire, was published in 1770. Its manuscript, as Brummel points out,[1] was actually finished in November, 1768, before the publication of the *Lettre sur la sculpture.* This fact indicates that Hemsterhuis, while still occupied with the latter work, had begun to elaborate on some ideas contained in it. The result of these efforts, the *Lettre sur les désirs,* also dedicated to de Smeth, was intended to be a sequel to the essay on sculpture. Even many years later Hemsterhuis emphasized that both works could and should not be separated.[2] As a matter of fact, the very first sentence of the *Lettre sur les désirs* refers to a promise made in the preceding work, namely, to expatiate on the reason for the distaste that arises in us when we are exposed constantly to an object we deem beautiful or otherwise desirable. It is this observation that leads Hemsterhuis from the limited field of empirical esthetics to an investigation of the nature of human desire and into speculative philosophy. Another link between the essay on sculpture and its sequel is the definition of beauty, which is extended in a somewhat modified form beyond the realm of esthetic experience to describe and define a characteristic feature of the human mind as it becomes manifest in human desire. The essay under discussion marks a transition in Hemsterhuis' interests from esthetics to a Socratic concern for the study of man, which he shared with many thinkers and poets of the Enlightenment.

The nature of human desire is responsible for the distaste we experience after being habitually confronted with an object that we previously deemed desirable or beautiful. Human desire, Hemsterhuis asserts, is a phenomenon whose analogue is to be found in the power of attraction pervading the material universe.

He does not dwell here on this analogy, which had been pointed out by Hutcheson and Ferguson, both applying Newtonian physics to ethics. Hemsterhuis believes he has shown in his essay on sculpture that the mind has an inveterate tendency to gather a maximum of ideas in a minimum of time. The fulfillment of this desire is hindered, however, by the fact that man's ideas depend upon sense organs and succeed each other in time. If the mind could be directly affected by objects, without the interposition of sense organs, the time to obtain ideas of objects would shrink to an absolute minimum, i.e., zero. Furthermore, if man could instantaneously grasp the infinite number of ideas which constitute the totality of an object, the latter would be united with the soul in a most direct and perfect manner. The object and the soul would become one. It is characteristic of Hemsterhuis that he uses the word "âme," "soul," with its traditional metaphysical, even Platonic connotations, where we have hitherto employed the term "mind." The soul attains perfect enjoyment of an object only when any consciousness of the duality of both has disappeared. The highest goal of human desire is a most intimate, perfect fusion of the soul with the object desired. In his present state man cannot achieve such union, nor the perfect enjoyment derived from it.

Objects are either homogeneous or heterogeneous to the soul, and this in varying degrees (I, 54). The more homogeneous an object is to the soul's "essence"—Hemsterhuis uses here certainly Platonic terminology—the greater our desire for a union with this object and the greater the possibility of such a fusion. One loves, for example, a statue less than a friend, the latter less than one's beloved, and most of all one loves God (*ibid.*). The constant contemplation of a beautiful object soon arouses surfeit in people endowed with finest sensibility because they are quickest to realize that their desire for a perfect union with the object cannot be fulfilled. In friendship the obstacles toward union seem to be greatly diminished. As to love, nature deceives us for a moment when the lover believes he has achieved complete fusion with the beloved, but the surfeit following physical union—Hemsterhuis quotes the dictum *Omne animal triste post coitum*—evinces its imperfection. Our love of God, the contemplation of the "Great

Being" ("Grand Etre"; I, 55), should not give rise to surfeit, since the possibility of a perfect union cannot be denied. There seems to exist a perfect homogeneity between the soul and God. We know of God's existence through an inner feeling ("sentiment interne"; I, 55) or through irrefutable proofs. While His attributes may be anthropomorphic creations of our reason or imagination, this Immense Being is, philosophically speaking, simple and infinite. God, Hemsterhuis seems to imply, is most homogeneous to the soul because the latter is also simple in substance and infinite in the sense of *capax infiniti,* i.e., desirous and capable of embracing infinity in thought.

Hemsterhuis arranges objects of desire in a scale which indicates their degree of homogeneity with the soul and at the same time the intensity of desire for union as well as the feasibility of a perfect fusion of the soul with its desired object. It has been pointed out that this scale has no longer any relevance for the realm of esthetics, from which Hemsterhuis started, but that it is of a purely speculative character.[3] The work of art takes the lowest place in the scale because it is thought to be least homogeneous with the soul. The experience of the beautiful, bound to time and the senses, appears now as a mere substitute for or adumbration of an experience of the highest value that transcends the limitations just mentioned.[4] The maximum-minimum formula is still used, but now in a different context, so that it no longer defines the specific character of esthetic experience.

As to the scale proposed by Hemsterhuis, we may agree that a work of art is in a sense less "homogeneous" to the "soul" than a friend or the beloved. On the other hand, however, the latter often present more obstacles to the soul's desire than a work of art, which can be grasped more easily, since it is less complex and has no will of its own. It is somewhat surprising, furthermore, especially in view of Hemsterhuis' praise of "la Céleste Amitié," that friendship ranges below physical love. To be sure, the intensity of desire is greater in love than in friendship, the union achieved by lovers seems to be more complete; but at the same time Hemsterhuis looks at love as a sort of ruse of "Nature" to further procreation of the species through the momentary illusion of an apparently perfect union. On the basis of Hemsterhuis' own presuppositions, the scale proposed by him can hardly be called consistent.

When Hemsterhuis ranks nondiscursive, instantaneous intuition and the union of the soul with God highest he seems to come close to mysticism. But his "Grand Etre" is the God of the philosophers. He admits himself that he wants to speak of God "en philosophe" (I, 55). The "homogeneity" between the soul and God is expressed in purely conceptual terms. The wealth and depth of mystic experience is conspicuously lacking.

The manifestations of love, Hemsterhuis continues, arise spontaneously in all human beings. They show that the soul seeks all kinds of ways and means to become united with the desired object. And not only with *one* object, but with everything outside the soul, desire thus being an analogue to attraction in the material universe. The soul desires always. We are reminded of the Platonic doctrine of Eros or desirous love in the *Symposium*,[5] which Hemsterhuis combined with the results of Newtonian physics and the psychology of his time. His emphasis on desire brings also to mind the role assigned to the *conatus*, the *appétition*, and uneasiness, respectively, in the philosophical systems of Spinoza, Leibniz, and Locke.

In the *Lettre sur la sculpture* Hemsterhuis had hinted at the aversion that the soul, eternal and indivisible in essence, feels toward succession and duration. Now he elaborates on this point, arguing that the union of soul and body remains imperfect because they are heterogeneous in essence. The knowledge the soul has of its conjugate body is not more certain than that of other bodies. Knowledge is in both cases gained through the medium of our sense organs. From the dubious assertion that while we were reading this printed text we were not conscious of our body, Hemsterhuis concludes falsely that its nonexistence would not have made any difference to us as we were engaged in the act of thinking. He voices here an extremely dualistic view of body and soul, going back mainly to Neoplatonism, but perhaps also influenced by Cartesianism. This dualism is the basis for the soul's aversion toward the temporal to which the body is bound.

The soul achieves union with the desired object in two ways: either physically or intellectually. Concerning the first way, Hemsterhuis maintains that sexual desire is the most intense manifestation of the soul's striving to be united physically with the object desired. There is a mutual interaction between the sex organs and our ideas. The passionate fervor evinced in religion, love,

friendship, and even in the desire for material goods is connected
with the parts of our body in which Plato located concupiscence.
Sexual abnormalities, such as pederasty, sodomy, etc., arise when
the soul is unable to direct and regulate the "universal power of
attraction" (I, 59). Such a directing power is as necessary for the
moral world as the existence of a power that counterbalances
universal attraction for the maintenance of the physical universe. In
view of Hemsterhuis' dualistic views concerning body and soul it is
somewhat surprising to see him concede to the body so much
influence on the mind. Nowhere else in his writings do we find
such a frank acknowledgement of the role of sex in man, even in his
mental makeup.

Discussing the intellectual way of achieving union with the
desired object, the author turns above all to friendship, which is
directed to persons with whom we can share a maximum of ideas in
a minimum of time. There is a constant endeavor to become more
homogeneous, together with a striving for mutual self-perfection.
These are the workings of eros as described by Socrates in
Xenophon's *Symposium*. The ideal of mutual self-perfection
became a leitmotiv of Hemsterhuis' friendship with his Diotima as
well as for her and Fürstenberg, in the latter case tinged by
Leibnizian ideas and assimilated into a Christian context.

At this point of the *Lettre sur les désirs* its author takes the
opportunity to expatiate on the differences between the Greeks and
the moderns. The former are praised for their tact and extreme
sensibility, for their spirit of legislation that allowed the individual
to pursue civic virtues and to direct his actions to the furtherance of
the greatest good of his particular society. While Hemsterhuis
bestows excessive praise on the Greeks, he is critical of the moderns,
and that means above all of Christian religion. Under its influence
the individual, assured of eternal life, no longer sought the greatest
good in this temporal world. Consequently, civic virtue declined.
Inactivity and brutishness grew, the fruits of the revealed religion
we "enjoy," as Hemsterhuis writes ironically (I, 64). In his negative
attitude toward Christianity, partly determined by his Grecolatry,
he voices opinions and biases widely current in the Age of
Enlightenment. As a matter of fact, he notices with obvious
satisfaction that some more enlightened minds have begun to
separate religion and civic virtue.

Returning to the main theme of his essay, Hemsterhuis thinks he has shown that it is in the very nature of the soul to unite its essence in the most intimate and perfect manner with the essence of the object desired. Everything in the world known to us shows a tendency toward union or unity, manifested in matter as the universal power of attraction. And yet, the universe is composed of absolutely isolated individual essences, which in spite of the semblance of a chain of beings (I, 67) exist only for their own sake. Hemsterhuis concludes from this that the world is in an unbalanced, strained state ("état forcé"; I, 68). The power that has decomposed the unity of the whole into individuals is outside of nature, and this power is God.[6] While the attempt to grasp the essence of this impenetrable Being would be folly, it is evident that individuation implies coexistence of individual entities, which in turn is the source of *rapports*, i.e., of inalterable laws. These can and should be investigated.

From a consideration of human desire Hemsterhuis has moved on to metaphysics. This movement of thought is also apparent in the General Remark (I, 70—72), which he appended to the *Lettre sur les désirs* in order to give the reader a résumé of its argument. There are in it, however, some ideas not previously expressed. Restating the thesis that the soul desires to obtain the greatest number of ideas of an object in the shortest time, the author carries this principle to its extreme. In this case the number of ideas will be infinite, while the span of time necessary to grasp them will shrink to zero. Time being reduced to an absolute instant, the soul is equidistant from all parts of the object, which are now equally present to the soul. If the number of ideas becomes infinite, it is claimed, the idea of the soul's existence or its consciousness must be included. A mind capable of grasping an infinite number of ideas instantaneously will therefore be truly one with its object. It would follow then, according to Hemsterhuis, that God, who has this postulated perfect intuition of all objects, would be one with them. To the author of the *Lettre sur les désirs* the conclusion he reached concerning God seemed to be stringent enough. Nevertheless, he denounces it as "absurd" (I, 71), since it implies an identification of the Maker and Sustainer of All with the things He made and sustains. Being afraid of the pantheistic consequences that seem to follow from his own premises, he rejects as "manifest contradiction" *(ibid.)* the identification of Creator and creation, while he saw no logical difficulties in the coincidence of knower and object known, of desire and desideratum.

Admitting that a perfect union or identification of the soul with its desired object cannot be realized under present conditions, Hemsterhuis emphasizes once more the ineradicable desire of the soul to achieve such a fusion, a goal that can only be reached by a process of continual approximation, which he compares with the hyperbola and its asymptote. The comparison just mentioned appealed especially to some German romantics, like Novalis and Friedrich Schlegel, who interpreted Hemsterhuis' *désir* in terms of their own *Sehnsucht nach dem Unendlichen*, a longing for the infinite which can never be satisfied by any finite experience. In the preceding generation Herder had been impressed by the emphasis on desire as the fundamental characteristic of the human mind because this agreed with his own voluntaristic tendencies during his *Sturm und Drang* years. He shared with Hemsterhuis the conviction that there exists a fundamental homogeneity or analogy between soul and world, as well as a yearning for a knowledge in which the knower and the known will be fused, a longing also apparent in Goethe's Faust and Werther.

Herder read the *Lettre sur les désirs* in 1772, the year the *Lettre sur l'homme* was published; he planned immediately a translation of both works, but after 1773 his interest in the project abated.[7] Almost a decade later he returned to it, however, and his translation of the *Lettre sur les désirs* appeared in the November, 1781 issue of *Der Teutsche Merkur*, a journal edited by Wieland.[8] In a short preface he emphasizes the scarceness of Hemsterhuis' opuscule, which deserves more publicity in Germany than its brevity would seem to warrant. He praises the work for its wealth of ideas and its beauty. There is perhaps no one since Plato who has discussed the nature of human desire in such a substantial and subtle manner, Herder writes in an enthusiastic panegyric so typical of him. He notes, however, that Hemsterhuis' use of the idiom of French metaphysics has caused certain obscurities, and announces his intention to clear them up in his translation. This means, of course, a reinterpretation of Hemsterhuis in Herder's own terms, a method that he followed also with regard to Spinoza.[9]

In the preface Herder had spoken of the necessity of a commentary to the *Lettre sur les désirs*. Such he furnished in the essay entitled *Liebe und Selbstheit* (Love and Selfhood), which appeared in the December, 1781, issue of *Der Teutsche Merkur*.[10] The first German translation of Hemsterhuis' writings in 1782 contained in its first volume Herder's essay, a French translation of which was included by Jansen in his edition of Hemsterhuis' *Oeuvres* (1792), an example followed by Meyboom. Thus this little work, expressly designated a supplement to the *Lettre*, became attached to the Dutch philosopher's writings.

The very title of Herder's *Liebe und Selbstheit* indicates his intention to underscore the limitation of love by selfhood, its correlate. Characteristically also, Herder speaks of *Liebe* rather than *Verlangen*, desire. The latter and longing ("Sehnsucht") are the bridesmaids of love. While Hemsterhuis had pointed out that attraction and inertia, desire and individuation coexist in the universe, Herder puts more emphasis on selfhood as the necessary correlate of love. He is aware of their dialectical interplay. Without consciousness of self man would not enjoy the existence of other beings. If the self would lose itself in God it would no longer enjoy the union with the Divine Being. Agreeing with Hemsterhuis on the impossibility of a perfect fusion of soul and object, accepting also the analogy of hyperbola and asymptote, Herder goes further and rejects the very desirability of such a union. As Herder points out, the melody of life consists of consonant and not of unisonant notes. Siding with Leibniz, he affirms here, as elsewhere in his writings, the supreme value of individuality or selfhood, while he reproaches Hemsterhuis for seeing in individuation merely a limitation of desire.

Regarding some specific points, it seems that Herder would range friendship above love because the former is purer. Even marriage, of which Hemsterhuis has too low an estimation according to Herder, must partake of friendship. The culmination of love is not attained in the moment of physical consummation but rather in that instant when two persons become aware for the first time of their mutual love. Herder also criticizes the assertion that Christian religion has weakened the pursuit of civic virtue. He agrees emphatically, however, with Hemsterhuis' view that religion is "a free relation of every individual to the Supreme Being," a view to which the Greeks, as the philosopher concedes, hardly rose.

While Herder ranked the author of the *Lettre sur les désirs* in style, scope, and depth with Plato, Shaftesbury, and Diderot,[11] Hamann found it difficult to follow Hemsterhuis' arguments. In a letter to Herder, written April 20, 1782, he professes with his usual irony that he can neither understand the reasoning in the *Lettre sur la sculpture* nor see what the maximum-minimum formula could contribute to an understanding of desire ("des Verlangens"). According to Hamann, the explanation of desire and surfeit is based on paralogisms concerning unity and the impossibility of achieving it.[12] The inveterate opponent of rationalism and Enlightenment objected to Hemsterhuis' "algebraic prose" as a concession to these currents of thought. Lessing reacted more positively to the *Lettre sur les désirs*, which he read with extraordinary pleasure ("ungemeines Vergnügen"), though he had misgivings about the philosopher's views on love ("System von der Liebe"). They explained nothing and merely substituted one formula for another.[13]

Hemsterhuis' ideas on love apparently influenced directly or indirectly (by way of Herder) an anonymous article that appeared in 1796 in Niethammer's *Philosophisches Journal*.[14] In 1797, Novalis jotted down his "Hemsterhuis-Studien," which remained, however, unpublished for a long time and have only recently been adequately edited by Hans-Joachim Mähl, who has convincingly identified the references to individual works.[15] Novalis' entries concerning the *Lettre sur les désirs* consist mainly of quotes from it in German translation. Without dependence on sense organs, characterizing the present state of man during which ideal enjoyment remains an unattainable idea, the whole soul would be instantaneously penetrated by its infinite object. Man has an incessant desire to appropriate or assimilate everything. Adding his own comment, Novalis speaks of a continual stimulation ("Reitz") that would cease only with the attainment of its goal. He writes of a subjective idea that grows as the soul expands, of an indeterminate problem ("unbestimmte Aufgabe") that can forever find only a relative solution, especially since a possible expansion of the object postpones a compete fusion with it to an indeterminate future.[16] While there are other excerpts from the *Lettre*, Novalis was mainly interested in passages supporting his own romantic longing for the infinite ("Sehnsucht nach dem Unendlichen"), strengthened also by his study of Fichte's philosophy. The poet was aware of that aspect of

Hemsterhuisian thought which Brummel calls "modern," akin to romanticism.[17] Hemsterhuis transcends classicism when he describes the soul in terms of restless, forever unsatisfied desire. Goethe, as indicated in the preceding chapter, referred briefly to the *Lettre* in his *Campagne in Frankreich*, but only to take issue with the philosopher's observation on distaste arising from a constant exposure to a work of art.

CHAPTER 5

The Letter on Man

THE *Lettre sur l'homme et ses rapports*, published in 1772, was written for François Fagel, the philosopher's young friend, who had asked for a "petit cours de philosophie,"[1] The discussion of human desire in the *Lettre sur les désirs*, still closely connected with ideas enounced in the *Lettre sur la sculpture*, had led to considerations concerning the nature of the human mind or soul. Stimulated by Fagel, Hemsterhuis proceeded to write a treatise on man in his relations to, or *rapports* with, the physical universe, other human beings, and God. The *Lettre sur l'homme et ses rapports* (henceforth referred to as Letter on Man), as the author entitled this long treatise with characteristic modesty, furnishes indeed a "petit cours de philosophie," a comprehensive statement of his views concerning epistemology, philosophical psychology, ethics, and religion.

Containing the results of sustained efforts to achieve a *Weltanschauung*, and at the same time adumbrations of ideas to be taken up again and elaborated on in his later writings, the Letter on Man occupies a central position in Hemsterhuis' oeuvre. On account of its scope as well as length, and since it deals with the philosopher's most thorough attempt to present his main ideas in a systematic fashion, this work has often been regarded as his most significant opus. But it is also the least felicitous and readable among his writings. Trying to emulate the rigorous, coherent reasoning of the deductive systems of the great rationalists or of Newtonian physics, and impressed by the *esprit géométrique*, Hemsterhuis encumbers his Letter on Man with a scaffolding of syllogistic ratiocination, hoping thereby to strengthen his arguments. Apart from the fact that one may disagree with their supposed cogency—an objection that can be raised against any system based on inferences from debatable assumptions—Hemsterhuis' argumentation is confused and cumbersome. Confused, because he does not adequately define the terms he uses, cumbersome within the context of the epistolary form that he chose to communicate his thoughts. The anonymous critic who reviewed the Letter on Man in the *Journal Encyclopédique* commented on the lack of elegance, the austere presentation of ideas in a work whose whole format indicated that it was directed at cultured readers rather than metaphysicians.[2]

If the Letter on Man has the character of an outline or sketch of a system this may partly be due to the fact that this work furnished a résumé of conversations that had taken place between the author and Fagel. More generally, however, Hemsterhuis lacked the sustaining power to develop a philosophical system. His forte were acute observations and *aperçus*. Here, as in the *Lettre sur la sculpture*, a multitude of topics are briefly touched upon so that the ideas seem to crowd each other. Any account of the contents of these and his other works must therefore at times appear unduly condensed. Hemsterhuis offers *fermenta cognitionis*, fruitful ideas capable of being elaborated, and this is what endeared him especially to such thinkers as Herder, Novalis, and Friedrich Schlegel.

The title of the work under discussion is representative of the central theme and concern of its author's thought. He shared this predominant interest in man with his revered master Socrates as well as with the philosophers of Enlightenment. Besides, the nature of man became an all-important issue in the dispute between philosophical materialism and its opponents, to whom Hemsterhuis belonged.

Soon after the completion of the Letter of Man, the author felt the need to supplement it with additions and elucidations. These "additions et éclaircissements" are mentioned by Princess Gallitzin in a letter of November, 1791, which contains a list of manuscripts bequeathed to her by her deceased friend.[3] For a while she planned to translate some of his works into German. Even after two volumes of his *Vermischte Schriften* had been published in 1782, she still thought of translating the Letter on Man, augmented by the philosopher's additions.[4] Nothing came of these plans. Jansen's posthumous edition of Hemsterhuis' works, however, contained copious notes to the Letter by Ch. W. F. Dumas, which Boulan found to be substantially identical with the above-mentioned additions. The latter form a section of a manuscript in the University Library at Leiden.[5] Brummel reported on a copy of the *Lettre sur l'homme* acquired by the Royal Library at 's Gravenhage containing additions in Hemsterhuis' own handwriting that are even closer to Dumas' notes than the corresponding sections in the manuscript investigated by Boulan, which was not written by the philosopher himself. The copy described by Brummel belonged most likely to Fagel. Of greatest importance is, of course, the discovery that the notes ascribed to Dumas actually go back to Hemsterhuis himself.

Since the short preface by the editor ("Avertissement de l'éditeur") appears even in the first edition of the Letter on Man, we may assume that it was authorized, if not written, by Hemsterhuis. In it the many then current publications attacking or ridiculing religion and morality are deprecated as a deplorable consequence of the otherwise commendable freedom of the press. The prevailing tone of the philosophers and the fashionable scientific jargon come likewise under attack. The Letter on Man will show that the use of reason per se does not lead to materialism or to a justification of libertinage. The preface clearly indicates what will henceforth be the principal aim of all Hemsterhuis' writings: to combat the materialism and atheism then widely current among the French *philosophes*.

Because the author failed to mark distinctly any subdivisions within the Letter on Man, Meyboom and May have given outlines of its contents.[6] It indicates a certain lack of clarity in the work itself that the two authors use partly different categories in their analyses. The following topics are treated, in this order: man as a sentient and thinking being; man as an active, acting being; the nature of the world in which man lives and his *rapports* with it: the physical world as perceived through the sense organs, and the world as known through the "moral organ"; society; human knowledge.

Hemsterhuis admits at the very outset that he might be reproached with obscurity. The latter he ascribes mostly to the nature of the subject treated, whose investigation will reveal "faces of the universe" inaccessible to our sense organs and lead to the very "abyss of beings" (I, 81). Passages like this express a new *Weltanschauung* and view of life which influenced German thinkers from Herder onward, while the syllogistic arguments left them cold.

Starting with a discussion of man as sentient and thinking being, Hemsterhuis asserts that any being capable of sensations ("de sentir"; I, 82) of other objects possesses these by means of ideas or images that arise out of the *rapports* between the objects and the organs of the sentient being. "Organ," it is pointed out, refers not only to the organ itself, but also to the medium intervening between object and subject, e.g., light, air. The sentient being, while receiving the idea of an object, is aware of being passive ("se sent passif"; *ibid.*) and "feels" therefore that there exists an external object or a cause for the idea. This conviction is strengthened by the fact that other sentient beings have substantially the same sensations. There are, then, objects that exist outside the sentient beings. Since the "idea" of an object is the result of *rapports* between the object and the modifications of the organs, it follows that among the many modes of being of the object there must also exist the one which corresponds to the idea or sensation in the sentient being. That is, the object really exists as it appears.

Hemsterhuis deals in these few, compressed paragraphs with epistemological problems on the solution of which other philosophers have expended sustained efforts: for example, the origin and validity of our conviction of the reality of an outside world, the reliability or "objective" character of sense perceptions per se, and the nature of objects of knowledge. Most significant perhaps is the thesis that objects of knowledge are defined by the *rapports* obtaining between them and sentient beings, which leads to the assertion that the appearance of an object is a real aspect of the object itself. Hemsterhuis thus avoids subjective idealism as well as an extreme form of phenomenalism. Objects have a real existence independent from being known, but what is known of them constitutes a real aspect of them.

The passages under discussion suffer from a certain vagueness, especially in terminology. The verb *sentir* is used vaguely in the sense of to perceive, to have sensations, to feel. The term "substances" appears in a context that hardly warrants such a concept. It is not quite clear whether the expression "ideas or images" implies an identity of these terms. The definition of "organ," including the medium between object and organ, is too wide and has given rise to misunderstandings.

Ideas which arise in sentient beings due to *rapports* between their sense organs and objects are called "primary ideas" ("idées primitives"; I, 82). Both animals and man possess such primary ideas, which disappear with the absence of their objects. It is therefore impossible to compare objects that succeed each other unless there exists a means of fixing their primary ideas. Signs, according to Hemsterhuis, fulfill this function. They are distinct symbols, each of them corresponding to one idea. Each idea evokes a sign and vice versa. The author of the Letter on Man emphasizes that he is not concerned here with signs as means of communication, but merely with their function of effecting a recall of ideas (I, 83). The primary natural signs are the effects of the objects on one organ. Animals also make use of such signs, which are bound to the presence of the objects and can usually not be evoked at will. Hemsterhuis uses the term "sign" in this context in a vague and unusual way. In his annotations on the Letter on Man, contained in a copy recently discovered and published by Georges May, Diderot maintains that memory or recall does not depend upon signs and that memory or imagination would suffice to compare ideas of objects.[7] This is correct if the word "sign" is taken in its commonly accepted meaning. It seems, however, that Hemsterhuis' *idée* refers to an immediate, momentary sense impression, while *signe* designates its fixed form in memory or imagination, its mnemogram. In any case, the terminology is muddled, the care with which Kant analyzes the cognitive process is lacking.

For reasoning beings, Hemsterhuis continues, another class of signs is available, which correspond to objects and can be evoked at will. These arbitrary signs, comprising sounds, gestures or other expressions of the emotions and semaphors, facilitate the comparison of ideas. They make possible what Hemsterhuis calls the "coexistence" of ideas in the mind, a term which must not be taken, as Diderot did, to imply that one can be fully conscious of more than one idea in one point-instant of physical time.[8] A sentient being that has the ability to acquire primary ideas possesses, according to Hemsterhuis, a "contemplative or intuitive faculty" (I, 84); beings that can recall ideas by means of arbitrary signs have that intuitive faculty which is called "reason"; its application to ideas constitutes "reasoning."

The degree of intellectual perfection is determined by the number of ideas coexisting in the mind that can be offered and submitted to the intuitive faculty. Hemsterhuis distinguishes four gradations of intelligence: genius, sagacity, wit or sense ("esprit"), stupidity. Most significant is the characterization of genius, which reminds us of the maximum-minimum formula used in the definition of beauty: genius, conscious of many *rapports* at once, is capable of grasping with ease great and remote truths. Adducing an algebraic problem as an example, Hemsterhuis points out that a genius will immediately realize its solution, without the aid of intermediary steps. He concludes: "c'est le génie qui sent" (I, 86). Although Hemsterhuis seems to refer in what he says about genius to an intuitive grasp of truth, relying on feeling rather than ratiocination, it must be emphasized that otherwise expressions like "sentir" or "faculté intuitive" have not yet in the Letter on Man the emotional, irrational connotations ascribed to them by later German readers. "Sentir" means to perceive, to be aware (*wahrnehmen*, in German terminology), while the "faculté intuitive" signifies a faculty of beholding, perceiving, but also "reason."[9] On the other hand, the attack on "artificial logic," inferior and posterior to the "true logic" of the intuitive faculty (I, 89) seems to vindicate readers who have emphasized the irrationalist tendencies in Hemsterhuis' thought.

In a long note appended at this point (I, 85-88), Dumas, or, as we know today, Hemsterhuis, defines perfect conviction as the perception or sentiment of absolute truth ("le sentiment du vrai absolu"; I, 85), which for us consists in the identity of the idea of an object with its essence. There are no degrees of truth, but only gradations of conviction. The latter is perfect when its objects are axioms.

There are three ways, Hemsterhuis continues his main topic, by which sentient beings receive ideas: (1) by the action of objects on the sense organs; (2) by their accidental movement; (3) by movements in the organs evoked through signs. Ideas in the first category are clear and not confused; those in the second group are less clear and often confused; the ideas caused by signs are even less clear, but not confused. Most significant is what the author has to say at this point about dreams. The ideas perceived in dreams have their origin in accidental movements of the organs. They possess a greater intensity than ideas evoked by signs. Observing that we sometimes find in dreams solutions to problems we vainly tried to solve while waking, Hemsterhuis goes on to assert that man is his true self in his dreams and that a faithful account of them will reveal his moral character. Diderot, who had written shortly before (1769) *Le rêve de D'Alembert*, is sceptical about the role assigned to dreams by the author of the Letter on Man, pointing out their frequently pathological character as well as the discrepancies between the conscious and subconscious.[10]

Drawing consequences from what has been affirmed before, Hemsterhuis proceeds to elaborate on the differences between animals and man. The former, he decrees, are unable to create arbitrary signs and therefore to recall ideas at will (I, 90). They depend entirely upon the accidental presence of objects or the laws of association ("idées accessoires"; *ibid.*). While their ideas can be as vivid as those of man, in some cases perhaps even more so, the number of coexisting ideas they can dispose of is much smaller. Intellectually, animals are infinitely inferior to man. While adopting a mechanical model for the explanation of sense perceptions and the association of ideas, Hemsterhuis ascribes to man *velléité*, or will as a distinctive feature, which enables the human mind freely to dispose of and compare ideas furnished by his sense organs. Diderot strongly protests the introduction of such an occult quality and maintains that man and animals do not differ radically from each other.

In dealing with man as thinking being, Hemsterhuis considers first "sentient beings" in general, a term that includes animals. Very likely this approach owes much to Condillac's sensualist philosophy, as expounded in the *Essai sur l'origine des connaissances humaines* (1746) as well as the *Traité des sensations* (1754). Hemsterhuis' classification of signs is similar to that given by Condillac. Both authors agree that signs are indispensable for the fixation and combination of ideas. Judgments consist of comparisons of ideas. Hemsterhuis parts company with Condillac's empiricist approach, however, when it comes to a discussion of man as an active, acting being ("être agissant"; I, 92). Here he adopts metaphysical terms, and starts a string of soritical arguments to prove that the "active principle" in man, the soul, and therefore also man's "essence," is immaterial as well as immortal.

Since bodies persist in a state of rest or uniform motion unless impelled by an outside force, and man passes by an act of will ("acte de sa velléité"; I, 92) from rest to accelerated motion, this moving principle ("principe moteur"; *ibid.)* can only be something different from any physical body, namely, the soul. This principle is also invoked to account for changing the direction of movement. According to Newton's first axiom any single uniform motion would continue forever. Since effect and cause are equivalent, the soul as the cause of motion is also one, uniform and eternal. It has often been said, Hemsterhuis points out, that a thing is eternal when it exists through itself. In Spinoza's terms: the eternal substance is *causa sui,* its own cause. While it is true, Hemsterhuis maintains, that a thing existing through itself would necessarily be eternal, it does not follow that everything eternal exists through itself. He sets out to prove that matter and motion, while eternal, do not exist through themselves, that they had a beginning and since then have continued in being. Hemsterhuis distinguishes two orders of eternity: an eternity of infinite duration that had a beginning and, on the other hand, an eternity out of time without beginning or end. The last-mentioned concept of eternity, corresponding to Spinoza's notion of it, applies only to essences whose very nature involves existence. Of such essences it is self-contradictory to think that they could exist in any other mode than they do. Evidently this cannot be asserted of matter. Its essence does not involve existence, matter is not a *causa sui.* In the notes ascribed to Dumas, Hemsterhuis adduces some variations on the "proof" that matter does not exist through itself. They all start out from the fact that its modifications are subject to change and logically speaking contingent. The whole argument hinges on Hemsterhuis' definition of the *causa sui,* which he, like Spinoza, defines in purely logical terms of the principle of contradiction. Physical cause and logical ground are not clearly distinguished. Diderot maintained that the actual modifications of matter, though logically contingent, are necessary and determined, i.e., subject to causality.[11] He might have added explicitly what he tacitly assumed—that matter could very well exist through itself eternally as *causa sui,* provided this expression is not taken to imply logical necessity.

We have dwelt on Hemsterhuis' arguments at some length because they are characteristic of his thought and his position in eighteenth century philosophy. On the one hand, he adopts the empiricism of Condillac's psychology of knowledge and Newtonian physics. On the other hand, he uses terms and argumentations that belong to the deductive reasoning of the great rationalist systems, without attaining the grandiose consistency of Spinoza, of whose philosophy there seem to be faint echoes, although his name is never mentioned. In some notes, ascribed to Dumas (I, 93 f., 96), Hemsterhuis tries to prove the immateriality of the soul and its immortality as a consequence of its unity or indivisibility, much in the manner of the then prevailing rational psychology. He makes much use of the concept of an essence involving its existence. Though open to empirical philosophy and science, his reasoning shows all the characteristics of Pre-Humean and Pre-Kantian rationalist metaphysics.

After the digression on matter and eternity, a necessary part of his refutation of materialism, Hemsterhuis returns to a consideration of the soul. The latter is not aware of its own separate existence unless it acquires ideas of external objects by means of organs, which the soul needs in order to have ideas, to think, and to act. However, even if there is no reaction from outside objects, *velléité* or the faculty to be able to act ("la faculté de pouvoir agir"; I, 98) exists potentially. It seems that with the emphasis on *velléité* Hemsterhuis moves away from the deterministic consequences that his sensualistic starting point implied, according to which the soul becomes aware of itself only through ideas derived from objects outside of it.

Hemsterhuis concludes this section of the Letter on Man with some answers to objections that might be or actually were made. Most important is what he has to say in this connection about *velléité* or, as he here paraphrases it, "la spontanéité de l'homme" (I, 101), man's ability to act spontaneously. *Velléité* is a crucial concept, strongly rejected by Diderot.[12] To those who want a proof that there is such a thing as *velléité*, Hemsterhuis answers: "To want to prove man's *velléité* means wanting to prove his very existence" (I, 102). Diderot remarked that while the fact of willing needs no proof, the meaning of "to will" ("vouloir") should be defined; he maintained that "I will" ("je veux") means no more than "I am such as I am" ("je suis tel"), i.e., determined in character and will.[13]

Sensing that many philosophers would hardly accept his assertion that one's *velléité* is as evident as one's existence, Hemsterhuis sets out to convince them and other doubters of its existence. To prove that, he says it suffices to consider a case in which our will does not immediately achieve its goal. From the observation that our will grows with the obstacles it meets in order to overcome them and from the fact that there seems to be no quantitative equivalence between the will as moving power or cause and the effects it achieves—the will of one person can move a whole empire into action—Hemsterhuis concludes that the nature of *velléité* is contrary to all we know of the essential properties of matter and motion. Acknowledging this, he continues, the freedom of will—at this point he substitutes *volonté* for *velléité*—should no longer be as incomprehensible as it seemed (I, 104). Hemsterhuis' arguments are, as so often, not cogent at all. Diderot objected that the author of the Letter on Man approaches these problems in terms taken from the mechanics of brute, inert matter, while we deal in reality with active, sensible, organized matter.[14] Hemsterhuis does not and cannot prove that *velléité* is not a modification of organized matter. Even if *velléité* cannot be described in terms of mechanics, it does not follow that it invalidates the laws of physics or that human will is free.

As to the vexing problem of free will, Hemsterhuis suggests that one should consider the moment before a choice has been made, when there is still freedom, rather than the moment after, when the freedom of choice can no longer be shown. The wise man makes the right choice because he wants to. While there is no effect without cause, it has not been proved that every cause is effect. Human will, here called *volonté*, is, according to Hemsterhuis, a spontaneous cause exempt from the chain of causation, a position that bears some analogy to Bergson's in our century as well as to Kant's noumenal causality of freedom. Diderot categorically rejects the possibility of a break in the causal chain; man's mind is moved by ideas which cannot be evoked at will, is passive before it becomes active,[15] a tenet from which Hemsterhuis himself had started out.

Turning to a consideration of the external world, the author of the Letter on Man points out that man can manipulate things, has discovered the laws of motion, and has thus been enabled to foresee many events. But he still does not know the essence of matter, the mechanism underlying changes, or the origin of motion. Acting on matter, man perceives reaction. In gravity, inertia he sees constant action and reaction. He concludes that the universe is to be likened to a taut spring ("ressort"; I, 105 f.). In a strange mixture of Newtonian physics and Spinozistic metaphysics, Hemsterhuis defines inertia as that which makes a thing what it is, (I, 106), while attraction determines its location and relations to other things. Attraction and inertia, though apparently acting in opposite directions, are in reality manifestations of only one attractive force, either acting between the parts of a body as cohesive force, (Hemsterhuis' "inertia"), or between several bodies (attraction, gravitation). The universe would soon be reduced to amorphous unity if inertia and attraction alone prevailed. According to Hemsterhuis, there must exist another, centrifugal force (I, 109), counteracting the centripetal tendency. He had alluded to the necessity of such a power, a sort of analogue to the force of repulsion invoked by Kant, in the *Lettre sur les désirs*, where he postulated an extramundane agent causing and maintaining individuation against the universal power of attraction.[16] To be more convincing, he introduces in the Letter on Man a spurious ontological argument: since it is self-contradictory that an essence existing through itself should exhibit two opposite principles, it must be concluded that the actual universe, the result of two opposite principles, does not exist through itself. Experience shows, according to Hemsterhuis, that motion "originates" only through the *velléité* of an animated being (I, 111). Arguing by analogy, we must conclude that, even where we cannot observe the beginnings, all motion is due to the *velléité* of such a being. The manifestations of purposefulness and adaptation in nature, for example, in the animal eye, prove that the "author of the physical universe" (I, 112) is an intelligent being, infinitely superior to man in intelligence.

This is all that man could know about the Creator if his knowledge were limited to ideas derived from the sense organs alone. Man would realize that an infinity of worlds is nothing if compared with their Creator, that the infinite universe with its infinite aspects is only one thought of the Supreme Deity. The awareness of such a dreadful power would fill man with awe and make him feel his nothingness. Such obscure, sterile, depressing knowledge of God, Hemsterhuis writes, would render man the unhappiest of beings, ignorant of the attributes of the Immense Being as well as of his *rapports* with God and the duties resulting from them (I, 112 f.). The author of the Letter on Man describes here the notion of God entertained by some deists that allows no place for a uniquely personal relation to God.

Fortunately, however, Hemsterhuis seems to say, man's knowl-edge is not thus limited. While the sense organs, each in its way, furnish knowledge about the physical aspects of the universe, the heart or conscience (I, 113) discloses its moral aspect. Between the latter and the aspects of the world revealed through the sense organs there is as little incommensurability as between the infor-mations rendered by the various senses. All "faces" of the universe, to use Hemsterhuis' expression, are equally valid elements in the structure of man's world, whether reacted upon contemplatively or actively. The ideas of love, hate, envy, esteem are as clear as those of tree, star, cold, sweet, soft, etc. If there exist differences in the precision of our perceptions they are due to the varying strength and training of our organs. In our present society, for instance, the organs of vision and hearing are much better trained than all others.

Before entering upon a discussion of man in society, Hemsterhuis wants to examine more closely the organ that hitherto has not received a suitable name and that is usually designated as heart, conscience, sentiment or feeling (I, 114). A little further on in the Letter on Man, the author suggests for it the name "organe moral" (I, 124). This organ, which discloses the richest, most beautiful aspect of the universe, makes us aware of our existence, our rapport to things, while the other organs cause us to perceive the *rapports* of things to us. Diderot maintains that these two kinds of *rapports* are inseparable from each other and really identical.[17] He is, of course, right. Hemsterhuis should rather have spoken of a differing emphasis on the subjective or objective side of *rapports*. As vision and hearing depend upon light or air, the moral organ depends upon the presence of other animated beings endowed with *velléité*. It is only in society, through communication with other willing and thinking beings, that the moral organ is developed and becomes ac-tive. The latter discloses an aspect of the world to which man's soul belongs as a part. Thus his own self becomes an object of con-templation. From an awareness of man's *rapports* with things, es-pecially, however, with other moral beings, the notion of duties arises. It can be seen now that man's sense organs may lead him to an idea of a Deity, but that only the moral organ will tell him of his duties toward God.

While animals may have organs that man does not possess, they seem to lack any perception of the moral side of the universe. They also lack arbitrary signs, which play such an important role in human communication. It is in this connection that Hemsterhuis discusses language. He notes that expressive gestures, involuntarily and without being learned, accompany ideas. Such gestures and sympathetic movements (crying, contagious yawning, the compulsion to keep in step) furnished the basis for communicative signs, complemented by the association of certain articulated sounds with a certain idea, of thought with verbal action. Hemsterhuis presents a physiological model for the processes underlying language (I, 117 f.) in terms similar to those developed in Hartley's associationist psychology. The original, "natural" language which was only *one*, understood by all men, has not been preserved. Social conventions have changed and diversified it radically. "Sublime music" still gives us an intimation of the original language (I, 122), which was not onomatopoetic, as has often been asserted, but rather the result of movements in the sense organs stimulated by objects and of corresponding movements in the vocal organs. In the *Réflexions sur la République des Provinces-Unies*, written many years later, Hemsterhuis pointed out that a language is rich in proportion to the wealth of signs it possesses to express ideas and sensations clearly, which in turn depends upon the number of ideas of things and *rapports*. Linguistically, this wealth finds expression in the vocabulary as well as in the positions and relations of words. The perfection of a language consists in the energy and precision with which the most subtle nuances of ideas are rendered. It progresses with the increase of knowledge and is the most faithful mirror of the intellectual level attained by a speech community.[18]

Returning from his digression on language to the main topic of the moral organ, Hemsterhuis observes that an isolated individual would not have any idea of what is morally—and, strangely enough, physically—good, though the feeling of pain may have given him an idea of what is bad (I, 123). From the idea of good followed necessarily ideas of better and best, of goodness as the cause of good, and a notion of infinite goodness. The sense of touch results in the sensations of impenetrability, heat, the pleasing; that of hearing in those of measure, sound, harmony; through vision we perceive contour, color, beauty; through the *organe moral*—the term is introduced at this point for the first time—we obtain sensations of motive or desire, duty, virtue (I, 124). Virtue, beauty, harmony, and the pleasing ("l'agréable"; *ibid.*) are very closely related to each other, just as are vice, ugliness, dissonance, and the disagreeable. From this can be concluded either that the moral organ communicates with the sense organs or that the various faces of the universe are not as heterogeneous as they appear at first sight. The moral organ must not be confused with the intellectual faculty which forms general concepts. All men, regardless of education, have of love, hate, esteem as evident a perception as of ideas derived from the sense organs. Hemsterhuis regards this as proof that the first-mentioned ideas are also received through an organ, the *organe moral*. However, such notions as justice and prudence, for instance, do not enjoy the same status of immediate evidence, because they are modifications of the general idea (I, 125) of virtue, which results from the use of the intellectual faculty.

We note at this point a lack of clarity concerning the relation of desire, motive, virtue, designated as "sensations" resulting from the moral organ, to love, hate, esteem, etc., which are called "sensations" of the same organ (I, 114 and 125). While the relation of virtue to the moral organ poses no question once we admit the existence of such an organ, Hemsterhuis might have explained why he considers motive and desire likewise sensations resulting from the *organe moral*, since they are not *eo ipso* and indisputably moral phenomena. Objections of a similar nature could be raised concerning the ideas ascribed to the other senses. That beauty, for example, is relegated to visual perception alone cannot be justified.

The moral organ shows greater homogeneity with the essence of the soul than the sense organs. It is therefore likely that it will never be separated from the soul. From everything that has been said about the *organe moral*, Hemsterhuis concludes that the rapport of each individual with the Supreme Being or with other human beings depends upon the degree of sensibility or perfection of this organ. On its perfection depend also the duties of the individual. Since the perfection of the *organe moral* varies individually, each individual has different duties to fulfill. When Hemsterhuis speaks of duties he does not mean actions that conform to what he calls the factitious, mechanical laws of a given society (I, 130), but to acts that are in accordance with the laws of nature and the eternal order of the universe based on the coexistence of all things. There are people, it is pointed out, whose moral organ is so sensitive that they do not fit into any actual society. Brutus, who committed a crime in the eyes of society when he killed Caesar, undoubtedly thought that he acted in conformity with the eternal order of things.

These views have caused some embarrassment among the early admirers of the philosopher, who were eager to present him as a gentlemanly conformist. Actually, these views involve no sceptical denial of duty or complete relativism even when he asserts in a somewhat obscure passage that good and bad are not diametrical opposites, but rather determined by society (I, 126). On the contrary, he advances an idea of duty that is independent of varying social conventions of morality or legality and seeks to anchor it in the individual's conscience, the awareness of his *rapports* with the world. Such emphasis on the role of the person is an expression of a *Lebensgefühl*, a feeling for the value of individual life, which appealed to Herder, Jacobi, Friedrich Schlegel, and Novalis. On the other hand, Hemsterhuis' assertion that a person with the least-developed moral organ has the fewest duties to fulfill (I, 130) tends to limit personal freedom, which the philosopher otherwise tried to defend. Crime and vice, as Grucker pointed out, appear as natural effects of a feeble moral organ.[19] Duty, and with it man's moral life, is not conceived in terms of an imperative, but rather as being linked to a given individual disposition or, as Diderot would say, to the good fortune of being well-born.

Hemsterhuis concludes what he has to say at this point about the *organe moral* by asserting that man's greatest happiness lies in the growing perfection of this organ, which results in a greater enjoyment of his own self as well as in closer *rapports* with other human beings and with God. Supreme wisdom consists in making all actions or thoughts conform with the impulses of the moral organ, without bothering much about human institutions or the opinions of other people.

Besides the definition of the beautiful in the *Lettre sur la sculpture*, there is nothing that has aroused as much attention or criticism as the notion of the *organe moral*. Its description is a cardinal point of the Letter on Man. While Hemsterhuis uses at first the terms "heart," "conscience," "sentiment" (I, 113, 114) to describe what he names a little later *organe moral* (I, 124), he introduces this phenomenon from the very beginning as an analogue to the sense organs, as another organ (I, 113, 114). He is convinced that the moral organ actually exists, and claims to have demonstrated the great probability of its real existence (I, 127). It is this insistence on an "organ" for the moral side of the world that has called forth criticism even from such admirers of Hemsterhuis as Meyboom. The latter argues that there is no need to assume a specific organ to explain "moral" ideas, and asks what is meant by an "organ" that cannot be located anatomically.[20]

The discovery of Diderot's commentary on the Letter on Man sheds new light on a letter quoted in excerpts by Meyboom (III, 155 ff.). In this communication, written to Diotima in the fall of 1779, Hemsterhuis refers to critics who have either denied the existence of the *organe moral* or objected to the term *organe* as not suitable. Admitting that this word is "somewhat too much in the figurative style," he suggests a new expression, namely, "sens moral," moral sense (III, 159), but insists on the real existence of a means or medium ("moyen") that conveys sensations of the moral side of the universe. We can be sure that Hemsterhuis' letter to Diotima was written under the influence of Diderot's outspoken censure of the terminology and mode of argumentation employed in the Letter on Man. There are some passages in this section of the work that find Diderot's approval: the emphasis on the various aspects of the world disclosed through the different senses; the immediacy of the ideas of love, hate, etc., the observations on expressive and sympathetic movements.[21] But he objects to Hemsterhuis' figurative use of the word *coeur*.[22] As to the *organe moral*, Diderot asks where this "organ" is located and criticizes the figurative meaning attached to the term.[23] Both *coeur* and *organe moral* need not be assumed to explain the sensations relegated to them by Hemsterhuis; perception, recall, association, reasoning suffice for an explanation, and there is no use for an imaginary sixth sense.[24]

Undoubtedly, the expression *organe moral* was open to criticism, as Hemsterhuis himself came to admit. He used the term "organ" much too vaguely when he spoke toward the end of the Letter on Man even of the "organ of the intellect" (I, 160). He never thought, to be sure, that the moral organ could be anatomically identified, and while Diderot's insistent questioning about the location of this organ in the human body was in line with his philosophical materialism, which made him ask the same question concerning the soul, he clearly made no effort to show understanding for what Hemsterhuis really meant. The explanation for the notion of a moral organ is to be sought in the sensualistic position taken in the beginning of the Letter on Man. Starting out from the thesis that all primary ideas or sensations are derived from the *rapports* between an external object and the modifications of our sense organs, the author finds that we possess some ideas which carry with them the same degree of immediacy and clarity as the ones derived from sense perceptions, although they cannot be attributed to any one of our sense organs. Love, hate, esteem, envy are adduced as examples of such ideas, and it is important to notice that these phenomena are considered here as ideas in the Lockean sense of the word, that is, as contents of our consciousness. The ideas just mentioned relate to that aspect of our *rapports* with the world around us which has moral significance. It was for Hemsterhuis a plausible, though not logically cogent, step to trace them back to a moral organ. Using this term, he could stay within the framework of a sensualistic position concerning the nature and origin of our primary ideas and suggest that what he calls the moral face of the universe enjoys epistemologically speaking the same status and validity as those faces of the universe that are disclosed by our sense organs.

Hemsterhuis referred moral ideas to a special organ in order to maintain the independence, irreducibility, even superiority of the moral side of the world against Neo-Spinozism, radical sensualism, materialism.[25] The doctrine of the *organe moral* served approximately the same purpose as the theory of a moral sense advanced by Shaftesbury, Hutcheson, and others, namely, to assert the immediacy of moral ideas and judgments. The author of the Letter on Man might have availed himself, of course, of the term "moral sense," with which he was perhaps acquainted through Shaftesbury, Adam Smith, and Hutcheson. He may have felt, however, that the commonly accepted meaning of the expression "moral sense," which referred to inborn altruistic inclinations, was too limited for what he really meant: an awareness of the moral aspect and significance of the world around us, to which we react not only as physical but also as moral beings, in a positive or negative way. The moral organ per se does not guarantee that we act in accordance with moral norms, nor does it furnish a sanction of morality or legality, both of which are explicitly mentioned as resulting from a weakened *organe moral*. The latter's domain comprises moral and religious sentiments, conscience, duties, as well as the phenomena of sympathy and empathy. Unlike Shaftesbury or Hutcheson, Hemsterhuis makes no attempt to establish a closer link with the realm of esthetic experience. He is above all interested in the *rapports* of man with other human beings and with God. The emphasis on sentiments, sympathy, empathy indicates an awareness of the irrational factors in human experience which appealed to Herder, Jacobi, and Novalis. They did not quibble about the literal, anatomical meaning of the term *organe moral*, but understood it in the general sense of "ein Organ haben für . . . ," i.e., possessing an awareness of or a sensibility for the moral or any other aspect of the universe.

Announcing his intention to turn to a consideration of man in society, Hemsterhuis expatiates again on the moral organ, without which a sentient active being would remain isolated, as it were. By dint of the moral organ man multiplies his ego (I, 131), so that he becomes a truly social being. Let us suppose a primitive society, the author continues, in which all members are equal and endowed with a perfect moral organ. Such a society would exhibit a perfect equilibrium because every individual would be aware of the joys and sufferings of others as much as of his own. Obviously influenced by Rousseau's *Discours sur l'origine . . . de l'inégalité parmi les hommes* (1755), Hemsterhuis sees in the notion of property, the origin of harmful inequality among men. Before that notion took hold of man, he was able to satisfy all his needs easily and naturally. An individual endowed with great physical strength, but with a very imperfect moral organ, could not cause any great inequality or disorder. After the "false and ridiculous idea of property," (I, 133), of self-aggrandizement, had arisen, equality disappeared and the "mechanism of legislation" *(ibid.)* furnished the only means to prevent the total destruction of man. The *organe moral* became useless and unused after it was replaced by laws. The latter could limit evil as far as effects are concerned, but not remove its cause. Men, born free, turned into slaves of legislation, which acknowledges only the physical aspects of *rapports* while disregarding the inner well-being of the individual. If men had consciously striven to establish a society with a minimum of religion and virtues, the result would have been very much like our present society, an observation quoted with approval by Herder and Jacobi.[26] In these passages Hemsterhuis combines, like Rousseau, a penchant for a rationalistic construction of history with a tendency toward primitivism, the latter apparent in the preference given to the "natural," original *organe moral* over derivatory, "artificial" morality or legality.

The legislators saw too late that the moral organ had become atrophied. To remedy this situation to a certain extent, they made use of institutionalized religion (I, 136) or supposed revelations. In its true form religion results, as Hemsterhuis had pointed out in the *Lettre sur les désirs* (I, 63), from the *rapports* of each individual with the Supreme Being. This definition is taken up again in the Letter on Man (I, 135), but now in connection with the moral organ, which discloses our *rapports* with God according to its degree of individual perfection. Religion thus understood is entirely different from the "obscure, sterile, depressing knowledge of God" mentioned earlier in the Letter on Man (I, 113), a knowledge consisting of a purely intellectual notion of a Supreme Being. A truly personal rapport with God can only be established by means of the *organe moral*, which will also tell us about our duties toward God. First among these is the cult or worship derived from our admiration and love for the omnipresent Supreme Being. Besides, there is an obligation to place all our thoughts and desires before God as well as to conform to the eternal order as it is known to us in our conscience. Disregarding any special revelation, the cult we owe to the Supreme Being should consist only of acts of gratitude (I, 138). Concerning prayer, first rejected as absurd, then readmitted in an ambiguous deference to revelation, Hemsterhuis shows little insight into this basic religious act. He justifies prayer by its beneficent psychological effects but hints that truly enlightened persons can dispense with it. There is an indication, however, that the author of the Letter on Man had experienced himself the fervors of a quasi-mystical religious enthusiasm when he refers to the violent sensations and amazing effects on the whole person which are felt while the moral organ is actively turned toward the Supreme Being (I, 139). Since the author gives no more than this hint, we cannot decide how much of what he writes is based on genuine experience and how much of it is literary cliché, derived from Plato, Neoplatonism, and perhaps Shaftesbury.

Turning to a discussion of established cults, Hemsterhuis deems it necessary to begin with a consideration of their supposed basis, i.e., revelation. The latter, which presupposes that man is not in all respects what he should be, may disclose either an aspect of the universe not known through his organs, or *rapports* to God that relate to an unknown face of the world, or, finally, obscure truths regarding the universe we know. According to Hemsterhuis, no individual, even if laying claim to revelation or miracles, has any right to influence the faith of another person, since the *rapports* with the Supreme Being are a matter of each individual. If one wants to pass judgment on the actually existing religions, often mixed with political or legal institutions, it must be kept in mind that they do not present religion in its pure form. Illustrating his thesis, the author refers to be sure also to the disfiguration of ancient polytheism by the poets, but then takes, as so often, the opportunity to attack the barbarian Christian Middle Ages, the stupidity of the monks, and the bastardized Platonism prevailing in Christian doctrine. While it is almost impossible to obtain an idea of this religion in its original purity, it would be most absurd to judge it by the way it is practiced at present. If one could remove everything that is false in Christianity one would find that this religion comes closest to a genuine revelation. Christianity alone summons man to find individual happiness, frees him from the bonds of an artificial society in order to be himself, and makes him consider his societal duties in the light of those toward the Supreme Being. These considerations together with the fact that Christianity still furnishes the mainstay of society in Europe should suffice to render this religion at least respectable in the eyes of unbelievers.

Hemsterhuis' remarks on Christianity are followed by the general assertion that all sane and well-formed human beings have a more or less distinct sensation of the real and necessary existence of the Deity, that there exists no man who is truly an atheist. While the sensation of a Divine Being is extremely weak in the isolated individual, religion grows with the unfolding of the *organe moral* in society. Far from extolling the isolated savage, Hemsterhuis, like Rousseau, emphasizes that society is the *conditio sine qua non* of any truly human existence, but at the same time the source of many evils.

A review of the Letter on Man, often ascribed to Herder, praised the "magnificent vistas" of religion offered in this work; the critic felt that Christianity could not lose anything by Hemsterhuis' remarks.[27] Herder's Letters concerning the Study of Theology (1780—81) contained excerpts from the *Lettre sur l'homme* dealing with the corruption of religion, and the superiority of Christianity as revealed religion.[28] According to Meyboom, a pious spirit of morality and religion prevails in the Letter on Man (III, 154), although he regrets that its author writes about revelation without mentioning Christ (I, 144 f., n. 2). We are not surprised to see Diderot applauding those passages in the Letter on Man which are critical of Christianity. Everything else, however, that is said on religion comes under attack. Naturally, he questions the assertion that there are no real atheists.

It is noteworthy that Hemsterhuis approaches the subject of religion in connection with man's existence as a social being and with the *organe moral*. To the subject he contributes hardly anything original or significant, except perhaps his definition of religion, which remains a mere *aperçu*, a *fermentum cogitationis*. Most of what he has to say about religion concerns its abuses or disfigurements by a "mechanical society," in which the moral organ has become atrophied. Faith is defined in terms of purely notional assent. There is no reference to any unique historical event, nor to Christ or Moses, and Lessing's problem of reconciling historical fact with rational truth in regard to revelation does not exist for the author of the Letter on Man. As he himself emphasizes, he discusses religion as a philosopher, for whom the light of reason is the sole guide (I, 136). Indebted, no doubt, to deism, Hemsterhuis develops a concept of natural religion based on the activity of the *organe moral*.

Turning to a consideration of our present society, Hemsterhuis asserts that it evinces an extreme state of imperfection and inequality. A large part of the imperfection goes back to the discrepancy between religion, aiming at the eternal bliss of each individual, and the demands of civic virtue, concerned with the temporal welfare of society (I, 150). The most dangerous evil besetting the age he lives in, Hemsterhuis continues, is the strife between the so-called orthodox theologians and the so-called philosophers who preach irreligion and atheism with the same zeal, vanity, and ignorance as the orthodox clergymen their doctrines. The victory of the *philosophes*, who have a better chance to win by using witty ridicule, offers the prospect of future generations without religion and morals. Hemsterhuis pleads for enlightened, humane theologians on the one hand, and for philosophers, on the other hand, who do not cater to popularity by employing miserable sophisms. It may at first appear odd that he calls the strife between orthodoxy and atheism the greatest evil of his age. To be sure, the wording is strange, but if we consider the intellectual history of the entire modern era, the struggle between religion and a non- or antireligious world view is of epochal significance.

The reflections on society are followed by some further thoughts on human knowledge, a subject that already had been treated at the beginning of the Letter on Man. The faculty of communicating ideas to homogeneous beings, it is pointed out, led to language and writing. Rhythm or, as Hemsterhuis writes, *mesure* (I, 153) seems to be one of our very first, even prenatal sensations. In one brief paragraph of hardly ten lines he states that the idea of harmony was derived from the combination of sound and rhythm, and that these together with gestures led to the arts of vocal music, poetry, rhetoric, dance. These arts are older than what is commonly called "science" (I, 153). A rudimentary "knowledge" ensued. Rhythm, harmony, and melody, which had been essential features of original language, receded into the background or were lost. That the arts preceded science and that language was originally poetic in nature had been maintained long before in Vico's famous treatise on the theory of history, the *Principles of a New Science* (1725), and was asserted later by Hamann and Herder. As to the imitative arts, whose perfection depends upon a peculiar property of the soul, Hemsterhuis refers to a recent work on sculpture, without mentioning its title or that he is its author.

The total of man's knowledge is made up of ideas acquired by means of the senses plus the ideas of the *rapports* obtaining between the former ideas. If man had only ideas of the first category, i.e., of isolated objects, he would not possess real knowledge. If he had ideas of all *rapports* of all objects he would resemble God in his perfect knowledge of the universe. The perfection of human knowledge is measured by the number of primary ideas of objects multiplied by the number of ideas of *rapports*. This product varies in the course of human history. Since our mind cannot grasp all ideas together in their remotest *rapports*, the various branches of knowledge arose. On the other hand there is a tendency to overcome this separation, to apply one science to others. Democritus, Hippocrates, Plato, Archimedes made endeavors along this line, but the imperfect state of mathematics prevented them from attaining the "great truths" of modern science. Hemsterhuis refers briefly to mathematics as the only science furnishing perfect knowledge because its objects are of our own creation or construction (I, 156), so that the object and its idea are identical, a thesis advanced previously by Hobbes.

At this point Hemsterhuis turns to some reflections on the progress of human knowledge that evince a mixture of observation and speculation. They contain a typically Hemsterhuisian *aperçu*, probably the nucleus from which the discussion of human knowledge in this section of the Letter on Man started out. Man's knowledge, or rather his mind, seems to move around a point of perfection like comets around the sun, in an eccentric orbit which has likewise its aphelia and perihelia. The part of history really well known to us comprises only two perihelia with one aphelion separating them. In each perihelion an *esprit général* prevails that imparts a characteristic "color" or tinge to all cultural activities. Our perihelion is characterized by the prevalence of the "esprit de géométrie ou symétrique," while the preceding perihelion, the age of Greek culture, was dominated by an "esprit moral ou de sentiment" (I, 156). The spirit of the marvelous (I, 157) prevailed among the Egyptians and Etruscans, if we may judge by the style of their artistic productions. Under the rule of each particular *esprit général* some activities of the mind are favored while others are stunted. Astronomy, optics, mechanics, economics, that is, branches of knowledge that have been subjected successfully to mathematical treatment, find in our perihelion extremely favorable conditions for their perfection. The Greeks, on the other hand, had as clear, definite, and perfect notions of moral phenomena as we have of geometrical entities. Morals, politics, the fine arts, these tender flowers once so brilliant under the Athenian sun, wither in our arid climate, Hemsterhuis asserts in a florid prose inspired by Grecolatry.

In each perihelion one branch of knowledge ranks above all others because it is most closely related to the *esprit général* of the epoch. This particular way of knowledge is applied to the most heterogeneous phenomena, often resulting in false or too farfetched explanations. As these accumulate, the mind becomes sceptical of them, despairs of finding truth, and sinks into indolence. Thus the perihelion turns into an aphelion, an assertion which shows the purely speculative character of Hemsterhuis' pretended "explanations."

For the notion of an *esprit* that is manifested in the cultural achievements and the institutions of an age Hemsterhuis was probably indebted to Montesquieu. In the Letter on Sculpture (I, 43) the concept of an *esprit général* had been applied mainly to the visual arts to account for changes of styles. Now it was linked with newly developed ideas concerning the *organe moral* and the perihelia to form a theory of history. While the theory of alternating perihelia and aphelia excludes any assertion of a unilinear, continual progress in history, it accounts for the conviction that the Greeks had achieved perfection in their own way long before our civilization. The theory also supports the observation, emphasized before by Caylus, that the arts had gone through times of flowering and decay.[29] Furthermore, it excludes the notion that the Greeks had reached an acme of absolute pefection never attained again, so that all subsequent history was decay, a view which might have easily resulted from Hemsterhuis' tendency toward Grecolatry. The theory of perihelia presents a new way to solve the quarrel of the ancients and moderns by insisting that both are capable of reaching perfection. Any extreme doctrine of relativism that might have been evolved from the thesis of a prevailing *esprit général* peculiar to each age is avoided by holding on to a standard of perfection and to a distinction between perihelia and aphelia. Since the perfection attained in each perihelion is one-sided, no age can lay claim to absolute excellence. Far from absolutizing or glorifying the spirit of his own epoch, as many popularizers of Enlightenment were wont to do, Hemsterhuis pointed out that the rule of the *esprit géométrique* entails a neglect of the *organe moral*, of the heart and the feelings. Like Rousseau, he warned against this prevailing tendency of his age and became the spokesman of a new *Lebensgefühl*, transcending the confines of doctrinaire Enlightenment. It is an important consequence of the theory of perihelia that it allows for the prospect of an ever-growing perfection in the future, an idea Hemsterhuis took up again in his dialogue *Alexis*.

Surprisingly enough, Diderot did not object to the theory of perihelia. He even applauded some observations made in this connection.[30] In the "Letters concerning the Study of Theology" Herder quoted, obviously with approval, some passages relating to the perihelia.[31] He shared Hemsterhuis' penchant for *aperçus* and for analogies that link the physical universe with the life of man's soul. Having read Herder's excerpts from the Letter on Man, Hamann confessed that he was puzzled by the perihelia, a statement perhaps indicating his disagreement with a secularized view of history in which Christ was not even mentioned.[32] Novalis translated rather long passages concerned with Hemsterhuis' theory of history, including the notes ascribed to Dumas; while he did not make any comments, he jotted down in connection with these excerpts some reflections on the perfectibility of our present organs and the possible existence of some still undeveloped organs in man[33]

In the last few pages of the Letter on Man, Hemsterhuis sets out to sum up his findings, not without adding some new thoughts, however. Man's soul is an eternal, indestructible essence created by God. By means of bodily organs it obtains sensations or ideas of the faces of the universe which are analogous to these organs. The soul, which possesses an intuitive faculty whose activity consists of comparing sensations, is also endowed with a principle of activity, or *velléité*, that seems to be limitless, but whose intensity depends upon the capability of the organs. Without these the soul loses all sensations of the universe. Most likely, however, the soul is attached to several organs which will serve it better after being separated from the body. The moral organ as well as the "organ of the intellect" (I, 160), or the faculty to reflect and compare, adhere to the soul, which has an insatiable desire to behold rather than to know ("plutôt pour voir que pour connoître"; *ibid.*). Being made to contemplate rather than to know, it seems likely that the soul will pass all of eternity in the contemplation of the infinite faces of the universe.

This upsurge of quasi-mystic speculation, indebted to the heritage of Neoplatonism, provoked Diderot's opposition. Novalis, on the other hand, was fascinated just by this divinatory facet of Hemsterhuisian philosophy, which agreed with his own thought and longings as well as his penchant for attaining the suprasensual through the senses. When the author of the Letter on Man claims that man is not made to know, a thesis rejected by Diderot, he means that man will never fathom the essence of things, of God, and of the world, a knowledge his French critic deemed chimerical or useless. Jacobi and the members of the Münster circle gathered around Princess Gallitzin agreed, however, with their friend that it is man's vocation to behold, which implied for them a confirmation either of a philosophy of faith *(Glaubensphilosophie)* or of the joys expected from an afterlife spent in the contemplation of God.

The soul, Hemsterhuis continues, bears heaven or hell in itself. We are reminded here of the famous lines from Milton's *Paradise Lost:* "The mind is its own place, and in it self / Can make a Heav'n of Hell, a Hell of Heav'n" (I, 254 f.). Actually, the author of the Letter on Man merely denies that heaven and hell are physically existing places of reward or punishment meted out by the Deity: The role of judge is assumed by the moral organ. Paradise or inferno are necessary consequences of an individual's constitution. While legislators will punish or reward, God does not try to correct the universe by such acts. We can speak of crimes only with reference to a given society. Before God there are neither crimes nor vices. Hemsterhuis expressed this conviction repeatedly and acted accordingly when his official duties required him to pass judgment on offenders of the law. No denial of human freedom is implied, however; on the contrary, the existence of active and free beings is explicitly affirmed as constituting the life of the universe. Although their freedom is limited, since only a finite number of *rapports* can be realized by each of them, no fatalististic consequences should be inferred. While *sub specie aeternitatis et universi* virtue and vice do not exist, it matters infinitely whether an individual's activity is directed toward the Supreme Being and the order he knows through his conscience, or whether he takes an opposite direction. A person called "virtuous" is in harmony with the laws governing the coexistence of things and therefore happier and more perfect. Man would not have succumbed to vice and crime if he had not tried to aggrandize his physical being, thereby neglecting the moral organ. One might answer that then the arts and sciences would not have arisen, nor the prodigious number of ideas they called forth. "This I admit," Hemsterhuis writes, but then asks whether man might not have made as many discoveries relating to the moral face of the universe or the *rapports* with the Supreme Being as he has actually made concerning the sensory aspects of the world.

Adumbrating a change in the manner of presentation, the passage just discussed (I, 163) approaches the form of a dialogue, in which Hemsterhuis answers in the first person objections that could be raised against his tenets. His view is similar to the one expressed by Rousseau in his First Discourse. Arts and sciences have grown at the expense of the cultivation of the *organe moral*. The former led to man's constantly enlarged domination over the physical world, while moral and spiritual values were neglected. Diderot, who objected to this Rousseauistic antithesis, maintained that the moral sense had reached in his times a perfection formerly unknown.

Having criticized the smug self-complacency with which some Enlighteners gloried in the achievements of civilization, Hemsterhuis concludes the Letter on Man with an inspired, quasi-mystical flight of speculation about the prospect of transcending the limitations of our earth-bound senses. In the feeble light of dawn, he writes, we hardly perceive the things around us, which the sun will soon unveil. After the twilight of our life the moral organ will perhaps be more powerful, since the "organs of the heart and conscience" (I, 164) cannot unfold beneath the coarse encrustation of the body. They are the still shapeless wings hidden below the integument of the chrysalis. Hemsterhuis resumes here an image that he had used before in the Letter on Man when he spoke of the caterpillar's unawareness of its future beauty and happiness as a butterfly (I, 99). He designed a signet for Diotima, showing a butterfly just emerging from the shell of the chrysalis and the inscription "Sume Psyche immortalis esto" ("Take courage, soul, be immortal!").[34]

At the end of the Letter on Man its author turns almost completely away from the sensualistic position he seemed to have adopted at the beginning of the work. He enters into speculations concerning the possibility of obtaining after death a knowledge of yet undisclosed facets of the universe through hitherto unknown or undeveloped "organs." The *organe moral* furnishes during our present existence on earth an example of an incorporeal "organ," disclosing suprasensual, spiritual aspects of the universe. Locke's emphasis on the role of the senses for human knowledge as well as subsequent sensualistic tendencies in epistemology had led to a widespread in-

terest in the contributions of the various senses to the form and content of our knowledge. Diderot's *Lettre sur les aveugles* (1749)
testified to this interest. It was only natural to proceed to
speculations about the possible existence of more than the five
known senses as well as about the effects such additional "senses"
would have on our world view.[35] Influenced perhaps by the ideas
the Genevan philosopher Charles Bonnet had enounced concerning
palingenesis and a concomitant widening of our knowledge after
death by newly acquired senses, Hemsterhuis insinuated rather
than affirmed an increase of knowledge along new lines after death.
While he shares the idea of progress with the Enlighteners, he gives
to it an otherworldly bent by applying it to the individual's existence after death. This appealed to some members of the Münster
circle as well as some early Dutch admirers of Hemsterhuis, who
were eager to harmonize his philosophy with Christian doctrine.
Novalis was attracted by the prophetic enthusiasm with which
Hemsterhuis expressed his hopes for a future unlimited increase of
man's divinatory knowledge.

We have seen that the Letter on Man was reviewed soon after its
publication. Although Diderot refers to a negative reception among
Parisian critics,[36] the one review known to us, in the *Journal Encyclopédique*, September, 1772, offered a summary of the main
points discussed without raising fundamental objections. The
anonymous reviewer criticized the unknown author for the lack of
elegance in style and concluded his critique with the remark that
some ideas were more striking for their novelty than convincing. A
review in the *Frankfurter Gelehrte Anzeigen* (November, 1772)
often ascribed to Herder was full of praise for the work and its
author, who was mentioned by name. The review contained a suc-
cinct summary of the Letter, showing a sure grasp of its essential
ideas and singling out passages which had a special appeal for the
reviewer. While Herder's planned translation of the Letter never
appeared in print, excerpts from it were incorporated into the
"Letters concerning the Study of Theology," surely a sign of approval. The beginning of Herder's essay *Vom Erkennen und Emp-
finden der menschlichen Seele* (1778) is not, as has been claimed,[37]
a résumé of Hemsterhuisian theories. Its earlier versions contain,
however, brief sentences or phrases definitely borrowed from the
Lettre sur les désirs as well as the *Lettre sur l'homme*.

Diderot's critical notes, written most likely in 1773—74, shed above all additional light on Diderot's thought. Although never used by Hemsterhuis, not even in his "Elucidations," they are also of great interest to anyone concerned with the author of the Letter on Man. They reveal the personal relations that existed between the two thinkers, show the points on which both agree as contemporaries in the Age of Enlightenment, but also their radical differences. Diderot represents exactly that tendency toward atheistic materialism which Hemsterhuis intended to combat in nearly all his writings. The former's assertions and critical observations elucidate by contrast the tenets held by the Dutch thinker. The latter denies that motion and sensibility inhere in matter, and therefore postulates an immaterial principle. For Diderot matter in motion is an indivisible datum. Sensibility, he says in agreement with speculations in Le Rêve de D'Alembert, is very likely a general property of matter. Hemsterhuis, it is correctly pointed out, talks only of inert, brute matter, neglecting its capability for organization in living beings.[38] Diderot questions the existence of the soul as an immaterial essence or substance, the cornerstone of Hemsterhuis' Platonizing philosophy. Other basic tenets of the latter's thought, such as freedom of the will, velléité, God, are either denied or rejected as superfluous hypotheses by the French thinker, who also engages in a spirited defense of atheists[39] against the reproach of immorality raised in the Letter on Man. It is deplored that the author of this work has deviated from the sensualistic position he apparently took up in the beginning of the work. When Diderot criticizes obscurities of style that have marred the Letter in the eyes of some Parisian thinkers, he actually registers discontent with the speculative bent of Hemsterhuis' thinking, the frequently manifest "effervescence of the imagination," and the tendency to indulge in a Platonizing jargon.[40] In his envoi Diderot acknowledges, however, that reading the Letter on Man has given him great pleasure and congratulates the author on his new and beautiful ideas.[41] Even so, Diderot thinks, the Dutch philosopher is another example of those who are forced by intolerance to dress their philosophy in the garb of a harlequin, a statement that refers to certain reticences and inconsistencies in the discussion of Christianity in the Lettre sur l'homme.

in this connection Hemsterhuis' remarks on Le Rêve de

D'Alembert are of some interest. Having received from Prince Gallitzin a manuscript of this work, never published during Diderot's life, he wrote immediately to the Princess about his impressions.[42] The dialogues, he maintains, preach philosophical materialism with all the persuasive power of an eloquent man, who has finesse, a profound knowledge of the human heart, but who is at the same time a pitiful psychologist, a superficial metaphysician, lacking entirely the *esprit géométrique* and with it sure tact. The *Rêve de D'Alembert*, evincing a shocking lack of taste together with traits of genius, is the most pernicious piece of writing among ancients or moderns. In another letter, written earlier in the same year (1784), Hemsterhuis admits, however, that he has learned much from Diderot, a "great mind" ("un grand esprit") quite unlike Voltaire.[43]

Novalis' excerpts from the Letter on Man deal with the perfection of the mind in proportion to the number of coexistent ideas it can grasp, with the gradations of mental power, with signs and language, as well as with the theory of perihelia. The poet also jots down that the soul's destination is to behold, and not to know. But of the greatest importance for him is what he calls the theory of the moral organ.[44] He interprets the latter as being not only a sense for moral distinctions, but also, herein agreeing with Hemsterhuis, an organ which discloses the spiritual aspects of the universe. He underscores the prophetic, divinatory character and function of the moral organ, which furnishes a prototype of future, new organs to be developed by the individual after death or by mankind in an infinite progress of knowledge that will reveal more and more of a noumenal world only dimly adumbrated at present.

As Hemsterhuis wrote to Diotima, the *Lettre sur l'homme et ses rapports* contains basically all he knows and all the great truths of which he is thoroughly convinced.[45] Many of the themes which he was to treat in more detail in his later writings are touched upon in the Letter on Man, his most significant, though by no means most impeccable, work. Its form is marred by the fact that too many heterogeneous themes are crowded into the compass of the Letter without any consistent principle of arrangement and with too many digressions from the main thread of argumentation. This lack of form betokens a limitation of Hemsterhuis' thought, an inability to develop *aperçus* or *fermenta cognitionis* into sustained efforts of conceptualization. More specifically, the Letter on Man, the first and perhaps most ambitious attempt of its author to present his philosophical views, shows an unresolved conflict between the sensualistic assumptions made at the beginning and subsequent metaphysical arguments in favor of an immaterial soul, its immortality, and free will. As Brummel has pointed out, the Letter on Man reveals more than any other work the transitional character of Hemsterhuis' thought, here still deeply indebted to leading ideas of the Enlightenment, but at the same time trying to express a new *Lebensgefühl*.

CHAPTER 6

Some Minor Works

T HIS chapter will deal with five opuscules, written after the completion of the *Lettre sur l'homme*. Differing widely in content as well as form, they comprise a eulogy of Hemsterhuis' friend François Fagel, a letter on the subject of atheism, a fragment of a treatise on the Republic of the Netherlands, a draft of recommendations to the State Council of the Republic, and an unfinished dialogue concerned with the choice of a military career by a young man. Of these works, only the eulogy and the letter on atheism were finished for publication during Hemsterhuis' life, whereas the others did not appear in print until long after the philosopher's death. The dialogue is discussed together with the minor works because its briefness does not warrant treatment in a special chapter. Regardless of strict chronological considerations, the two finished works will be taken up first, then the political treatises, and last the dialogue.

I *In Praise of a Gentleman-Virtuoso*

Soon after the death of François Fagel in 1773, Hemsterhuis wrote the *Description philosophique du caractère de feu M. F. Fagel*, commemorating his younger friend, and in some respects even his disciple, for whom he had written the *Lettre sur l'homme*. This eulogy, which was translated into Dutch at least twice (III, 125 f.), seems at first glance to be of a purely personal concern. But the very title, *Description philosophique* . . . , hints at a wider significance of this opuscule.

Though by no means superficial in the study of the sciences and humanities, Fagel never aimed at becoming a specialist. His ideal was rather one of versatility and universality as much as these were consistent with a predominant concern for man and with the formation of a many-sided, well-balanced, strong personality. Such a goal could only be attained by the happy few who had the means and leisure for a thorough, nonprofessional education. The latter was neither meant to prepare for a successful career as a courtier, nor did it aim at a merely esthetic self-perfection. Fagel exemplified for Hemsterhuis a tradition that reaches from the *uomo universale* of the Italian Renaissance, the ideal scholar of the Humanists, to Shaftesbury's *virtuoso* and the various forms the ideal of a perfect gentleman assumed in Europe after the Renaissance.

II   *The Letter on Atheism*

In this brief treatise, probably the last one written for the Princess and known as *Lettre de Dioclès à Diotime sur l'athéisme*, Hemsterhuis reverts to the epistolary form used by him in the beginning of his literary career. Diocles and Diotima, familiar to us as personae in several of his dialogues, appear in the title of this work, which in its present form, as Brummel has shown in detail,[1] is a considerably changed version of an essay on atheism contained in a letter actually sent by Diocles-Hemsterhuis to his Diotima on September 7, 1787.

The treatise, henceforth referred to as Letter on Atheism, was apparently intended to fulfill a promise to write on religion. At the same time it was to be an answer to Jacobi's insistent inquiries about Hemsterhuis' attitude toward Spinoza. Somewhat perturbed by Lessing's opinion that *Aristée* was a document of manifest Spinozism, Jacobi had asked Hemsterhuis as early as 1784 to clarify his position on this philosophy, but had received only an evasive answer. When Jacobi prepared a new edition of his book on Spinoza, he thought of the Letter on Atheism and asked for permission to publish it. In a letter to Diotima of December 8, 1788, he indicated that he would welcome more detail on the third form of atheism. Hemsterhuis, who admitted that the Letter was hastily written, emphasized that he would not like to be drawn into the controversies about Spinoza[2] then taking place among German intellectuals. After parts of the Letter had been rewritten, a revised copy was sent to Münster in February, 1789, of which Jacobi published a German translation in the second edition (1789) of his book on Spinoza as "Beylage II. Diokles an Diotime [*sic*] über den Atheismus." Jansen, who printed the French text in 1792, acknowledged that he had obtained the Letter from Jacobi.

Very likely, neither the Princess nor Jacobi was entirely satisfied. For Diotima, who had already rejoined the Catholic Church, the Letter on Atheism came too late; besides, little was said about the positive role of religion proper, and nothing about a specifically Christian life, based on biblical revelation. Jacobi, who had hoped to find in Hemsterhuis an ally against Spinozism, could hardly claim that the Letter, in which Spinoza was not even mentioned by name, supported his cause. But Jacobi was glad to see atheism refuted and praised the Letter as an excellent tableau of the whole history of philosophy, executed with a few strokes by the mind and hand of a master.[3]

The Letter on Atheism is actually a very sketchy, highly subjective, schematic survey of the history of atheism in occidental thought. History teaches, we read, that religion and worship, both based on human nature, preceded atheism, the result of derivative reflection. Adhering to the notion of a natural religion as it was advanced by Herbert of Cherbury, Grotius, and the deists, Hemsterhuis rejects some theories current in his time which asserted that fear or the cult of the dead is the source of religion. It was rather the magnificent spectacle of the firmament and other natural phenomena that caused wonderment which, joined with the idea of number and greatness, led man to the adoration of a vastly superior Being and a feeling of dependency (II, 203). This vague emotion eventually crystallized into the notion of "God." As moral ideas developed, they were connected with the Deity, but also gave rise to anthropomorphic polytheism. Rather surprisingly, Hemsterhuis states that he will not speak about the contribution of the "moral organ" to our knowledge of the Deity, as he had done before in the *Lettre sur l'homme* and *Aristée*. He now admits that this phenomenon has been little analyzed; even its very existence has been questioned.

Reviewing the history of atheism, Hemsterhuis points out that its first form, expounded by the Greek atomists and the product of rudimental enlightenment, soon gave way to Socrates' serious contemplation of the moral world. The second form of atheism, based on an incredulity, often reasonable, which easily degenerates into indifference, can be healed by true philosophy (II, 209). According to Hemsterhuis, the materialistic atheism of his own time, the "gigantic son of our foolish pride" *(ibid.)*, will only be overcome when one realizes the incontestable truth that "matter" ("matière") is a term that designates essences inasmuch as we are in rapport with them through the medium of our sense organs. If these would change or increase in number, entirely unsuspected attributes of matter would be disclosed.

In view of Hemsterhuis' supposed indebtedness to Spinoza, suspected by Lessing and recently asserted by Vernière,[4] it is significant that Spinoza's putative "atheism" is only obliquely referred to and criticized in the Letter. Its author directs his main attack against the French materialists, who in his eyes represent the most consistent, virulent, and disconcerting type of atheism. If he was aware of the link that exists according to Vernière between Spinoza and the French materialists, Hemsterhuis did not explicitly refer to it.

Many of the ideas and attitudes expressed in the Letter on Atheism were widely current in European Enlightenment: for example, the sketch of a "natural history" of religion, the hypothesis of a primitive monotheistic deism preceding polytheism, religion as an instrument of state- or priestcraft, the praise of God as Supreme Legislator, the negative stance toward the Middle Ages. It was certainly not for these ideas that Hemsterhuis was so highly esteemed by the Princess, Jacobi, or some German romanticists. What attracted them was his opposition to a dogmatic, materialistic atheism. To refute this philosophy, he made use of a concept of "matter" that he had elaborated previously and according to which this idea is a function of the advance in our cognitive faculties. "Matter" is forever more than we know of it at any given time. This concept of "matter" was employed to oppose a dogmatic *Weltanschauung* that claimed to have solved the riddles of the universe by reducing them to "matter in motion." To the Princess and Jacobi the Letter furnished a rather satisfactory refutation of atheistic materialism. Strangely enough, Novalis' notes on the Letter contain no reference to a connection of Hemsterhuis' ideas on "matter" with Kant's *Ding an sich* or Fichte's infinite process of cognition.[5]

The undogmatic character of Hemsterhuis' philosophy found expression at the end of the Letter on Atheism in the words addressed to Diotima, who had by that time become a Catholic again: "Que le seul Dieu nous bénisse avec tout ce qui nous est cher" (II, 210). This wish to be blessed by God implied that although Diotima and her Socrates had adopted different creeds here on earth, they were still united in their love of the one God they worshipped.

III   *Two Political Treatises*

A number of Hemsterhuis' writings, above all the dialogue *Alexis II*, deal with man as a *zoon politikon*, but only two works treat explicitly political themes. Both were published long after the philosopher's death by Halbertsma.[6]. One of these, the *Ebauché* [sic] *d'un avis du conseil d'état* (henceforth cited as *Avis*), is a draft of a counsel concerning the government of the seven provinces composing the Netherlands and drawn up in connection with Hemsterhuis' official position in the State Council. The other work, the *Réflexions sur la République des Provinces Unies*, was written for and dedicated to Princess Gallitzin and Franz von Fürstenberg, "couple sage et illustre." Of the two works, both evincing Hemsterhuis' concern with his own country, only the *Avis* was finished. The *Réflexions*, intended, as he wrote to Diotima on December 11, 1780 (III, 100), to be an outline of a "philosophical" history of the Dutch Republic, remained a fragment.

The *Réflexions* never got beyond general speculations about the origins of human society — a theme treated by Vico, Rousseau, Kant, Herder, as well as many other thinkers of the eighteenth century — and a discussion of the ways in which social groups acquire a distinct character. According to Hemsterhuis, it was not the sex drive or the care for infants and the aged that induced man to live in society but rather a moral principle, peculiar to man, by dint of which he shares the joys and sufferings of his fellow creatures. Hemsterhuis adds to this assertion, which reminds us of the role assigned to the moral sense by Shaftesbury and Hutcheson, a pronouncedly Platonic tinge: the moral principle shows that man is only a sort of migratory bird on earth, an essence linked temporarily to a specific modification of matter. The author of the *Réflexions* is aware of the fact that the "moral organ" is neither manifest in isolated individuals nor in groups as such, the latter being merely "robust animals."[7] Inequalities in natural endowments led to differentiations within groups and with it to ambition, the source of many evils but also an indication of man's greatness. Powerful, ambitious individuals and legislators shaped groups into states. According to Hemsterhuis, there are only two basic types of government: republican or monarchical. Republics further the well-being of the individual, monarchies, that of the state. Like Montesquieu, the author of the *Réflexions* correlates forms of government with patterns of thinking and linguistic expression. Although he refers to the state as "the greatest and boldest product of man,"[8] his attitude toward it is predominantly negative. States, lacking any "moral organ," are mere "animals," whose relations are described in Hobbesian terms.[9] A perfect society, made up of individuals linked by no other bond than the "moral organ" and the "golden chain" forged out of their essences by God, would not need political organizations.

The last sentence of the *Réflexions* asserts that the history of the Netherlands became of interest to philosophers at the moment when the yoke of tyranny was shaken off and the Dutch Republic with its unique form of government came into being. The *Avis* contains some specific proposals on how to preserve and further it.

IV   *Alexis II, or on the Military*

Hemsterhuis' dialogue *Alexis ou du militaire* was published for the first time in 1924 by Émile Boulan. Its manuscript had been acquired by the Library at Leiden in 1866, too late for inclusion in Meyboom's edition. Hamann reported during his stay in Münster (1788) that he had read in manuscript "Alexis II du Militaire."[10] Diotima, who considered for a while a military career for her son, had asked her Socrates to write on the "esprit militaire." He obliged immediately and sent parts of the work to her in February and May, 1783. As she became preoccupied with other things, Hemsterhuis' interest in this work also slackened and it remained a fragment. Although lacking the wealth of ideas of Hemsterhuis' other dialogues, *Alexis II* has the Athenian *couleur locale*, the graceful conversational tone and simple diction that characterize his later works.

In the scheme of history the philosopher had expounded in *Alexis*, the "military spirit" belonged to the "iron age." It was natural, then, to discuss the military and war in a sequence to that dialogue. The interlocutors are again Diocles and Alexis. *Alexis II*, which ends somewhat abruptly with Diocles' assertion that divine Justice is the daughter of Jupiter and Love, is certainly not intended to inspire enthusiasm for war or to serve as a manual for a young man contemplating a military career. A motto from Theocritus, which precedes the dialogue, expresses the hope that the very word "war" may disappear and that cobwebs will cover all arms. What Hemsterhuis aimed at was to dispel a notion of "false glory" and impart an idea of "divine justice." War and its concomitant, the "esprit militaire," as well as so-called justice, whose purpose is to maintain an existing social order, belong to mankind after it has fallen away from a "golden age" of harmony and love. Both Alexis-dialogues end with a tribute to the power of Love as it is manifested throughout the universe: in the earlier dialogue, Alexis vows to sacrifice in the temple of Love; in *Alexis II* Diocles reveals Love as the source of Justice. This indicates that, although unfinished, the latter dialogue had conveyed its main message.

A letter written to the Princess on May 2, 1785, contains remarks on love for one's fatherland that show some connection with *Alexis II*.[11] Hemsterhuis' attitude toward patriotism is ambiguous. Faulty education engenders an exclusive affection for one country, for a mere "modification of artificial society," and fills a child's mind with such words as "foreigners," "enemies," and the like. Hemsterhuis proposes an instruction that would banish the word "fatherland," and teach universal instead of national history, a proposal the Princess followed in the education of her children. But the philosopher also confesses that he is a Frisian, filled with love for his people and pride in their glorious past. The outcry about the "maladie mortelle" of his country, at the beginning of the letter, shows Hemsterhuis' genuine patriotic concern. Love for one's country, as it is manifested in its true heroes, such as Miltiades or Themistocles, seems to be no more than love of justice and defense of the oppressed. Only this kind of patriotism can be justified before the forum of reason. Hemsterhuis indicates to the Princess that these remarks are not to be taken as the investigation of the "Amour de la Patrie" which he had planned to write for her. The emphasis on love of justice forms the connecting link between the letter of May 2, 1785, and *Alexis II*. It is not unlikely that the discussion of the "esprit militaire" would have gone on to a consideration of patriotism.

Hamann, who read, as we mentioned above, a manuscript of

Alexis II, wrote to Jacobi on May 16, 1788, that this dialogue made him aware of the radical difference between himself, the "hyperborean Socrates," and the "Socrates from The Hague." The letter consists of quotes from *Alexis II* and somewhat obscure but definitely sarcastic comments, directed against the style and content of the dialogue.[12] The inveterate opponent of Enlightenment saw in Diotima's Socrates only another representative of it.

CHAPTER 7

Sophylus, or on Philosophy

S IX years after the publication of the *Lettre sur l'homme et ses rapports*, Hemsterhuis returned to the subject of philosophy in *Sophyle ou de la philosophie* (1778), this time using dialogue, a literary form that had been adumbrated in a passage near the end of the Letter on Man. During the years intervening between the two publications, important events had taken place in the philosopher's life. He had lost his young friend François Fagel. Around the time of his death, or shortly after, he had met Princess Gallitzin, who soon became his friend, disciple, and even symphilosopher, to whom he directed his further writings. In a letter to her he acknowledged that *Sophyle* as well as *Aristée ou de la divinité* (1779) would not have been written without her encouragement or help.[1] As Brummel points out, these two dialogues were at first perhaps planned as one work; this conjecture is supported by the fact that Cornelis Ploos van Amstel published, without ever mentioning the philosopher's name, translations or adaptations in Dutch of the *Lettre sur l'homme* and *Sophyle*, the latter bearing the title "Aristeus."[2] Boulan found that the "Traité sur l'immatériel," listed by Princess Gallitzin as one of the writings bequeathed to her by her friend, was incorporated into the final section of *Sophyle*. Soon after Boulan's discovery Brummel identified the later parts of the "Éclaircissements" to the Letter on Man with the above-mentioned "Traité" and a sequel to it.[3]

Most likely, the Princess had more influence on the form than the actual content of *Sophyle* and the writings which were to follow.[4] She shared with her "Socrates," who soon started calling her "Diotima," an admiration for Plato's dialogues, which induced Hemsterhuis to cultivate from then on the more lively, colorful form of dialogue instead of writing learned treatises, somewhat ineptly entitled "Letters," which dealt with their subjects in a staid, often scholastic manner. Portions of *Sophyle,* to be sure, are still written in this style. They contain chains of argumentation, with the individual steps numbered consecutively (I, 187 f., 194 f.), a procedure befitting a treatise, but hardly appropriate in a dialogue.

While the *Lettre sur l'homme et ses rapports* is of greater length and treats a larger variety of themes than any other of Hemsterhuis' writings, *Sophyle* is the shortest of his published dialogues. Both works are intended to give accounts of their author's philosophy. In the Letter on Man this is accomplished by dealing extensively and somewhat diffusely with man and his relations to the world in which he lives, whereas *Sophyle* concentrates on some basic tenets and discusses a number of problems touched upon in the *Lettre sur l'homme.* Some of the arguments advanced in the last-mentioned work are almost literally reproduced.

Sophylus, whose name appears in the title of the dialogue, defends a materialistic, sensualistic world view against Eutyphron, the author's spokesman, who assumes the role of convincing his opponent that the latter's views are indefensible. The conversation starts *in medias res* with Sophylus praising philosophy for freeing man from prejudices and pointing out the limitations of his knowledge. When Eutyphron adds that philosophy also discloses new, hitherto unknown aspects of the world, his adversary insists that experience must remain the base of all philosophy. Eutyphron agrees, but asserts that there are many different modes of experience, some of them transcending the knowledge obtained through the five senses, which are for Sophylus, on the other hand, the only source of all cognition. Such a position, Eutyphron admits, had formerly been also his own. He tries to support his claim that we can obtain knowledge that is independent of our sense organs by referring to a spider throwing its web unhinderedly even across a stream. Sophylus objects, however, to the use of poetic similes or fables by a philosopher. Besides, all the books he has read insist that matter in motion is the sole and ultimate, eternal reality.

Eutyphron admonishes him to leave aside all books and turn to the study of man, which together with the use of *bon sens* will lead to a sound philosophy. Expressing a sceptical distrust of "systems," which are nothing but gratuitous, unwarranted combinations of often merely supposed truths, Eutyphron maintains that there are

only two philosophies that convey truth in an unbastardized form:
the Socratic and Newtonian. The latter is not really a system, but
merely a branch of philosophy, dealing with mechanics insofar as it
is amenable to pure geometry (I, 172). It should be remembered
that Newton's main work bore the title *Philosophiae naturalis prin-
cipia mathematica* (1687) and that during the eighteenth century
the term "natural philosophy" was used with reference to physics as
well as chemistry. Turning to Socrates, Eutyphron asserts that the
Athenian alone, who made us believe that man resembles God, gave
us a true and full idea of philosophy instead of preaching a narrow,
subjectively biased "system." He taught that philosophy, far from
being the daughter of wit ("esprit") or imagination, dwells in every
sane head and upright heart and that it is the source of universal,
lasting happiness. While there were many authors besides
Hemsterhuis who used Greek names for the interlocutors in supposedly "Platonic" dialogues whose thought was thoroughly
modern, the author of *Sophyle* heightened the contrast between
Greek costume and post-Cartesian content by his explicit juxtaposi-
tion of Socrates and Newton as exemplary thinkers. Neither of the
two had been accorded such an eminent place in Hemsterhuis'
previous writings.

Eutyphron's philosophy is, as he says, that of Socrates and of
children, a philosophy which could be found in the depth of our
heart and soul if we would take the trouble to look for it there. The
emphasis is plainly on the needs of the heart. Although Eutyphron-
Hemsterhuis maintains that he prefers truth above all, he confesses
that he would be saddened if the pursuit of knowledge led to the insight that there is no afterlife (I, 171).

At this point, Sophylus is eager to know more about a philosophy
so different from the one he is familiar with. Eutyphron, of course,
obliges. Everything that is passive, he begins, *is;* I perceive, have
sensations; that is, I am passive; therefore I am ("Tout ce qui est
passif, est: je sens; ainsi je suis passif: par conséquent je suis"; I,
173). If I tell you, "I am," and you *are* ("si vous êtes"; *ibid.*) and
believe me, Eutyphron continues addressing Sophylus, I am convinced that you believe the truth; consequently, if you tell me that
you *are*, I believe you and have the same conviction of believing a
truth. Having established the existence of one "thou," I can assure
myself in the same way of the existence of other "thous," and then

of things outside myself. Hemsterhuis offers here a dubious analogue to the Cartesian *cogito (ergo) sum*. Like Descartes, he proceeds from the evidence of "I am" to a "proof" of the reality of other beings and things. Not content, however, with the immediate evidence of *sentio (ergo) sum*, "I feel, I am," he tries to deduce this proposition from a more general one. But "everything that is passive *is*," must be considered a completely arbitrary assertion. What Hemsterhuis had in mind most likely was that we become aware of our existence while passively receiving sense perceptions. This psychological interpretation, however, does not remove the element of arbitrariness. There is no reason for not substituting "I will," "I act," etc., for "I perceive" and then conclude "I am." Hemsterhuis got entangled in difficulties when he tried to improve on the evidence of the Cartesian *cogito sum*, which embraces, if the *cogito* is understood to mean "I am aware (conscious)," such variations as "I am aware I feel, I am," etc. It is characteristic for Hemsterhuis, nevertheless, that he replaced the Cartesian *cogito* by "je sens," a fact that indicates, as Brummel points out,[5] a shift toward an irrational feeling of existence, a *Daseinsgefühl*.

Sophylus is amazed that Eutyphron deems it necessary to prove his own existence as well as that of things outside the self. But Eutyphron insists that nothing should be taken for granted without proof, and enters into a discussion of the question of how we know that objects exist outside ourselves. The idea or sensation we have of an object by means of the senses, he says, is the result of the *rapports* between the object, our sense organs, and the intervening medium. Assuming and maintaining that the subject, the organs, and the medium remain constant while the ideas change when we turn from one object to another, Hemsterhuis asserts that the cause for the difference between the ideas must be in the objects. That is, the object is the cause of the idea we have of it. The differences perceived between the ideas of a cube and a cone, for example, are due to diversities in the essences of the objects, since the other factors intervening between subject and object remain the same. Our ideas of objects correspond to real objects outside of us. The *rapports* between our ideas are analogous to the *rapports* between their corresponding objects. Our senses do not deceive us about the order of things.

Eutyphron introduces at this point of the dialogue the term

"essence" for that entity or reality which corresponds and gives rise to our ideas of beings and things. Any essence may possess a large number of "modes of being" ("manières d'être"; I, 175) unknown to us. Hemsterhuis had referred to the "manières d'être" of an object in the *Lettre sur l'homme* (I, 82) and pointed out that among all these there may be one "manière d'être" of which we have an idea through our sense organs. Eutyphron maintains that things are to a certain degree really what they appear to be (I, 176). In other words: their appearance is a mode of being of their essence, and our ideas of objects correspond to real aspects of them. To support this view, Eutyphron asserts that a watchmaker could not construct a watch unless his ideas conform to real aspects of things as well as to the *rapports* existing between them.

When Sophylus ventures the opinion that our ideas allow us to draw reliable inferences concerning the essence of things, he is told that he is going too far. To illustrate his own view, Eutyphron-Hemsterhuis refers to a block of marble covered with inscriptions in several languages. Only those who master all these idioms will understand all messages. Others will comprehend merely a part or none of them. Only those aspects of an essence for which we have an organ are grasped by us and enter into our idea of the essence. This expression applies first of all to our actual anatomically identifiable sense organs. Beyond that it may be understood in the general sense of "ein Organ haben für," i.e., an awareness of any other, nonsensory aspects of the universe. An essence may have, as Eutyphron says, a hundred thousand aspects (I, 180), while only three or four of them are perceived by us. The conclusions we can draw from our ideas as to the essence of things are limited to that part or "face" of them which can act on our organs.

It has become clear why Hemsterhuis introduces the term "essence." He does so to indicate that reality is inexhaustible and much more than can ever be known about it. Being or essence has an infinite number of attributes or aspects of which man knows only an infinitesimal portion. "Matter," as the term is usually understood, designates merely those aspects of Being or essence which are disclosed by our sense organs, and can therefore not be considered synonymous with all of reality, as a naïve form of dogmatic materialism asserts. It is this materialistic concept of matter which Hemsterhuis attacks. While he has no quarrel with those scientists or philosophers who emphasize that matter may possess more properties than are or can be known by us, he chooses to speak of "essence" rather than "matter" because of his own metaphysical position, his conviction that reality has an immaterial side which is at least as "real" as so-called matter. For similar reasons he uses the term "essence" instead of "object" or "thing," since the last-mentioned concepts, as they are usually interpreted, are too circumscribed to allow for an infinite number of possible attributes.

Sophylus still wants a proof that immaterial essences really exist. In addition he would like to know how we can have an idea of them and how they can act on an essence which is disclosed to us through sense perception.

As one proof of the existence of immaterial essences, Eutyphron adduces the fact that a European prince can direct a battle in faraway India by means of an oral or written order. If everything were nothing but matter, one could not understand, it is argued, how a mere word or piece of paper could set in motion such masses and forces as are involved in this chain of events. Hemsterhuis had used a similar argument before, in the Letter on Man (I, 103), to prove that the effects of *velléité* cannot be described in terms of mechanics because there exists no quantitative equivalence of cause and effect. For further proofs of the existence of an immaterial essence, Eutyphron refers to the "discourse of our friend" (I, 187), i.e., those passages in the *Lettre sur l'homme* (I, 92 f.) in which Hemsterhuis had demonstrated the heterogeneity of body and soul. Since the arguments are almost literally repeated in *Sophyle*, the single exception being a slight change in one premise, they need not be discussed here.

When Sophylus asks how we can have an idea of immaterial essence, Eutyphron takes the opportunity to comment on the term "idea" ("idée"; I, 190) and asserts that the term *idée*, derived from Greek *eidos* or *idea*, is synonymous with *image* (I, 190). Having a perception of a statue means having an idea or image of it, i.e., a visual impression, so that the term "idea" belongs, properly speaking, only to material objects. It is clear that in this passage at least "idea" and "image" are declared to be synonymous, while in the Letter on Man this had not been unequivocally stated and ideas had been designated somewhat obscurely as means by which we have sensations (I, 82). Asked whether we have perceptions, though not ideas or images, of what is just, of a lie, crime, love, gratitude, goodness, Sophylus answers in the affirmative. Since, as Eutyphron claims, all these phenomena relate to the soul and its activities, it is apparent that we have perceptions of immaterial essences. Eutyphron is also quite explicit about the relation obtaining between sensations and perceptions, declaring that the latter arise from the former. This leads, of course, to the question of what sensations give rise to perceptions of immaterial essences. Eutyphron-Hemsterhuis, however, does not pose this question directly. Instead, he points out that sensations of external objects are caused by some action from outside upon a sentient being (I, 192). Sensations arise if and when the following conditions prevail: (1) an essence can act upon a medium intervening between essence and sentient being; (2) there exists such a medium, which Eutyphron calls a "vehicle of action" (I, 194); (3) there exists an organ capable of receiving impressions from object and medium. If one of these conditions is not fulfilled there will be no sensation. The example of blind and deaf persons shows that there exist properties of matter of which they are unaware. By analogy we can conclude that the human species may lack organs for actually existing properties of essences.

At this point, Eutyphron wants to demonstrate how an essence that is not disclosed to our sense organs can become known to us by acting on an essence for which we possess an organ. As an illustration, he chooses a person without the sense of touch but endowed with that of hearing. For such a person matter lacks the essential property of impenetrability or solidity. However, when a hammer strikes a bell, the person will hear a sound which arises from the impact of two solid bodies. All that is known, then, is the audible effect caused by a property which cannot be directly known by any being that lacks the sense of touch. This example suggests the conclusion that we can know and perceive effects of essences or causes of which we have no direct sensory impressions. While it is true that we cannot have sensations or "ideas," as they are defined by Eutyphron, of essences for which we possess no organ, it does not follow that we can have no notion at all ("ni la moindre notion quelconque"; I, 196) of such essences or causes, unless "notion" is taken to mean "sensation" or "idea." Eutyphron-Hemsterhuis goes too far when he maintains that the person in the example cited above will forever search in vain for the cause of the observed phenomenon (I, 196). Even that person might arrive by inference from observations he can make at a notion of impenetrability or solidity, although he will not connect it with haptic qualities. Hemsterhuis seems here to disregard the role of constructive models and hypotheses. He is right, however, when he insists on the fundamental place of sensations in our knowledge of the external world. To these our models must refer and against them they have to be tested. Hemsterhuis is also right when he emphasizes that there are many essences or causes which have an effect on our sense organs but whose nature remains unknown because it bears no relation to our mode of perception (I, 197). He comes close to asserting that all we can know are the effects of an unknown substratum underlying all phenomena.

Eutyphron sums up his argument by stating that an essence can act by dint of a property for which we lack an organ on another essence in such a way that the effect on the latter becomes manifest to our senses. It is possible, then, that an immaterial essence, which has no rapport with our sense organs, can act on a material essence which has this rapport. It becomes apparent at this point that Hemsterhuis' real interest is to solve the problem of how the immaterial soul can act upon the body. An essence can influence another essence only if there exist *rapports* between them, which in turn presuppose the existence of some qualities, modifications, or modes of being common to the essences involved. Since soul and body, considered to be totally different by Hemsterhuis, act upon each other, they must share some quality unknown to us which makes it possible that they interact in such a way that the effects of this interaction become manifest to our sense organs. The property shared by both must pertain to the neural system and the brain only; otherwise the soul could act directly on any piece of matter. With the decomposition of the neural system and the brain after death, their rapport with the soul ceases, but the soul, Eutyphron-Hemsterhuis claims, will continue to exist.

The foregoing arguments present Hemsterhuis' solution to the vexing problem of the interaction of soul and body, bequeathed to modern philosophy by the Cartesian dualism of thinking and extended substance (*res cogitans* and *res extensa*). The author of *Sophyle*, who shares with Descartes the conviction that matter and soul are completely heterogeneous in essence, assumes that a real interaction takes place between them. The solution that a monistic materialism offers to the problem of body and soul, however, is completely unacceptable to the author of *Sophyle*, whose philosophical thinking derives its main impulse from the desire to refute materialism. Nor is he content with Spinoza's theory of psycho-physical parallelism, but tries to "explain" the assumed real interaction of matter and soul by positing a "quality" common to both of them. The assumption of such a hidden quality, inaccessible to empirical verification, seems hardly less speculative than Descartes' claim that the interchange between the two substances takes place in the pineal gland or the solutions proposed by the Occasionalists and Leibniz. Hemsterhuis' "explanation" is, however, less fanciful than Descartes' and less dependent on theological presuppositions than the Occasionalistic or Leibnizian doctrines. Holding on to Cartesian dualism as a secure basis for an antimaterialistic philosophy, Hemsterhuis attempts to bridge the gap between matter and soul in his own way by staying close to the sensualistic position from which he started out, but at the same time transcending it in a manner consistent with its tenets.

Eutyphron's final words state the aims of his philosophy, namely, to free physics from errors or doubtful presuppositions and to strive for a moral philosophy that is consoling, of lofty principles, and worthy of persons who are aware of all their potentialities (I, 198). These aims indicate the motives of Hemsterhuis' philosophical efforts: to combat the consequences that materialist thinkers drew from Newtonian physics (I, 193) as well as the ethical theories advanced by the same philosophers, who extolled hedonism or wellunderstood self-interest as the source of all human actions and denied the existence of an immortal soul. Eutyphron's final words are certainly directed at Princess Gallitzin, who for a while had been deeply impressed by the materialist doctrines of Helvétius, but who had soon realized that she needed a philosophy more in accord with her deeply felt moral convictions.

Sophylus, thoroughly persuaded by Eutyphron's arguments, sums up the results of their dialogue: (1) Our organs do not deceive, but inform us of real properties of the essences and of the rapports between them, insofar as they are disclosed to our organs. (2) What we call "matter" is essence insofar as it becomes manifest to our sense organs. (3) There exist essences that are different from matter.

(4) Our perceptions of immaterial essences are as certain as our ideas of material essences. (5) We can understand how immaterial essences can act on matter.

Sophylus' final vow that henceforth he will let himself be guided by the genius of Socrates underscores once more Hemsterhuis' admiration for this thinker, and expresses the conviction that Eutyphron, by following the dictates of the heart and good sense, has acted like the Athenian, whose philosophy was described in these terms earlier in the dialogue (I, 172). Obviously, the actual content of *Sophyle*, with its indebtedness to Cartesian dualism and Newtonian physics, is thoroughly un-Socratic. As to the claims of the heart, they are perhaps satisfied by some results arrived at in the course of the dialogue, namely, the proof of the existence of an immaterial soul—by implication considered also immortal—as well as the refutation of a materialistic notion of matter. Actually, the *Lettre sur les désirs* or even the *Lettre sur l'homme* contained more that appealed to the heart than the reasonings concerning knowledge or the interaction of mind and matter which take up such a great part of *Sophyle*. Although the context would certainly warrant a reference to the *organe moral*, there is no mention of it in the dialogue, an omission which is due perhaps to Diderot's criticism of this notion in his notes to the Letter on Man. When Eutyphron-Hemsterhuis claims that he follows the dictates of *bon sens*, he thinks most likely of the realistic position he defends in his epistemological arguments, which is bolstered by a pragmatistic appeal to practice as proving the agreement between objects and our perceptions, ideas, or notions of them. The philosophy expounded in *Sophyle*, however, is certainly not the philosophy of children that Eutyphron earlier in the dialogue (I, 172) had declared to be his own. Far from embracing a naïve realism, Eutyphron-Hemsterhuis argues for a kind of critical realism that asserts the existence of a real world of which we can discover some real properties and relations (*rapports*). But these are only selections from an infinite number of actually existing qualities of essences, and render aspects of a reality that is always more than we can know of it.

While it is true that some of the epistemological arguments and especially the proofs for the existence of an immaterial soul had been presented before in the *Lettre sur l'homme*, Hemsterhuis' first dialogue, *Sophyle,* focuses more sharply, without the digressions of the Letter on Man, on such problems as the reliability of our sense organs with respect to a dependable knowledge of the external world, the nature of matter, and the certainty of our knowledge of immaterial essences. New in this dialogue is Hemsterhuis' theory by which he tries to "explain" the possibility of an interaction between material and immaterial essences within the framework bequeathed by Cartesian dualism. Although the title of the dialogue would lead us to expect to hear more about the nature of philosophy, Hemsterhuis merely indicates a few traits of his own philosophy and then proceeds to expound some of its basic tenets, implying no doubt that his is the right way to philosophize.

CHAPTER 8

Aristaeus, or on the Divine Being

I *The Argument*

IN 1779, only one year after the publication of *Sophyle,* there appeared another dialogue by Hemsterhuis, entitled *Aristée ou de la divinité.* If both works, as it has been argued, were originally planned as one,[1] the author may have realized that the form of the dialogue imposed some limitations on the variety of topics treated. He decided therefore to publish two separate works. But even so, *Aristée,* the longest of Hemsterhuis' dialogues, contains a wealth of themes that might have been dealt with more conveniently in a treatise. These themes are listed in Meyboom's synopsis (II, 2—5) as follows: The problem of order in the universe, the existence of God, the nature of good and evil, the nature of the Divine Being, and man's relations with God.

It is for the variety and significance of the problems treated that *Aristée* has been considered the author's most important work,[2] the most complete expression of his thought.[3] This dialogue opens the series of works that represent the height of Hemsterhuis' achievement. The somewhat confused, strained systematizing of the *Lettre sur l'homme* has yielded to a more natural, personal expression of thought, and a warmth exhibited before only in those passages of the *Lettre sur les désirs* and the *Lettre sur l'homme* dealing with man's relations to God.

Aristée is prefacd by an "editor's note," written by the author himself, and Diocles-Hemsterhuis' brief dedicatory epistle to Princess Gallitzin, whom he addresses here publicly as "Diotima." In the editor's note, which testifies to the importance that Hemsterhuis attached to *Aristée,* this dialogue is referred to as a "metaphysico-moral" work (II, 6). Its manuscript, the editor pretends, was found on the isle of Andros, several years ago when the Russians undertook a military expedition against the Ottomans in the Greek Archipelago. The fictitious translator states that he has dealt freely with the corrupt Greek text. To help modern readers, he has substituted for the undecipherable "jargon" of ancient physics, the terminology of "our physico-geometry" (II, 6), of Newtonian physics. According to the editor, the author of the manuscript seems to be an Athenian of the late fourth century B.C. who belonged to the Socratic School. His dialogue exhibits traits of Socrates' good sense, Plato's poetry, and Aristotle's exactness. Since the manuscript was allegedly written long after Socrates' death, the Diotima to whom the work is dedicated cannot have been the divinely inspired woman who taught the philosopher all he knew about the nature of friendship. Like some novelists of his time, the German writer Wieland, for example, Hemsterhuis refers to a fictitious source to add credibility to his re-creation of a Greek setting, knowing, of course, that his sophisticated readers would never take this seriously. We detect in the preface of the feigned editor with its display of antiquarian learning an irony that was hardly present in any of Hemsterhuis' previous writings. This ironic detachment allows him to characterize his own style of writing and thinking without being immodest, since he hides behind the editor's persona. With the fiction of an ancient manuscript and its translator, the author of *Aristée* gives a playful explanation for the fusion of elements of ancient and modern speculation that can be observed in all his works. Diocles' dedicatory epistle to Diotima is a sincere tribute to Princess Gallitzin, who had inspired him to write this dialogue. In *Aristée*, Diocles writes, he has tried to expound those convictions which have guided Diotima in the conduct of her own life and the education of her children.

The dialogue starts out from a concrete situation that motivates the ensuing discussion. Diocles meets Aristaeus, who has been watching for a while an earthworm being attacked by an insect. The spectacle of the writhing worm has aroused disagreeable, somber thoughts in the observer. When Diocles crushes the insect to end the worm's suffering, Aristaus sees in this act another instance of cruelty. Asked what his thoughts are, he answers that the just observed "disorder" (II, 10) seems to prove that, instead of being the creation of God, the world exists eternally through itself, its modifications being the result of blind chance. Such thoughts may suggest, as Vernière maintains,[4] that Aristaeus, like Sophylus, represents views similar to those argued by Diderot. Both figures lack, however, the latter's acumen and strength of conviction, thus becoming easy targets for Diocles' arguments. As the German poet Wilhelm Heinse remarked in his diary, Aristaeus is a "poor sinner," treated by Diocles like a boy in a "miserable dialogue."[5]

The beginning of *Aristée* touches upon the problem of theodicy, which occupied so many thinkers and poets during the Age of Reason, all of them trying to "justify the ways of God to man" before the forum of human reason and attempting to reconcile the evil and suffering found in the world with the existence of an omniscient, omnipotent, benevolent Supreme Being. Hemsterhuis focuses his attention on the "suffering" that seems to result from the struggle for existence in the animal world, a phenomenon that furnished arguments against the existence of a Supreme Being. Such arguments, involving the "pathetic fallacy" to a certain extent, were advanced during Hemsterhuis' life by Diderot and Voltaire, and later in the nineteenth century by, among others, the German poet Büchner in his drama *Dantons Tod*, or Tennyson, who referred to nature as "red in tooth and claw."

Aristaeus' assertion that the sufferings of sentient beings suggest a fundamental disorder in the universe is countered by Diocles' remark that what is evil for the victim is good for the aggressor. There ensues, however, a discussion in which Diocles tries to define "order" and defend it against his friend's sceptical objections. In a rather condensed argument that would need elaboration, Diocles maintains that the notion of order is based upon a certain "modification" or "disposition" (II, 11), inherent in a number of objects which happen to be considered by the human mind. This "disposition" makes it possible to perceive with a maximum of ease the whole formed by these objects. The degree of order that can be established among them is proportionate to the number of properties shared by them. Order presupposes on the side of objects similarity, proportion, regularity, uniform succession, and universal laws. On the subjective side, order relates to man's disposition to find pleasure in obtaining a maximum of ideas in the shortest possible time, an observation that formed a leitmotiv of Hemsterhuis'

Aristaeus, or on the Divine Being   111

thought after it was enounced in the *Lettre sur la sculpture*. The
perception of order presupposes an ability to connect ideas, which
varies in accordance with the intellectual powers of any given individual. To illustrate this, Diocles refers to the difference between
a savage and a profound "métaphysicien géomètre" (II, 12), the
latter seeing *rapports* where nobody had seen them before.

Man's knowledge is confined to a finite number of terms in an infinite series. Since he knows only a part of the world, the order he
may find there does not allow him to draw conclusions concerning
the whole universe or God. More specifically, Diocles maintains
that phenomena which man calls "good" or "bad" furnish hardly
any basis for assertions about order or disorder in the universe.
Agreeing with Aristaeus that such a view does not support a proof of
God's existence by arguments based on cosmic order, Diocles affirms that these arguments imply in any case an anthropomorphism
unworthy of God's majesty.

The order perceived by man is not necessarily identical or coex-
tensive with the one existing among things themselves, but is the
result of certain properties which are "analogous" to his faculty of
connecting ideas. This emphasis on subjective factors does not imply, however, as Aristaeus suggests, a denial of all order in the universe, although this order and man's perception of it may be entirely different (II, 14). Diocles' position can be summed up as follows:
things are susceptible of order if they share properties; the degree of
order increases with the number of properties shared and of *rapports* obtaining among things; to these conditions must be added
the provision that there exist beings endowed with the faculty of
perceiving order, a faculty showing widely different gradations.
Aristaeus, not yet convinced by Diocles' arguments, admits order in
certain creations of man as well as animals but denies that it pertains to things in general. Going back to the problem of order in the
universe, Diocles points out that everything in it possesses *essence*
(II, 18), or the power of being and of being what it is ("la force
d'être, et d'être tel qu'il est"; *ibid.*). Since all qualities are
manifestations of the common property of essence, Diocles concludes that the universe would exhibit to any being endowed with
complete knowledge of all essences the most beautiful order (*ibid.*),
i.e., the highest degree of order based on the greatest number of
common properties.

Urged on by Aristaeus, who still thinks that things are too heterogeneous to submit to order, Diocles gives another definition of the latter. Things are susceptible to order by dint of qualities they share to form a determinate whole; the disposition of parts to form such a whole makes for order.[6] From this definition follows: (1) Any subordinate whole perceived by the limited faculties of a finite being exhibits only an imperfect order, since the whole is constituted by merely partial aspects of the essence. (2) For any finite being there exists an infinite number of things which do not form a determinate whole, in other words, there is much disorder for such a being. (3) The universe is composed of essences, which form a whole in an absolute sense, determinate in infinite ways (II, 20), and admitting no disorder. Aristaeus was wrong when he asserted that so-called evil reveals a fundamental disorder and constitutes proof that there is no God. On the other hand, the order that inheres in the essences could also be found in a world existing through itself and therefore does not prove the existence of a Creator. While the fact of order furnishes no proof of an intelligent Creator, the belief in the latter entails the presumption of order in the created world.

In keeping with his epistemological position, Hemsterhuis maintained that the notion of order depends upon objective as well as subjective factors, the most important among the latter being a disposition toward orderliness inherent in the human mind as it is constituted at present. The last-mentioned restriction, though alluded to only in passing, is characteristic of the author of *Aristée*, who envisaged the possibility of a future development of man's mental capacities far transcending their present state. What he had in mind was hardly the progress of the human species, one of the favorite topics of Enlightenment, but rather the unfolding of the individual mind in the course of an existence extending beyond this life. Such speculations must have appealed not only to Princess Gallitzin but also to Lessing, who expressed similar conjectures, coupled with then widely current ideas about palingenesis, continued rebirths, in his work *Die Erziehung des Menschengeschlechts* (The Education of the Human Race). It was published in 1780, the same year that Lessing met Jacobi and obtained from him copies of the *Lettre sur l'homme*, of *Sophyle*, and of *Aristée*.[7] Both Hemsterhuis and Lessing expressed independently of each other similar thoughts, derived partly from Leibniz and more specifically from the *Palingénésie philosophique* (1769) of the Genevan naturalist Charles Bonnet.

The insight into the limitations of the human mind led Hemsterhuis to conclude, like Hume in his posthumously published *Dialogues concerning Natural Religion* (1779), that order as it is perceived by man furnishes neither a proof for God's existence nor a basis for safe inferences with regard to things in themselves. This reasoning also applies, of course, to our perception of disorder and any dogmatic conclusion drawn from it, for instance, Aristaeus' assertion that the universe is ruled by chance only. Though the refutation of such a view was of greatest concern to Hemsterhuis, he did not place as much emphasis as we might expect on an argument, be it sceptical or critical, Humean or Kantian, against a dogmatic affirmation of disorder. The author of *Aristée*, who was unwilling to embrace a sceptical attitude, set out to give what he considered a "proof" that the universe taken as a whole exhibits a maximum of order. The assertions, however, that being or existence can be included among the properties of essences and that the degree of order depends directly upon the number of properties shared remain highly questionable. Hemsterhuis' reasoning strikes us as too remote from facts and lacks on the metaphysical level the acumen of Leibniz' arguments concerning compossibility and the best of all possible worlds.

There are still three difficulties Aristaeus wants to have cleared up: (1) The order of the universe, as defined by Diocles, seems to exclude any change. (2) It has to be shown that apparent evil is not really evil. (3) God's existence has not been proved yet. Diocles proposes to begin with the first point, then proceed to the third. After that, it should be easy to find out what is meant by "evil." He rejects any attempt to deny apparent evil as such.

Concerning the first point, Aristaeus concedes that cosmic order does not mean that everything is in its place in a universe conceived as a "block of marble," but rather that everything exists in an order to which it belongs (II, 24). His insistence that immutable, eternal, and necessary are synonymous leads to a discussion of these concepts.

More important than Diocles' ensuing definitions and arguments is the direction of Hemsterhuis' thought manifested in them. What he opposes is not so much rationalistic metaphysics in general but rather Spinoza's system, as he understood it, and philosophical materialism. He derives from the principle *ex nihilo nihil fit* (out of nothing comes nothing), on which Lucretius based his conviction that matter has always existed without ever having begun, the notion of a Being existing through itself without beginning or end. This uncreated Being is either God, the Creator, or the universe existing through itself. The latter alternative, which hardly differs from Lucretius' concept of matter or Spinoza's God-Nature *(deus sive natura)*, is preferred by Aristaeus as being more in line with our sense experience than the idea of an "unseen" Creator-God. Diocles-Hemsterhuis, however, makes every effort to convince his friend that the universe has been created and cannot be an essence involving existence or "une existence par essence" (II, 27). To make his point, Diocles proposes in a somewhat pedantic fashion to consider the universe under six aspects.

The universe considered as an aggregate of physical bodies, which are all determinate and finite, is not truly an infinite like space and time. Both of them have no parts. Bodies and events are located in space and time, but form no parts of them. The "true infinite" (II, 27) is *one* and not constituted by an indeterminately large number of finite bodies or events. The universe regarded as organized (II, 28) shows an organizing power, i.e., a tendency of its parts to form what Diocles calls "substances." Hemsterhuis thinks above all of the processes of generation and growth. Nature produces real "substances" to be what they are, whereas man can only modify them to realize circumscribed effects. According to Diocles, "organization" manifests a purpose or "end" ("un but"; II, 28), which in turn *seems* to presuppose some "ideal" *(ibid.)*. While Diderot adduced the fact of organization to defend a naturalistic world view that denies final causes as well as an extramundane divine purpose, it constitutes for Hemsterhuis no proof that the universe exists through itself.

The physical world exhibits everywhere motion and rest, action and reaction. Since the latter are equal according to the well-known principle of Newtonian dynamics *(actio = reactio)*, it would follow, if we believe Diocles-Hemsterhuis, that the material universe should be in a state of perfect rest and true inertia (II, 30 f.). But since we observe motion everywhere, Diocles concludes that an active principle prevails over the balance of action and reaction. This principle cannot be an inherent property of inert matter. To keep motion and organization and the formation of substances going, a continually active outside force, a "puissance etrangère," as Diocles calls it (II, 31), is necessary. The notion of a world soul, which might favor a pantheistic conception of a universe existing through itself, is rejected by Diocles, who denies any analogy between the human soul and the active principle prevailing over a world of inert matter. While the soul acts on man's limbs and organs to produce effects on external bodies, there are no bodies outside the universe. Furthermore, the constant struggle going on in nature indicates that there exists no prevailing "general will" (II, 33) or *hegemonikon* that establishes unanimity.

Looking at the world from what Diocles calls rather infelicitously the "intellectual" side ("en tant qu'intellectuel"; II, 33), we perceive relations and *rapports* instead of isolated phenomena. Hemsterhuis most likely means to say that *rapports* are established by the activity of the intellect, which can create a universe conceived by the power of imagination. After this cursory observation, Diocles proceeds, strangely enough as part of his consideration of the intellectual aspect of the universe, to a discussion of the active principle in nature, which, as he had previously shown, prevails over inertia. Finding everywhere in nature directed action, Hemsterhuis draws from this spurious premise the conclusion that the ultimate cause of all the action in the universe must be an infinitely great and powerful intelligent will (II, 37). He claims to have given another proof that the material universe cannot exist through itself, this time using the traditional argument from a contingent to an ultimate, absolute cause which obviates an infinite progression within the realm of merely contingent facts. Seeing that the discussion of action leads to intelligent will as ultimate cause, we understand now why Hemsterhuis included this topic in the section dealing with the intellectual aspect of the universe.

Diocles opens the examination of what he calls the "moral aspect" of the universe with the surprisingly direct question of whether Aristaeus has ever been in love. The latter answers that he has experienced the overwhelming power of this passion, which he describes as a desire to possess, admire, embrace, even devour its object. Diocles remarks that such a desire destroys its own objective and results in a merely momentary and imperfect enjoyment, whereas true desire or love aims at a perfect union of lover and

beloved. Asked whether the desire for a union of essences is the
same as the tendency to procreation in organisms, to the "formation
of substances," as Diocles-Hemsterhuis calls it somewhat prudishly
(II, 40), Aristaeus denies vigorously such identification, although he
admits that human desire is never entirely free of such a tendency.
To make this point clear, he gives an account of his own experience.
It convinced him that the drive toward procreation has nothing in
common with the desire for a union of essences, or *Seelenliebe*, the
love of souls. While the former has a definite goal—the propagation
of the species—the latter reaches its objective only by an infinite
process of approximation. The two kinds of desire seem to coexist to
a degree. Only a few people can keep them apart and legal institutions have tried to join them together. But the mixture of both
entails a corruption of the higher form of desire.

Aristaeus describes the difference between the two kinds of love,
which Spinoza had distinguished as *amor* and *cupiditas* or *libido*, in
terms of his own lived experience, thus making the distinction more
convincing. We are somewhat surprised, though, that it is Aristaeus
who gives expression to a dualistic conception of love, which is more
in accordance with Diocles-Hemsterhuis' *Weltanschauung*.
However, if Diocles, who voices throughout the dialogue its
author's views, had told Aristaeus' story, the readers, including the
Princess, might have seen in it a "confession" of the philosopher's
erotic experience. Furthermore, by ascribing a dualistic view of love
even to Aristaeus, with whom Diocles agrees in this point,
Hemsterhuis may have thought to strengthen his own arguments.

While the author of the *Lettre sur l'homme* had asserted that union with the object of our desire can be achieved either physically or
spiritually, he suggests in *Aristée* a radically dualistic view according to which sexual intercourse and what he calls love or desire are
totally different. In line with a long tradition of Neoplatonism, he
maintains that the former corrupts the latter and makes man a
prisoner of finitude. Hemsterhuis directs his attacks above all
against marriage. Far from beholding in it or desiring it to be an
organic fusion of body and soul of the partners, he sees in it only a
legal institution, a product of artificial society, resulting in the con-
tamination of two totally different "principles," the "marche
organique" (II, 42) toward the propagation of the species and the
desire for a fusion of essences. Both are grounded in human nature,

which would cease to exist if *Seelenliebe* were to replace sexual love. Hemsterhuis argues, however, for keeping them apart, and attacks the attempt to bring them together in the institution of marriage, which corrupts love by linking it with the purpose of begetting offspring. Marriage has produced a monster of shame, pudency, and humiliation (II, 43), unknown to man in his natural state. We observe here a curious blend of Neoplatonism and Rousseauistic primitivism. In the spirit of the latter, the artifices of immoral society with its proprietary rights are blamed for destroying the natural innocence of sex. The Neoplatonic strain is vividly represented in Aristaeus' account of his "fall" from *Seelenliebe* into sensuality.

Hemsterhuis vindicates a distinction that was of great personal significance to him as well as to Princess Gallitzin. The philosopher, as we have seen, never married, while *Seelenliebe* and friendship toward women played an all-important role in his life. His Diotima, to be sure, was married, but found no fulfillment in marriage. After she had children, they became her main concern. Besides, there was *Seelenliebe* for her Socrates and later for von Fürstenberg. The word "husband," she wrote to Hemsterhuis, belongs to a social institution that has nothing to do with the sacred bond of spiritual love; in a later entry in her diary she blamed bad customs and poets for having confused sexual love with the purest desire of the soul, with true love.[8] Triangular arrangements based on the coexistence of marriage and *Seelenliebe* were not too rare during the latter part of the eighteenth century among intellectual circles in Germany.[9] The life of F.H. Jacobi furnishes an example for such an arrangement, comprising in one household his wife and his young aunt, for whom he felt *Seelenliebe* and friendship. In his novel *Woldemar*, the hero is happily married, but also bound to another woman in a relation that could never exist between persons of the same sex, although it is totally different from what is commonly called "love" and has nothing to do with sex or marriage, nor with that form of self-deception known as "Platonic Love."[10] *Aristée* was published too late to have influenced the first versions of *Woldemar* (1777, 1779). But before that, Hemsterhuis had expressed similar views on the difference between true desire and sexual love in the *Lettre sur les désirs* (1770) and the *Lettre sur l'homme* (1772). After reading *Woldemar*, Lessing wrote to Jacobi that Hemsterhuis' "System von der Liebe," his theory of love, really does not explain anything and amounts to a mere substitution of one formula by another.[11] This remark refers to the *Lettre sur les désirs*, but would, of course, also apply to *Aristée*.

An interesting commentary on Hemsterhuis' theory of love in *Aristée* can be found in the diaries of Wilhelm Heinse. This German writer became notorious as the author of *Ardinghello* (1787), a novel that champions esthetic immoralism and free love. In drastic, downright obscene terms Heinse rejects Hemsterhuis' spiritualizing views on love, which are taken to imply that one could have sexual intercourse only with the *canaille* among women, certainly a misrepresentation of the philosopher's ideas. Heinse, who asserts emphatically that physical and spiritual attraction are not mutually exclusive, shares Hemsterhuis' critical attitude toward marriage, but for an entirely different reason: copulation may become unattractive when enjoined in a legal institution.[12]

An anonymous article in the *Berlinisches Archiv der Zeit und ihres Geschmacks* of 1796, dealing with the idea of love in the works of Pope, Wieland, Fielding, and Hemsterhuis, indicates the interest that the latter's views on love found in Germany. Hemsterhuis' dualism, the anonymous author asserts, proves only that sexual desire can exist without love.[13]

The discussion of love, Diocles claims, will facilitate an understanding of the moral aspect of the universe. Individuals manifest virtue or vice proportionate to their desire for fusion with other essences. By dint of the "moral principle" (II, 45) a person identifies with another essence and sees himself as other individuals would see him. The ideas of pity, justice, virtue, and vice are grounded in this principle, which makes us judge ourselves and urges us to strive for perfection. If such a moral principle dwells in our limited minds, it is hardly conceivable that it would be lacking in the Supreme Being, of whose existence we are convinced by other arguments. It is noteworthy that Hemsterhuis no longer speaks of an *organe moral*, but rather of a *principe moral*, a change in terminology most likely due to Diderot's critical annotations to the *Lettre sur l'homme*. Furthermore, Hemsterhuis distinguishes now a passive and an active manifestation of the moral principle. We are not only passively attracted toward other essences, feel their joys and sufferings like our own, but adopt an active attitude when we become judges of our *rapports* with or actions toward other individuals, and judge ourselves as others would.

Diocles is now ready to consider the last of the six aspects of the universe that he proposed to discuss. Speaking of the laws that seem to govern the world, he distinguishes two kinds of them. One set is based upon the nature of the material universe. The other comprises laws imposed from outside ("de dehors"; II, 47). Without an immaterial principle of action, the universe would be *one* inert mass. The material world, which is to be likened to a spring whose tautness is maintained by an external force, could never exist .through itself. While the active principle underlying all motion can produce organization and modify relations between existing things, it cannot really create the latter. We are, therefore, led to assume the existence of a productive power that creates (II, 49) and that is the cause of action and inert mass.

At Aristaeus' request, Diocles elaborates on the concept of activity, which he defines as the faculty of a being to act on things. Such activity appears either as indeterminate, undirected *velléité* or as directed *volonté*, the latter receiving its direction from the intellect. Without the *principe moral*, *volonté* would aim merely at the preservation of the individual and never attain nobility or greatness. The moral principle, however, can only modify what exists, but never create. The existence of a creative power, infinitely superior to human intelligence, is as certain as that of the universe. Diocles-Hemsterhuis finds in this power the Deity (II, 51) Who has created everything, continues to bring forth substances, and has peopled the universe with free beings, capable of happiness. But also beset by misfortune and plagued by unhappiness, as Aristaeus hastens to add, and he wonders how we can ascribe to God justice, goodness, and other similar attributes that do not even pertain to the essence of man, and what we can expect of an omnipotent Being that is the author of evil as well as good.

This question leads Diocles to a discussion of what is good and bad or evil, of the nature of happiness and unhappiness. Things are good or bad not in themselves but only relatively so. Furthermore, good and evil exist merely for sentient beings endowed with consciousness. Volcanoes, floods, epidemics are scourges and men are cruel or vicious only by their effects on sensitive creatures. When Aristaeus remarks that according to this view human beings cannot be reproached for being cruel, Diocles answers that they are endowed by nature with intellect and the moral principle, although in various degrees. The finest feature of man is his capacity to correct and perfect himself, to modify his actions so that they contribute to the greatest possible good for himself and others. Of the two kinds of human imperfection, one is due to a deficiency in natural endowments, for which the individual is not responsible, while the other arises from a bad use of his capacities. To ascertain which kind of imperfection underlies any given action is well-nigh impossible, since we are very incompetent judges of others. The courts of justice in any case judge only infractions of the law and not the degree of perfection of which individuals are capable. Hemsterhuis expresses here convictions that made him advocate leniency in cases that came under his jurisdiction in connection with his official duties.

Evil, Diocles continues, arises from obstacles encountered by directed will (*volonté*). The Supreme Being encounters no obstacles and therefore does not have to choose between good and evil. The latter distinction with its concomitant gradations pertains exclusively to beings endowed with limited intellect, activity, and freedom. As to physical pain, Diocles maintains, it also arises from obstacles met by the will. Since the intensity of pain is proportionate to individual sensitivity, it was erroneous to describe a worm's pain in terms derived from human experience. When Aristaeus mentions the sufferings of Socrates, condemned to drink hemlock, Diocles points out that the philosopher's great soul was far above the pains his adversaries tried to inflict on him. Even Tantalus would have been happy without the desire to drink. If man's free will would be directed toward goals above the ways of the world and the common passions, there would be no obstacles and therefore no evil. Aristaeus concedes that such an optimistic view might apply to Socrates and other wise men, but hardly to Hecuba or Oedipus, nor to the innumerable, nameless downtrodden and miserable creatures who lack the consolations of philosophy. They will doubt that life is a boon and ask whether the Deity ever cares for them. When Diocles refers to the immortality of the soul, his friend suggests that misery and a disposition toward evil will remain with some souls even in an afterlife. To which Diocles replies that a potential for the good will also endure and that evil is based on the changeable *rapports* we have with other things or beings, while what is good pertains to our very nature and stays with us forever. Evil must be considered a passing phenomenon, like a meteor. Such hopeful views, Aristaeus interposes, will hardly console people overwhelmed by real, present calamities. Diocles retorts that man projects himself constantly toward the future, be it good or bad, in hope or in fear.

Convinced now by Diocles' arguments, his friend offers a résumé of them: Man, being essentially good and capable of perfection, can at least partly overcome evil, which is entirely due to accidental factors, by training his imagination. It is only the latter that has created the "monstrous gradations of good and evil" (II, 63).

There still remains one major question to be discussed, the nature of God and man's relations to Him. Diocles opens the discussion with a preliminary statement about the two kinds of conviction man can hold. Convictions rest either on "inner sentiment" or on reasoning (II, 64). Diocles had previously emphasized that both kinds of conviction are equivalent (II, 46). Now he asserts that all reasoning must ultimately go back to axioms grounded in the "pure conviction of sentiment" (II, 64). Diocles-Hemsterhuis' dictum, "La conviction du sentiment vaut bien celle de l'intellect" (II, 46), was quoted with approval by Jacobi in a tractate written against Moses Mendelssohn,[14] after the latter had attacked the *Spinoza-Briefe*. Engaged in polemics against Spinozism, which he considered the epitome of rationalism, Jacobi welcomed Hemsterhuis' acknowledgement of sentiment as a source of evidence. He also cited with approval Diocles' further observation that a single sigh ("un seul soupir") uttered from time to time by a well-constituted person to express the yearning for betterment and perfection amounts to more than a "geometrical" demonstration of the nature of the Divine Being.[15] Seeing here a support for his *Glaubens — or Gefühlsphilosophie*, extolling faith or sentiment above reason, Jacobi referred to this passage as a dictum of a sublime mind and quoted it at the end of a letter to Hemsterhuis, a copy of which was incorporated in the Spinoza-Briefe.[16] We may safely assume that the praise of the "seul soupir" must have appealed strongly to the religious yearnings of Princess Gallitzin.[17]

It must remain doubtful whether the emphasis on feeling represents the "genuine" Hemsterhuis, as Brachin has maintained.[18] As a matter of fact, Diocles-Hemsterhuis argues that the convictions based on inner sentiment have lost their original hold on man. As his needs and intellectual powers grew, he came to prefer precise rational demonstration to the simplicity and vagueness of feeling. Reasoning is better adapted to commonly shared sense experience, and therefore more communicable than the convictions of feeling, which are grounded in the ineffable "essence" of the individual.[19] For this reason, Diocles chooses the way of rational demonstration to expound the nature of God. Jacobi objected to this line of argument, pointing out that the conviction of God's existence is based on a feeling shared by all mankind.[20] In the *Lettre sur l'homme*, Hemsterhuis himself had asserted that all sane, well-formed human beings possess a "sensation," i.e., a perception of or feeling for the necessary and real existence of the Deity (I, 146).

The only real infinite in nature, Diocles claims, is space, being *one*, without parts, comprising everything that is either actual or possible. To assert the nonexistence of space would be absurd. Space must be of infinite duration. Two or even more than two distinct, absolute infinites cannot exist, since their coexistence would presuppose limits, i.e., imply a negation of absolute infinity. According to Diocles, we have thus arrived at a "geometric and perfect conviction" (II, 65) of the existence of *one* God-Creator, existing by essence and His own power. Space, merely one of the infinitely many attributes of the Deity, is the only one by which we know the Great Being. The entire universe, in actuality as well as potentiality, is less than a mode or atom of this infinite Deity that is completely and perfectly present in everything throughout the universe. It seems inconceivable how anyone could doubt his relatedness to the omnipresent Deity. When Lessing referred to the Spinozism manifest in *Aristée*,[21] he had most likely this part of the dialogue in mind.

Aristaeus, confessing that he feels bewildered by Diocles' views concerning the universe and the Deity, wonders whether there can be any close relations between the "Dieu infini" and man, who seems to be reduced to absolute insignificance. To dispel these doubts, Diocles points out that man can rise to a contemplation of the infinite universe and a knowledge of its laws. Furthermore, the afflictions humans suffer concern only the body, i.e., some arrangement of matter, and cannot destroy what Diocles calls "l'humanité." Aristeus still wants to be convinced that God is really concerned with human affairs. Advancing a thesis common to most theodicies, Diocles admits that God does not interfere with general laws in favor of particular cases. But all things and beings in the universe have *rapports* with the omnipresent Creator proportionate to their homogeneity with God and their degree of organization or, as Hemsterhuis writes, "à proportion de la richesse de leur composé" (II, 69). Free beings, especially humans, can increase or diminish their *rapports* with the Deity. They should, therefore, aim at increasing their knowledge of God. And the only way to do this is to follow the advice of the Delphic oracle: "Know thyself." While we are in rapport with the Creator even in our physical makeup, the latter can hardly be changed. Consequently, we must concentrate on *rapports* that can be improved at will ("à volonté"; II, 70). It is in our power to enhance the faculties of the soul and to aim at their harmony.

Diocles proceeds to argue that our faculties of willing and acting as well as our intellect find their analogy ("homogénéité") in God and differ only in scope from the attributes of the Deity. There exists, then, no unbridgeable gulf between God and man, a fact which becomes even more apparent when we consider the "moral principle," especially its active aspect, as it has been described by Diocles. The voice of conscience, which passes judgment on our actions and urges us toward moral perfection, is grounded in the essence of our immortal soul, bestowed upon us by God. Through the moral principle we are linked in empathy to beings homogeneous with us and attracted to the sublime, beautiful, divine. It is our task to turn the moral organ steadfastly toward the divine, to purify this faculty to such a degree that virtue is practiced with ease, becomes our very nature, instead of being the result of sweat and toil. The lives of Epaminondas, Timoleon, and Socrates above all manifest, according to Diocles, such effortless virtue, which is accompanied by an imperturbable happiness. Hemsterhuis expounds here a notion of virtue that bears resemblance to the ideal of the "beautiful soul" (*schöne Seele*) which the German poet Schiller opposed to the rigorism of Kant, whose ethics is based on a radical dualism of duty and inclination.

After man has attained a perfect harmony among his faculties, be it by exerting himself or mainly by dint of his natural disposition, other, hitherto unknown faculties will develop and man's homogeneity with God (II, 73) will increase still further. While it might be doubted whether God concerns Himself with petty human affairs, it is certain that man has the ability to move closer toward the Divine Being. The pilot who steers his ship in conformity with the mainstream and not against it, even more the eagle adapting his seemingly effortless flight to the currents in the air, are symbols of the virtuous person who no longer encounters any obstacles on the way to true happiness because he proceeds in accordance with the Supreme Will. Hemsterhuis drew a vignette showing an eagle in flight to adorn the last page of *Aristée*.

Remarking that night is approaching, Diocles expresses the opinion that the questions raised during the course of his conversation with Aristaeus have been answered to the satisfaction of both. Seen with the eyes of God, it was found, the universe exhibits a perfect order. This "grand total" (II, 74) does not exist through itself, but is the product of an infinitely intelligent creative power. Infinite space gives us a measure of the immensity and omnipresence of God, to whom man is related by dint of homogeneity. In order to realize this relatedness more fully, further "developments" *(ibid.)* are necessary. The soul must shake off its rind of matter; it needs death to perfect itself ("il faut secouer l'écorce matérielle; il faut la mort"; II, 74 f.). As long as man is limited to discursive thinking, bound to space and time, he cannot know how many deaths and "developments" will be necessary to attain greatest perfection. It suffices, however, to realize that we start our flight ("notre essor"; II, 75) toward it in this life, that death speeds up the progress in perfection, which depends entirely upon the efforts of beings endowed with freedom and perfectibility. We are reminded of Socrates' words near the end of Plato's *Apology* that, provided the soul is immortal, he would wish to die again and again in order to be able to continue the search into true and false knowledge.

II *Summary*

Aristée occupies a very important place among Hemsterhuis' works because it deals, as we have seen, with the problem of evil, with the nature of the Deity, and man's relations to God—perennial questions to which the human mind has tried to find answers in religion or philosophy. In an age when Christianity was losing its hold on many minds, it became urgent to supply new solutions, independent of revealed religion. The ways of God had to be justified before the forum of human reason, an undertaking known as theodicy, of which *Aristée* furnishes an example. Diocles and Aristaeus start out from the observed fact of preying and killing in the animal world, which they interpret in terms derived from human morality as a manifestation of "evil." Although vaguely aware of the "pathetic fallacy" involved in his argument, Hemsterhuis begins with "evil" in nature rather than the ills engendered in human society. The latter could be redressed by man's efforts, whereas the former raises the question of how evil and disorder can be reconciled with the conviction that the universe is ruled by a Supreme Being. Hemsterhuis solves this problem by denying the ultimate reality of evil in the world. Though admitting that the perception of order depends to a certain extent upon the percipient, he still believes, unlike Hume or Kant, that order can be shown to pertain to the universe itself, which would exhibit, as a matter of fact, a most perfect order if we could behold it with the eyes of its Creator.

Aristée was written as a refutation of atheistic materialism, according to which "matter in motion" suffices to explain the world as it is. Apart from denying that motion inheres in matter, Hemsterhuis claims that both owe their existence to a Creator. While this implies a rejection of pantheism, the author of *Aristée* does not believe in the God of revealed religion, especially of Christianity. He wavers between a theistic, deistic, and pantheistic notion of the Deity, between ratiocination and the immediacy of inner sentiment as sources for the conviction that everything owes its existence to a Creator. Though *Aristée* contains no references to God as the Supreme Judge, or to God's love for mankind, Hemsterhuis tries to show that there exist analogies between man and the Deity, that the latter, being omnipresent, is not absolutely remote from human concerns. There is nothing said, however, about what God does for mankind. All the emphasis is on man's endeavor and obligation to strive for greater homogeneity with the Divine Being. Man, being endowed with an attraction toward the sublime, beautiful, and divine, is thought to be infinitely perfectible through the cultivation of intellect, will, and the "moral principle." Hemsterhuis' shift from revealed religion to ethics, from the Christian view of fallen man to perfectibility, is typical of

Enlightenment. But he does not engage in vituperations against the Church or the political establishment and attacks the atheistic materialism of the radicals among the Enlighteners.

Obviously, evil and suffering are minimized in *Aristée*. Moral evil is not a manifestation of the corrupted nature of man but an accident of his condition, due to obstacles which can be overcome by directed effort. While vice reveals only an infirmity or imperfection for which the individual is not really responsible, perfect virtue, on the other hand, appears as merely the outcome of an individual disposition. Each person is what he is and cannot change the nature of his endowments. This does not imply, however, that man's actions are completely determined. He can and even ought to strive for the harmonious development of all his faculties, a striving which will be continued in afterlife.

Hemsterhuis' arguments in favor of palingenesis, freedom, final causes, as well as his dualistic, Neoplatonist views concerning love, and his leaning toward transcendence and spiritualism make his ethic differ from that of Spinoza and also from the hedonism of the French materialists. The emphasis on individual character as the basis of moral conduct and on happiness as the desired result of virtue distinguishes Hemsterhuis' ethical views from those subsequently advanced by Kant, who insisted on obedience to universal law and duty and denied any moral significance to individual inclinations. Hemsterhuis' emphasis on individual morality and on the harmonious development of all human faculties proved attractive to a number of German intellectuals who espoused neither the hedonistic doctrines of Helvétius or Lamettrie, nor Kant's rigoristic ethics.

III   Reception of Aristée. *Its alleged Spinozism*

Aristée found considerable attention among German writers. Princess Gallitzin, who did so much for spreading Hemsterhuis' fame in Germany, had given a copy of the dialogue to Jacobi while he was visiting her in the spring of 1780. In July of the same year, he met Lessing. Pantheism became the subject of a lively debate, during which the latter expressed great sympathy for Spinoza's philosophy. Seeing in Hemsterhuis' writings an antidote against Spinozism, Jacobi, forever bent on finding allies against the supposed atheism of this philosophy, lent the *Lettre sur l'homme*,

Sophyle, and *Aristée* to Lessing, hoping most likely that he would be convinced by Hemsterhuis' arguments and reconsider pantheism. As it turned out, however, Lessing was "completely enchanted" ("ganz bezaubert") by *Aristée* because he found here, as Jacobi reports,[22] an expression of manifest Spinozism in such a beautiful exoteric guise that the latter contributes in turn to the elucidation of the central doctrine.

We can understand that Lessing's remarks engendered in Jacobi a special interest in *Aristée*. Far from agreeing with the former's findings, he adduced this dialogue repeatedly as an aid in his refutation of Spinozism. His *Spinoza-Briefe* include the copy of a letter to Hemsterhuis,[23] which contains a fictitious dialogue carried on by Spinoza with Hemsterhuis and Jacobi. There are numerous footnotes referring to *Aristée*, which the great defender of pantheism is supposed to have read. The passages quoted from Hemsterhuis' dialogue assert that any determinate act shows direction and presupposes an intelligent cause, that action and reaction would cancel each other out in nature if there did not exist an active principle transcending the physical universe. These arguments are rejected by Spinoza, who affirms that no action can have an absolute beginning, "out of nothing," as it were. Admitting his inability to refute pantheism on merely metaphysical grounds, Jacobi turns to Hemsterhuis-Diocles' "single sigh" for perfection, in which he sees a support for his conviction that a leap of faith offers the only valid alternative to Spinozism. The sequel to the letters on Spinoza, *Wider Mendelssohns Beschuldigungen*, also contains many references to *Aristée*, from which Jacobi cites passages dealing with the two sources of certainty (inner feeling or reason), the "single sigh" for perfection, and the ability of free beings to improve their relations with the Deity; other citations concern man's homogeneity with God and his capability to acquire hitherto unknown faculties that will establish new links with the Supreme Being.[24] Hamann, who had criticized Hemsterhuis' speculations on perihelia and aphelia in the *Lettre sur l'homme*, raised no objections to *Aristée*. In 1785 he wrote to Jacobi that he had read this dialogue, which he thought necessary to understand the letter to Hemsterhuis in the *Spinoza-Briefe*, with much pleasure.[25]

In his notes to *Aristée*, containing also extensive excerpts written down between 1783 and 1786, Heinse not only criticized

Hemsterhuis' views on love (see above, p. 118) but also other points, for example, the assertion that order or beauty is relative to the ease of our apprehension and the assumption that action and inertia would cancel each other without an overruling extramundane active principle. As far as Heinse is concerned, matter and force suffice to explain all phenomena, including organization, for which we need not resort to ideas or ideals of a designing intellect. To argue whether the active principle in nature is endowed with intellect amounts to a verbal quibble. The author of *Aristée* demands belief in a Creator-God, who remains unthinkable since we cannot think the act of creation. Others will for that reason be satisfied with that which *is*. Heinse, whose criticism of Hemsterhuis' theism proceeds from a dynamic pantheism, admits that *Aristée* is in some respects a masterpiece, although he considers the dialogue as such to be miserable.[26]

Although Baron Fürstenberg ascribed a greater role to duty than Hemsterhuis did, he admired in *Aristée* especially the description of the completely virtuous person given in the part of the dialogue which deals with the "moral principle."[27] Novalis showed in his "Hemsterhuis-Studien" likewise an interest in the passages treating morality and the moral aspect of the universe. Being familiar with Kantian ethics and Schiller's attempt to overcome its rigorism by postulating a "beautiful soul," he took note of the contrast that Hemsterhuis established between Themistocles' heroic virtue and Socrates' effortless moral harmony. To an excerpt concerning the "moral principle," he added the comment that Hemsterhuis "explains" our sublime pleasure in benevolent acts and virtue by relating it to metaphysics and what Novalis calls "higher physics." The fusion of moral "significance" and laws of nature was one of the poet's favorite projects. His quotations from *Aristée* refer to the six aspects under which the universe can be considered, to the distinction between *velléité* and *volonté*, and to Hemsterhuis' conception of matter as being merely inert. To the excerpts dealing with order, the poet adds his comment that order as well as disorder exist only to the extent that we have an idea of them. Diocles' rather casual remark about man's ability to create a universe by the power of his imagination is cited, most likely because it agrees with the poet's own conviction. This is also true of the passage in which Diocles says that our flight toward perfection will be accelerated after death. Novalis' fascination with death found support in Hemsterhuis' speculations on palingenesis and in Aristaeus' remark that death becomes an object of most vivid curiosity.[28] Franz von Baader, the German romantic *Naturphilosoph*, quoted in his diaries from *Aristée* Hemsterhuis' thesis that without a directing force the world would be a lump of inert matter and that the universe must be likened to a taut spring, a passage also quoted by Novalis.[29]

Ever since Lessing's remarks on *Aristée*, the Spinozism which he believed to have found there has become a much debated issue. He thought that Hemsterhuis, who had not yet been clearly aware of his own Spinozism when he wrote the *Lettre sur l'homme*, had now become fully conscious of it. Jacobi's impression, confirmed by Diderot, as he assured Lessing, was that Hemsterhuis could not be considered an adherent of Spinoza.[30] Jacobi, who had not yet read *Aristée* or met its author, subsequently tried to obtain from the latter an explicit statement on the pantheist philosopher, which then could be published as an endorsement of the views presented in the *Spinoza-Briefe*. Hemsterhuis' communication of April 26, 1784, only known through Jacobi's reference to it, did not fulfill these expectations. The author of *Aristée* merely deplored that Spinoza had confused the formulas of geometry, applicable with success only to physical phenomena, with the *esprit géométrique*, the application of which to mataphysics would have had results more worthy of his fine genius. Jacobi answered in the "Letter to Hemsterhuis" that what mattered really was not Spinoza's method but rather his principle *Gigni de nihilo nihil*, nothing is created out of nothing, which implies the denial of an absolute beginning.[31]

While most subsequent critics believed that Hemsterhuis was no Spinozist, Heinse, apparently influenced by Lessing's opinion as reported in the *Spinoza-Briefe*, maintained that *Aristée* was written to expound the system of the pantheist philosopher without its alleged absurdities. According to Heinse, Hemsterhuis differed from Spinoza in the question of determinism and made concessions to those who need a theistic God. Oddly enough, Heinse detected Spinozism even in the Hemsterhuisian *principe moral*. He believed, like Lessing, with whom he shared a sympathy for Spinoza, that the latter's system was manifested in *Aristée* under the guise of exoteric accommodation.[32]

In his recent study of Spinoza's influence on French thought,

Vernière has maintained that Spinozism emerges everywhere in Hemsterhuis' oeuvre.[33] As to *Aristée*, we are referred to the passage (II, 26) where Diocles argues that asserting the existence of finite, contingent being necessitates a going back to a Being existing through itself, a *causa sui*, either a divine Creator or a universe existing through itself. The latter alternative could point toward Spinozism. Vernière also cites the passage in which Diocles states that space is the only attribute manifest to our senses among the infinite number of attributes of the Godhead (II, 74).

While Hemsterhuis was undoubtedly familiar with some tenets of Spinoza's philosophy, Lessing's assertion that *Aristée* is the work of a confirmed Spinozist proves to be untenable. Diocles insists that the material universe cannot exist by itself; its existence is due to a "puissance étrangère" (II, 31), an extramundane power, a Divine Creator (II, 26). In this, Diocles-Hemsterhuis plainly differs from Spinoza's pantheistic *deus sive natura*. The emphasis on divine omnipresence that we find in *Aristée* rules out a deistic idea of the Supreme Being, but furnishes no proof for a supposed pantheism. With the notion of an omnipresent Divine Creator, Hemsterhuis comes close to a *Weltanschauung* that German philosophers have called *Panentheismus:* everything partakes of God, Who suffuses the entire universe as an animating power and yet infinitely transcends it as the Creator. The productive power which creates (II, 49) is neither the world soul assumed by some philosophers nor Spinoza's *natura naturans*, the immanent creative power in nature; it is the manifestation of the Deity, who has created the universe ("le Dieu qui a créé l'univers"; II, 51). Hemsterhuis' notion of a Creator, to whom he attributes intelligence, will, and the "moral principle," is as un-Spinozean as his defense of final causes. He wavers, however, between free will, rejected by Spinoza, and a deterministic theory of human conduct. The assertion that space furnishes a measure of God's omnipresence may go back to Newton just as well as to Spinoza.

Jacobi was certainly right when he pointed out that the author of *Aristée* was no Spinozist. Vernière's thesis that *Aristée* and the other dialogues aim at a refutation of "Neo-Spinozism," i.e., atheistic materialism, on the basis of a meditation on Spinoza's *Ethica*[34] is misleading if it is to mean more than an assertion that Hemsterhuis was somewhat familiar with the arguments of this work as an ultimately unsatisfactory alternative to his own philosophy. The fact that he did not heed Jacobi's request to support an attack on Spinozism does not imply an endorsement of this philosophy. Hemsterhuis probably thought that he had done enough to disperse any idea that he secretly championed pantheism and simply did not want to be drawn into the dispute concerning Spinoza, whose name he never mentioned in his published writings, not even in the *Lettre . . . sur l'athéisme.*

CHAPTER 9

Simon, or on the Faculties of the Soul

A MONG Hemsterhuis' complete dialogues, *Simon ou des facultés de l'âme* is the only one whose French text was published posthumously. It appeared in Jansen's edition of the *Oeuvres philosophiques* (1792), ten years after a German translation had come out in Volume II of the *Vermischte Schriften des H. Hemsterhuis*. Work on this dialogue was begun before the Princess moved to Münster. In January, 1780, copies of the manuscript were sent to her and Fürstenberg in Münster. Hemsterhuis' concern with the style and language of his work, for which he solicited help from Diotima and others, led to constant scruples and delays. As a result, the French text of *Simon* remained unpublished during his lifetime.

The unauthorized German translation of 1782, which possibly contributed to the delay of publication, is obviously based on a handwritten copy that had circulated in Germany. Jacobi, who owned as early as 1780 a manuscript of *Simon*[1] and sent after Hemsterhuis' death a copy of it to Jansen for publication in the latter's edition of the *Oeuvres philosophiques*,[2] can hardly be the person who got involved in the German translation of that dialogue. In a letter written on March 16, 1781, to K. L. von Knebel, a courtier in Weimar, Jacobi wondered how *Simon* had come to be known in some circles of that town; two months later, Herder wrote to Hamann that a Hemsterhuisian manuscript, most likely of *Simon*, was circulating in Weimar.[3] A vague reference to a Platonic dialogue and von Knebel in a letter of Goethe to Charlotte von Stein, dated February 5, 1781, has been interpreted by some scholars as an allusion to *Simon*.[4] Wieland wrote on March 2, 1781, to J. H. Merck, a friend of young Goethe, that a Hemsterhuisian manuscript would be well received in Weimar, and Merck indicates in his correspondence that he sent there an unpublished Platonic dialogue by the Dutch philosopher, which he considered superior to all hitherto published works of that author.[5] In a letter of June 10, 1783, Jacobi told Princess Gallitzin that Merck, who had probably sought contact with Hemsterhuis, owned a manuscript of *Simon;* Merck himself, who never mentioned the title of the dialogue he sent to Weimar, had insisted in a letter to the Duke of Weimar (February 28, 1781) that the manuscript was not obtained from its author but from a person who wished to remain unknown.[6] While we cannot be certain at present whether Merck possessed a copy of *Simon* and even less so whether he furnished the French original for the German translation, there can be no doubt that at least *one* manuscript of this dialogue was circulating in Germany outside of the small group constituted by Jacobi and Hemsterhuis' friends in Münster. We also realize the great curiosity that any published or unpublished work by the Dutch philosopher aroused among German intellectuals during the 1780's.

Hamann, who had read the German translation of *Simon* in 1785, asked Jacobi impatiently whether its French original had come out, and praised to his friend Scheffner in Königsberg the progress in Hemsterhuis' ability to write Platonic dialogue.[7] Herder, on the other hand, had written some years before to Hamann that *Simon,* in which he detected nothing that Hemsterhuis had not expressed better in the *Lettre sur l'homme,* lacked stimulating ideas as well as the grace of Plato's dialogues.[8] In the next decade, when the German romantics showed a renewed interest in Hemsterhuis' writings, Novalis made excerpts from *Simon* and Friedrich Schlegel praised this work in his essay "Über die Diotima" (1795) as the most perfect dialogue of the philosopher, whom he called "seelenvoll," gifted with deep understanding of the human soul. The suggestion at the end of *Simon* that dithyrambic poetry is akin to philosophy was greeted with warm approval by Schlegel in his essay on the study of Greek poetry (1795—96). He saw in this dialogue a Socratic poem ("eine Sokratische Poesie"), dithyrambic in composition, an outpouring of sublime and good sentiments. As Schlegel points out in his discourse "Über die Diotima," the prophetess who inspired Socrates in the *Symposium* found renewed recognition in *Simon,* where the Athenian philosopher acknowledges his indebtedness to her insights.[9] While it is certain that Hölderlin knew Hemsterhuis' writings, the poet mentions none of them specifically. When he named Susette Gontard, the woman to whom he was bound in *Seelenliebe*, and the heroine in his novel *Hyperion* "Diotima," he may have thought, like Schlegel, not only of the seeress in Plato's *Symposium* but also of the Diotima of Hemsterhuis' dialogues.[10] Goethe, who addressed his beloved Charlotte von Stein, in a letter dated November 9, 1784, as "Seelenführerin," guide of his soul, explicitly alluding to Hemsterhuis,[11] most likely remembered the vignette at the head of Diocles' dedicatory epistle in *Aristée*. A Greek inscription on an altar refers to Diotima as *Psychagogos*. Her function as a guide of the soul became, to be sure, more apparent in *Simon*, but it must remain a matter of conjecture whether Goethe thought also of this dialogue when he called Charlotte von Stein his "Seelenführerin."

Princess Gallitzin was repeatedly asked by Hemsterhuis to contribute to the composition of *Simon*. Meyboom quotes (III, 181) from an undated letter in which the philosopher expresses his joy over her reflections on the faculties of the soul and urges her to think about her role in *Simon*. In another letter, dated January 28, 1780, he asks her to make suggestions concerning the style and form of the dialogue (III, 183). Her "Attic soul" is to judge whether the work has local color. The Princess, who has thought as much as the author about the theory they have worked out together, might find that it lacks detail concerning the education of children. The solicitude for the upbringing of Princess Gallitzin's children, in which the philosopher was to participate, played a very important role in the writing of *Simon*. It is characteristic of the Princess that she urged her "Socrates" from the very beginning to avoid any mysticism in the dialogue; Diotima's instructions concerning the faculties of the soul should be clear and not be mixed with "poetry."[12]

Simon is, like *Aristée*, prefaced by an editor's note by Hemsterhuis himself and a dedicatory epistle by Diocles to Diotima. The author says he is bold enough to offer a frivolous public for its amusement profound metaphysics in the form of a dialogue by Simon, an Athenian dealing in leather goods. This contemporary of Pericles and Socrates could remember whole conversations between distinguished Athenians. One of Simon's dialogues, hitherto supposed to have been lost, was allegedly found, like *Aristée*, during the recent Russian military expedition in the Greek Archipelago. Pretending to be unfamiliar with the "algebra" needed for the psychology expounded in *Simon*, the editor claims that he is merely an antiquarian, critic, and translator, unable to grasp the spirit of the whole and to comment on Socrates' or Diotima's arguments. The dialogue, which is said to further the cause of man's improvement, seems to be dated and useless in a century that has attained perfection. Hiding behind the persona of translator and editor, Hemsterhuis views himself and his dialogue, as in *Aristée*, with ironic detachment. In Diocles' dedicatory epistle to his wise and sacred Diotima, whose thoughts resemble those of her namesake in the manuscript found by him and his beloved at an altar dedicated to Eros, Hemsterhuis renders a sincere tribute to the inspiring friendship with Princess Gallitzin.

Though shorter than *Aristée* or *Alexis*, *Simon* represents in complexity of composition and number of participants in the dialogue the author's most ambitious attempt to emulate Plato's *Symposium*. Prominent figures of this work, such as Socrates, Aristophanes, and Diotima appear also in *Simon*. Like *Aristée*, the dialogue starts out from a concrete situation. While the preamble to *Simon* is much more elaborate and richer in local color, it lacks the direct connection with the subject of discussion that we found in *Aristée*. It is mere curiosity that impels Hipponicus to visit Simon, who satisfies it by reading an account of a conversation that recently took place at his home.

Before beginning with the dialogue itself, Simon describes the occasion that gave rise to it. Socrates, Cebes, Agathon, Damon, a musician, and Mnesarch, a sculptor, had all assembled at Simon's to admire a sculpture by Mnesarch, representing Prometheus as he contemplates man just after he has created him. The expression of profound thought in the genius contrasts with the naïve candor and wonderment of newly born man, who has not yet a spark of the fire Prometheus was to steal from heaven. Aristophanes, who joins the gathering, finds the sculpture worthless. His objections are not directed against its craftmanship but against Prometheus, who spent too much mental effort on a creature rather undeserving of it and concealed the essential character of man while bringing the inessential to the surface.

At this point, Socrates enters the discussion and the dialogue
proper begins. Against Aristophanes, who insists that the vices of
man and the labyrinthine recesses of his soul should have been
turned outside to be visible for all, Socrates defends man as he was
created by Prometheus: youthful, vigorous, beautiful, essentially
not vicious, gifted with equanimity and the desire for knowledge.
According to Aristophanes man was a rather stupid creature before
he received the celestial spark and is since that an absurd, impure
mixture. It would have been better if Prometheus had made man's
vices directly perceptible. Mnesarch interposes that sculptors and
painters can manifest the inward life of men by a faithful rendering
of their physiognomies and attitudes. Even poets rely on these out-
ward manifestations. Voicing a commonplace tenet of eighteenth
century criticism that can be traced back to Aristotle, Aristophanes
maintains that poets do not aim at factual truth but at verisimilitude
(II, 87 f.). Socrates finds that Mnesarch and Aristophanes in a way
really agree. Just as the latter defends his presentation of Socrates in
The Clouds, although it differs from the factual person, Mnesarch
will have to admit that he would not depict the real Orestes, whose
intentions remained hidden from his mother just before he
murdered her, if he were to present him in such a way that his
thought were visible to us. Mnesarch would in that case give us his
interpretation of Orestes. Socrates concludes that there are thoughts
that remain undisclosed to sense perception and therefore cannot be
rendered by the visual arts. According to Mnesarch, and
Aristophanes agrees with this, there are some palpable traits that indicate a permanent disposition toward certain kinds of action. Thus,
it should be possible for artist and poet to overcome the limitations
pointed out by Socrates. While the latter admits that emotions and
passions can find expression in the physiognomies or stances of
men, he insists that man can hide his inner life.

At this point, Aristophanes asks the philosopher what rank sculpture occupies in relation to poetry. To find an answer, it is necessary
to define the arts. Mnesarch, being the youngest in the group, is
questioned first. He replies that sculpture is the art of working in
stone. But Socrates points out that this definition lacks a statement
about the purpose of this art. A shoemaker, for instance, does not
only work in leather but aims at making good shoes. Mnesarch then
boldly asserts that sculpture is undeniably the most perfect art since

it addresses itself to the eye and the sense of touch at the same time. Sculpture is most perfect because it presents in a most perfect manner everything that can be presented and because it is the only art that can prevail over time by eternalizing a "happy moment" (II, 96). Furthermore, a sculpture can be viewed from all sides and lasts through ages to come. Socrates, finding this praise somewhat excessive, raises several objections. According to him, sculpture does not appeal to the sense of touch, but presents its object, solid bodies, to the eye more completely than all the other arts. Even so, Socrates insists, there are limits to what the visual arts can depict. Due to their very nature they cannot represent motion or a succession of actions, and reduce life to repose and inertia. Far from being more perfect than all other arts, sculpture and painting are subject to severe limitations. Poetry, on the other hand, as practiced by Homer, can represent actions of gods or men extending through space and time. The poets, then, command in their art a much wider scope, wealth of ideas, and power than the visual arts.

Socrates suggests that Mnesarch's praise of sculpture has sidetracked the discussion. To seek the excellence of an art in the number and diversity of objects treated would imply that arithmetic, the art of computation, ranks highest, a conclusion that Mnesarch considers absurd. The modern reader will remember that "art" *(techne)* had a wider connotation among the ancient Greeks and that arithmetic was part of the quadrivium, the four liberal arts, in medieval education.

From this point on, *Simon* ceases to be a dialogue. Apart from two short narrative sections that belong to Simon, Socrates is the only speaker, reporting on conversations he had at various times with a Scythian and with Diotima. The philosopher tells first how he met at Aspasia's home a venerable visitor from Scythia, who was asked what he thought of the Greeks, their arts and sciences. Hemsterhuis combines here the setting of a Platonic dialogue with a literary device often used in the eighteenth century, among others by Montesquieu in his *Lettres Persanes* (1719) and Voltaire in *L'Ingénu* (1767). A traveler from a country considered "under-developed" or semibarbaric visits a nation that boasts of its advances in civilization and refinement. As an "intruder" or "messenger from the outside world," the traveler, often a "noble savage," criticizes a sophisticated civilization from the standpoint of a naïve, ingenuous probity. The Scythian in *Simon* assumes this role. While he finds the Greeks more enlightened than he thought, he is critical of conditions in Greece, especially the political dissensions and overwhelming diversity of opinions. He admits that the Athenians show an unexcelled finesse and fastidiousness in the arts. However, being taken up too much with artistry, they have no idea of the role of the arts within national life. According to the Scythian, art should aim at producing effects that are useful and pleasurable. Man, he continues, is composed of body and soul. Since art has to cater to the needs of both of them, there are two main branches of art. The first group, comprising the noble or liberal arts of poetry, sculpture, painting, music, and rhetoric, aims at enriching the soul by furnishing or modifying ideas and sensations. The aim of the second group, which consists of the mechanic arts and the crafts, is to enhance the welfare of the body. A third division of mixed arts is constituted by architecture in all its applications to civil and military purposes (houses, temples, fortifications, shipbuilding, etc.) as well as the mechanic arts insofar as they allow ornamentation. "Art" is again taken in its widest sense, corresponding to the Greek term *techne*.

Only the first group of arts is to be discussed further. As a preliminary, Socrates-Hemsterhuis points out, in agreement with Locke, that all of our ideas are derived from sense perception or reflection on it. While all artists aim at furnishing us with ideas of their choice, sculptors, painters, and musicians present ideas directly derived from our sense perceptions, whereas poets and orators induce us to form ideas by means of signs that stand for objects and ideas. Hemsterhuis seems to come close to the rather questionable distinction between natural and arbitrary signs made in some esthetic theories of the eighteenth century.[13] Turning to the question of the ranking of the arts, the Scythian rejects such a notion, asserting that Homer's and Phidias' Jupiter have made an equally profound impression on him. All arts exert an overwhelming power, depriving man of his freedom.

When Socrates objects that there is nothing more free or liberal than the arts and that their flowering is based on the complete freedom enjoyed by the Greeks, the Scythian counters that freedom, while desirable, may go too far if extended to assassins, robbers, or tyrants. It has adversely affected all domains of civic life in Athens. Spartan simplicity, good sense, and obedience to the laws have given way to personal interests, envy, injustice. All this, the Scythian maintains, is an outcome of the Athenians' boundless admiration for art, the artistic, and the artful. Any argument is accepted as long as it is presented artistically. It would not help to ostracize the artists, because the real power and despot in Athens is the public, which is enlightened, to be sure, but also arrogant, cruel, suspicious, wicked, and forever open to flattery. Hemsterhuis' Scythian voices a criticism of Greek civilization, especially of conditions in Athens, which reminds us of the views expressed much later by the Swiss historian Jacob Burckhardt. Hemsterhuis was most likely influenced by Rousseau's First Discourse, asserting that the progress of the arts and sciences in Athens, for example, entailed a decay of moral values. In both authors the criticism of Greek Enlightenment implied a censure of its counterpart in the eighteenth century. Princess Gallitzin's growing preoccupation with Christian religion and morality possibly also had an effect on Hemsterhuis' attitude, although he never abandoned what she called his pompous Graecism. Considering his admiration for the Greeks, it is somewhat surprising that he gives so much weight to the Scythian's arguments, to which Socrates offers only rather mild objections. *Simon* is certainly not a panegyric on ancient Greece nor the expression of an infatuation with Greek art and culture as we find it in Winckelmann, Heinse, Hölderlin, in young Friedrich Schlegel's "Grecomania," or in parts of Lessing's, Goethe's, and Schiller's oeuvre.[14]

Amazed at the Scythian's boldness, Socrates interposes that the Greeks consider art to be divinely inspired. The visitor from Scythia rejects this belief and asserts that mythologically speaking any art is a hybrid resulting from the union of a deity with a human. Sublime poetry, for instance, results from the union of Apollo's soul with that of Orpheus, Homer, or others. But Pan, mischieveous satyrs, and infernal deities also unite with human souls. Low comedy, lascivious poetry or music issue from such unions. Trying to prevent such "marriages" would not help, since all human souls are tormented by an erotic desire to be impregnated. The good and beautiful souls turn to the Olympian gods, the ugly and vicious minds to evil deities. Harmful consequences of the arts, as Plato also suggested, can only be avoided by severe laws. A ruler will act prudently if he

restricts the freedom of the arts in order to protect his government.
A report by Simon prepares us for Socrates' next discourse.
Aristophanes, we are told, showed increasing uneasiness over the
Scythian's arguments and finally left the gathering. After that,
Cebes wanted to be enlightened about the faculties of the soul and
Socrates agreed to discuss this topic. From now on until almost to
the end of *Simon* the philosopher is the speaker. He points out that
he learned all he has to say about the faculties of the human soul
from Diotima, the renowned seeress, who taught him to know
himself and the meaning of love. This is, of course, a reference to
Plato's *Symposium*, but also Hemsterhuis' tribute to Princess Gallitzin. Socrates tells the gathering of a meeting with Diotima which
took place after he had just been reading in the writings of
Democritus, the atomist and defender of philosophical materialism.
Asked by Diotima what he has learned from these works, he tells
her that he read with amazement how our virtues, vices, and
passions are grounded in our physical constitution, in physiological
processes. The text indicates that Socrates-Hemsterhuis thinks
rather of such writers as Helvétius and Lamettrie than of
Democritus. While Diotima agrees that, as medicine shows, soul
and body influence each other, she finds that the philosopher of
Abdera lacks understanding for that side of man which is beyond
the ken of our physical senses.

When Socrates asks whether man has more than the five senses
generally known, the prophetess answers the question by starting
out with a mythological account of man's creation. Jupiter, she says,
after having decided to create the human race, formed the soul of
the first man. It was a pure essence, potentially susceptible of all
kinds of sensations and endowed with *velléité*, the ability to will and
to act. Prometheus added subsequently to these faculties the imagination, a receptacle for all kinds of ideas. Since this faculty, in
itself nonphysical, needed "organs" connecting it with the external
physical world, Prometheus furnished the imagination with an infinity of "organs." When Socrates points out that only a limited
number of them are known at present, Diotima answers that in the
course of time the soul will be informed by other "organs," in addition to our present five senses.

Resuming her story of the creation of man, Diotima relates how
Prometheus, fearing disorder among men, stole a spark of heavenly

fire to endow the human soul with the faculty of intellect, which establishes order between the ideas stored by the imagination. Even then, men were still very imperfect beings since there existed no moral bond linking men to each other. The faculties of willing, perception, imagination, and intellect served merely the needs of isolated individuals. Intelligence became the instrument of egoism, harmful to society. In a passage that reminds us definitely of Rousseau's Discourse on the Origin of Inequality among Men (1755), Diotima describes how the idea of property arose, which led to wars and the ruthless exploitation of the earth. Jupiter would have annihilated mankind if Venus Urania, heavenly Love, had not interceded on behalf of man. With Jupiter's permission she descended to earth to instill love and virtue into man. She endowed him with a new faculty, the *organe moral*, and as a consequence sympathy, justice, and peace began to rule among men. A golden age ensued, during which the gods descended from Olympus to mingle freely with humans. This happened in a distant past. Although man could not maintain the bliss of this golden age, he has preserved at least a germ of divine love.

Socrates, who likes Diotima's theory of man better than that proposed by Democritus, still wants to know, however, how our virtues and vices can be derived from the various mixtures of the faculties of the human soul. Diotima claims that it is very easy to answer this question. What she says about *velléité* and its determinate form, *volonté*, about imagination and intellect or reason need not be repeated here, since Hemsterhuis has dwelt on these distinctions in his previous works. The fourth faculty, the moral principle or *organe moral*, it is emphasized, shows two aspects. On the passive side it becomes manifest as love, hate, envy, pity, anger, etc. While it is somewhat surprising to see these affects listed as manifestations of the *organe moral*, such procedure is in keeping with the definition of this "organ." It furnishes the mind with "sensations de tout ce qui tient au moral" (II, 128), with sensations that have moral significance. On the active side, the moral principle judges, modifies, moderates or enhances these sensations, imposes order on them, much as the intellect establishes order among the ideas received through the sense organs and stored in the imagination. Functioning as conscience, the active moral principle judges whether the acts of *velléité* and *volonté* conform to the idea of justice or not. Injustice is as repugnant to the *organe moral* as contradiction to the intellect.

After these preliminaries, Diotima takes up the actual answer to Socrates' question. She maintains that there exist five basic "psychological types," as we would say, each of them characterized by the proportionate strength of the four basic faculties of the human soul. This "true theory" (II, 133) furnishes, as Diotima claims, an insight into the nature of virtue, vice, and defects of character. Supreme virtue is the manifestation of an extraordinarily endowed soul, characterized by the ease with which vague *velléité* issues in acts of *volonté*, by the strength of the passive as well as active manifestation of the *organe moral*, by a great agility of the intellect, a keen perception of truth, and a great wealth and clarity of the imagination. All these faculties, present in equal and proportionate perfection, are united into a harmonious whole. Vice results from too great a power of *velléité* or of moral sensibility and the bad use made of intellect and imagination. Defects derive from a feeble *velléité*, incapable of determining itself and swayed by imagination and moral sensibility. Diotima asserts that her "theory" helps us to advance our knowledge of man, to improve education, to better ourselves. It has been pointed out above that the upbringing of her children was one of Princess Gallitzin's main concerns. For her benefit the Diotima of the dialogue elaborates on the usefulness of her "theory" for education. In children the four faculties can easily be discerned and evaluated. They can be modified in such a way that the greatest possible good will be realized together with the least possible evil. Moral sensibility, the most beautiful but also most baneful gift of the gods to man, demands the greatest care. A vivid and strong moral sensibility, which rules more despotically over *velléité* than the strongest imagination, is turned just as easily to love, pity, benevolence as to hate or anger, and must therefore be guided into the right direction by strengthening the intellect and the active component of the moral principle. Only then can moral sensibility become the mother of all virtues. On the other hand, the active side of the *organe moral* depends upon sensibility, which can be enhanced by presenting suitably chosen objects to it. Insight into the proportionate strength of our faculties helps us to achieve self-knowledge and self-perfection. The latter is at first a strenuous task, but becomes easier as we get used to regulating our activity. None of our faculties must assume absolute dominion. They should progress in unison to achieve a harmonious whole, which marks the acme of moral perfection.

While all humans share the same faculties, it is the use they make of them that creates the tremendous differences among individuals. Some of them have improved more rapidly because they used all their courage and power of will to further self-perfection. The flight toward perfection is accelerated by the activation of new, hitherto unknown organs, which reveal the future. As a consequence, some persons become seers and prophets. The sun, which has not always been as bright as now and which was enveloped by a thick crust of opaque matter before fire and energy from the interior of the star consumed it, is the most perfect symbol of the human soul. Man must imitate the sun, get rid of the encrustations surrounding his soul so that it becomes nothing but "organ," i.e., entirely open to the infinite aspects of the universe. The soul will then no longer see God in the universe or the latter in God but apprehend the world in a God-like fashion.

After Socrates' account of his conversation with Diotima, culminating in an inspired flight of speculation, Simon reports soberly how the members of the group assembled at his home reacted to the philosopher's discourse and how the gathering finally broke up. One item in this report deserves special notice. When Agathon asks Socrates whether Diotima's speech has not revealed a close connection between the language of the dithyramb and philosophy, the philosopher affirms such connection. He points out, however, that dithyrambic poetry is inspired by Dionysus, whereas philosophy derives its inspiration from the Goddess of Wisdom.

Hemsterhuis aimed in *Simon* more than anywhere else at a tableau of Greek life, at vivid and convincing local color. As a result, this work shows a preponderance of report and reported dialogue over direct, "dramatic" presentation and a rather complex structure in which all these elements are combined. There is, to begin with, a brief direct dialogue between Hipponicus and Simon, furnishing the "frame," as it were, for what follows. Simon then reports about the persons who made up a gathering at his house. A direct dialogue ensues in which Mnesarch and Socrates are the main participants, while Cebes' part in it is negligible and Aristophanes recedes quickly into the background. Socrates soon becomes the only speaker, who reports a dialogue he had with a Scythian. Before the philosopher embarks on his second discourse, a report on a dialogue with Diotima, Simon briefly describes Aristophanes' reaction to Socrates' first discourse and summarizes a discussion that ensued between the remaining participants. At the end of the entire dialogue we return to its "frame." Simon tells Hipponicus about the further course that the gathering at his house took. As to themes treated, Simon seems to lack the unity and coherence of *Aristée* and even of *Sophyle*. A new work by Mnesarch furnishes the basis for a discussion of sculpture and the arts in general. The Scythian contributes to the latter topic, but deals besides with another, Rousseauistic theme: the ill effects of an exaggerated cultivation of the arts and the artful on the mores of a community. A further topic, introduced by Diotima when she expounds her "theory" of the faculties of the human soul, becomes, as the title indicates, the main concern of *Simon ou des facultés de l'âme*.

While we need not dwell on the Scythian's criticism of Athenian society, the other themes treated in *Simon* deserve some elaboration. Concerning sculpture, the visual arts, and poetry, there is little in *Simon* that had not been said in the *Lettre sur la sculpture*. Grucker's conjecture[15] that Hemsterhuis had learned meanwhile from Winckelmann and Lessing must remain highly questionable. Jansen added a long note to *Simon*,[16] taken over later by Meyboom, which contains an exposition of Lessing's *Laokoon*, then still largely unknown to the French public. Hemsterhuis, who hardly read German, may have heard, of course, about *Laokoon* through his German friends. But there is little reason to postulate such a knowledge. Brummel assures us[17] that the philosopher refers to Lessing only once in his correspondence and then merely mentions the name. As to a possible influence of Winckelmann, the *Lettre sur la sculpture* shows more points of contact with the German historian of art than *Simon*. Both works deal with the question of the scope and rank of the arts. That poetry has a wider scope than the visual arts is reaffirmed in *Simon*, but now more emphasis is given to the fact, also elaborated on by Dubos, Harris, and Lessing, that the visual arts can merely suggest motion or action, since they are restricted to the representation of *one* moment in time. With this observation Socrates refutes Mnesarch's bold assertion that sculpture is the most perfect art. To defend his thesis, the sculptor uses

essentially the same arguments that had been advanced by
Hemsterhuis before. In *Simon*, however, Socrates attacks the
proposition previously asserted in the *Lettre sur la sculpture* (I, 43)
that sculpture is superior to painting because it appeals to both sight
and touch. The Athenian philosopher, denying any role to the sense
of touch, maintains that sculpture addresses itself only to the eye,
though more completely than any other art. Hemsterhuis dis-
parages now the importance of the sense of touch for a discrimina-
tion of sculpture from painting, a point that Herder correctly
emphasized against Lessing, in favor of a less concrete, more
spiritual concept of art. In keeping with this spiritualizing tendency
in Hemsterhuis, which was probably encouraged by the Princess,
Socrates states that a considerable part of the inner life of the soul
will never find adequate representation in a work of art. Both
Socrates and the Scythian reject the notion that a higher or lower
rank can be assigned to the individual arts. When the Scythian
asserts that the skill with which Homer or Phidias represents Zeus
evokes an equally strong and deep impression, Hemsterhuis may
have had in mind the comparison of these artists by Dio
Chrysostomos. This rhetor set forth ideas about the differences
between the visual arts, especially sculpture, and poetry which are
similar to the arguments used by such eighteenth century critics as
Dubos, Shaftesbury, Diderot, Caylus, Harris, Batteux, and above all
in Lessing's *Laokoon*.[18] A possible influence of Dio Chrysostomos
on these authors, including Hemsterhuis, remains a matter of conjecture. As Brummel suggests,[19] Mnesarch's use of the term
"heureux moment" (II, 96) probably goes back to Caylus' expression "instant heureux" in his *Tableaux tirés d'Homère et de Virgile*
(1757). Socrates' objection in *Simon*, however, that not only "happy" but also "sad" moments are represented in the visual arts
misses the point that "happy" is to be interpreted as meaning
"felicitously chosen." When Caylus speaks of "l'instant heureux
d'une nature frappante," he indicates that the moment chosen by
the artist must be "striking." Socrates' interpretation of the
"heureux moment" bears no relation to Caylus' views concerning
the "instant heureux" or to Lessing's "fruchtbarer Augenblick," the
most pregnant moment which sculptors and painters must choose to
suggest succession in time or action. Grucker's and Bulle's contention that Hemsterhuis' discussion of the "heureux moment" was in-

fluenced by Lessing must be rejected. Summing up, we may say
that the observations concerning the differences between poetry
and the visual arts present nothing that was not current among the
above-mentioned critics. Hemsterhuis expounded these ideas in
Simon with less detail and elaboration than in the *Lettre sur la
sculpture*.

Diotima-Hemsterhuis' "theory" of the human soul comprises
mainly a rather cut-and-dried classification of man according to the
proportionate strength of the four basic faculties of his psyche as
they had been outlined in a footnote to *Aristée* (II, 45 f., n. 2). This
ambitious effort to lay the foundations for a systematic psychology
contrasts with one of the main tendencies of Hemsterhuisian
thought, namely, to emphasize the value of ultimately ineffable individuality. The philosopher's undeniable penchant for pedantry
prevailed here over his finer sensibilities. A characteristic example
of this pedantry is the idea of representing the four basic faculties of
the soul by means of a diagram, showing what Hemsterhuis calls a
"four leaf clover." In a recently published letter to Princess Gallitzin, dated April 18, 1778, we find such a diagram referring to Baron
von Fürstenberg.[20] Trying to emulate the exactness of science,
Hemsterhuis even assigns numerical values to the strength or intensity of each of the faculties, using a scale from 0 to 100. The evaluation is based, however, on intution and not on pointer readings on
calibrated instruments, and is therefore inaccessible to scientific
verification. As the letter shows, Hemsterhuis himself took this
pretense at "exact" psychology very seriously. Since he was more
interested in ethics and education than in psychology per se, his
classification aims rather at types of conduct than at a psychological
typology. In accordance with his theory of ethics, the author of
Simon emphasizes the role of the *organe moral* in its relations to the
other faculties of the human soul.

The core of Hemsterhuis' ethics is to be found in Diotima's thesis
that the highest virtue is based upon and manifested in an
equilibrium of all faculties. The demand for a harmony of all
faculties introduces a strong esthetic component into ethics.
Although Shaftesbury, whose works were in Hemsterhuis' library, is
never mentioned by the author of *Simon*, the English philosopher's
ideal of *kalokagathia*, implying a coincidence of moral perfection
with beauty and harmony, may have influenced the thought of the

"Batavian Plato."[21] The common source of inspiration for both Shaftesbury and Hemsterhuis was, of course, Plato. While some of Novalis' notes from *Simon* deal with Diotima's classification of moral types,[22] we may assume that he felt more attracted to the passages, likewise excerpted, in which the seeress expounds her ideal of harmony and virtue and asserts that man's striving for perfection will continue after death and issue in a disclosure of new aspects of the universe by means of still unused organs. Novalis and Friedrich Schlegel found here an idea that linked Hemsterhuis with another favorite of theirs, Fichte, and his doctrine of man's infinite, asymptotic progress toward perfection. In Hemsterhuis' emphasis on the harmonious development of all faculties of the soul, Novalis and Schlegel could find support for their own demand that the formation of the individual person should aim at "totality" (*Totalität*). The Dutch philosopher was also an ally in their opposition to Kant's rigoristic ethics, based upon the dichotomy of inclination and duty. Friedrich Schlegel, as we have seen, admired the composition of *Simon*, seeing in it an example of dithyrambic philosophy, and was deeply impressed by the role assigned to Diotima, the seeress. Herder, on the other hand, was right when he claimed that this dialogue contained only a few ideas not previously expressed in Hemsterhuis' writings. To be sure, the attempt to establish five basic types of man was something new, but this schematic classification had hardly any effect on Hemsterhuis' readers, except Princess Gallitzin, whose interest in education was responsible for this typology. *Simon* contains, however, a reference to the golden age, which became the theme of the next dialogue, *Alexis*, a work that exerted a strong influence on Novalis and others.

CHAPTER 10

Alexis, or on the Golden Age

I The Dialogue

W HILE still trying to put *Simon* into final shape, Hemsterhuis began working on *Alexis ou de l'âge d'or*, the last work to come out during his life. Its French original and a German translation by Jacobi, entitled *Alexis oder von dem goldenen Weltalter*, were published simultaneously in 1787 in Riga (Latvia) by Hartknoch, a publisher known to Herder and Hamann. The latter had written in July, 1787, on behalf of Jacobi to Hartknoch, urging him to print *Alexis* and its translation. This dialogue, Hamann maintained, was on a par with Hemsterhuis' masterpieces so much admired by Kant.[1] As early as November, 1780, Hemsterhuis had communicated to Princess Gallitzin an outline of his thoughts about the golden age (III, 86 ff.), as described by Hesiod in his *Works and Days*, and indicated that he would pursue these reflections, which then became the central theme of *Alexis*. She received a complete draft of this work in November of the same year and expressed great admiration for the "sublime" dialogue.[2] Corrected copies of *Simon* and *Alexis* were sent to her in March 1783.[3]

Jacobi had met Hemsterhuis in 1781, when the latter was working on *Alexis*. Its main theme became most likely a topic of discussion, especially since Jacobi had alluded to the golden age and Rousseau's ideas on man in the state of nature in his dialogue "Der Kunstgarten," first published in 1779 in the journal *Deutsches Museum*. In this work, later incorporated into his novel *Woldemar*, the author emphasized that it was man's obligation to supplement instinct with reason in order to become truly human. After having read *Alexis* in manuscript, Jacobi wrote to Princess Gallitzin on June 10, 1783, that this dialogue, which reminded him of his own "Kunstgarten," surpassed everything written by Hemsterhuis, and indicated that he would like to translate *Alexis* if the author would give permission and be more careful with copies of the manuscript than he had been with *Simon*.[4] The Princess wrote immediately to Hemsterhuis (June, 1783), suggesting that Jacobi would be just the right person to render this dialogue into German.[5] Several years elapsed, however, before *Alexis* and Jacobi's translation of it were actually published.

Hemsterhuis, besides always being hesitant to publish, became engaged in other writings. While the Princess was deeply involved in her religious scruples and the education of her children, Jacobi's time was taken up with his Letters on Spinoza and the subsequent controversies. He proceeded nevertheless with his translation of *Alexis*, according to him one of the most beautiful products of the human mind.[6] The dialogue is mentioned by Goethe, who had apparently received a manuscript of it, in a letter to Jacobi of January 12, 1785, in which the poet advised his correspondent, however, that he was not going to write about the *meta ta physica* before he had studied more of *ta physica*.[7] It seems that *Alexis* and its translation were ready for publication by August, 1787, when Hemsterhuis requested a certain number of French and German copies for himself. He also asked that a copy be sent to Goethe, Herder, Wieland, Christian Friedrich von Blankenburg, and August Wilhelm Rehberg.[8] The latter had written philosophical treatises influenced by Hemsterhuis, while von Blankenburg, known today as the author of an essay on the novel, the *Versuch über den Roman* (1774), was responsible for the anonymously published edition of the *Vermischte philosophische Schriften*. As Brummel points out,[9] Hemsterhuis had at first regarded this unauthorized translation with suspicion. But in 1785 he and the Princess had visited von Blankenburg. Realizing then how much he had contributed to spreading Hemsterhuis' fame in Germany, they included him in the list of persons to receive a complimentary copy of *Alexis*. The third volume of the *Vermischte philosophische Schriften*, which appeared in 1797, contained this dialogue in a translation based on Jansen's first edition of Hemsterhuis' *Oeuvres* (1792). Pointing out that even Hemsterhuis considered the German version of *Alexis* superior to the original in precision and lucidity, Jacobi regarded his translation

as a work of his own. Friedrich Roth, to whom we owe this information, reprinted it therefore in Volume VI of Jacobi's *Werke*.[10]

Like *Aristée* and *Simon*, *Alexis* is also preceded by a dedicatory
epistle, in which Diocles conveys greetings to his wise and blessed
Diotima. He tells her of a visit to the temple of Saturn, where he
was especially attracted by the paintings depicting a golden age of
peace and happiness. Living in an iron age, Diocles finds it difficult
to render the impressions evoked by the pictures of the Saturnian
age. Diotima's pure and pious soul, he asserts, still preserves a
genuine archetype of the golden age this side of Elysium. The fictitious dedicatory epistle, which serves as introduction to the
dialogue, contains at the same time Hemsterhuis' homage to
Princess Gallitzin.

In *Alexis*, the author returns to the simple form of *Sophyle*. There
is no editor's preface, which precedes the dialogue in *Simon* and
Aristée, no ironic display of antiquarian learning, nor any fictitious
account of how a supposedly real manuscript got into the hands of
the editor. From the complex structure of *Simon*, with its narrative
frame, its alternation of reported with direct dialogue, and its large
number of participants, Hemsterhuis reverts in *Alexis* to a dialogue
between two persons only.

At the beginning of the dialogue, Diocles and Alexis meet, ex-
changing greetings. Their small talk turns very soon to more serious
matters when Alexis avows that he has lost his former liking for
poetry ever since Diocles awakened in him the taste for the
"philosophy of Socrates" (II, 144). The suggestion that the Athenian philosopher was perhaps a poet, while Orpheus, Hesiod, and
Homer were also philosophers, is countered by Alexis' avowal that
he has no sympathy for them as poets. As such they fabricate fables
or lies in order to amuse instead of conveying pure truth, which
needs no ornaments. Alexis is willing to go along with the poets as
long as they present truth, even if it is no more than verisimilitude.
He will accept theogonies and stories about the gods, about whom
we do not know anything, but objects to extravagant fables about
matters known to us. As an example of these he cites Hesiod's
description of the Saturnian golden age, which seems to contradict
everything we know of man in his present condition. Is it possible,
Alexis asks, that man was ever the way he is described by the poet?

Diocles insists that human nature has not degenerated. Hesiod did not lie about the golden age. To prove this contention, which becomes the main concern of the dialogue, Diocles reconstructs a picture of life on earth shortly after its creation. Humans as well as animals peopled the planet. Man, who had at that time no advantage over animals, has since then grown immensely in power and sagacity (II, 149), due to an inherent principle of perfectibility. While even animals are urged by instinct to satisfy their needs and thus to better their situation, they differ from man greatly in the perception of what constitutes a better state ("la sensation du meilleur"; II, 150). With the assertion that desire entails the principle of perfectibility, Hemsterhuis establishes indeed continuity between animals and humans, but overlooks the fact that the adjustment at which animal instinct aims is in each case only temporary and lacks the intentional, accumulative, or progressive feature of human perfectibility.

Referring to Diotima's discourse on the faculties of the human soul in *Simon*, Diocles points out that animals and humans right after their birth possess only the sensation of want and of an object that satisfies it. Intellect and *velléité* have no more than these data to work on, while the moral organ as well as any notion of duty are completely lacking. However, as man's intellect develops, several ideas or sensations of about equal power occupy his imagination so that man feels free to choose among them. Although Hemsterhuis still alludes to the four basic faculties as outlined in *Simon*, he goes beyond this schematic categorization by introducing the concept of *personnalité* (II, 161). By dint of the "principle" which constitutes personality man discerns, weighs, judges his faculties and establishes harmony among them. Wisdom is measured by the independence as well as the strength of the principle of personality. Bulle and Brummel have emphasized the importance of this step beyond a *Vermögenspsychologie*,[11] a psychology concerned with separate faculties, to what Bulle calls a new, irrational concept of personality and individuality. In this, Bulle surmises, Hemsterhuis was influenced by Jacobi. Hamann, Herder, Goethe, von Fürstenberg, and Friedrich Schlegel had also abandoned *Vermögenspsychologie* in favor of a unified view of man that extolled *Persönlichkeit*. All of the persons just mentioned were familiar with *Alexis*. Of others, like Wilhelm von Humboldt and Schleiermacher, who both insisted on the supreme value of *Persönlichkeit*, we can-

not be sure whether they knew *Alexis*, of von Humboldt not even
whether he had a firsthand knowledge of Hemsterhuis.[12] Novalis is
the only one who took extensive notes from the writings of this
philosopher and referred in his "Hemsterhuis-Studien" of 1797 explicitly to the principle of personality as outlined in *Alexis*.[13]

Closely connected with the emphasis on *personnalité* is the conviction that ethics has to consider the interplay of all faculties
within a given individual and that highest virtue consists in their
harmonious equilibrium, which is the manifestation of personality.
Personnalité, Persönlichkeit has the additional connotation of an
ethical ideal which distinguishes personality from the merely psychological concept of "person": not every person is a personality. It
must remain a matter of conjecture how much Hemsterhuis' very
brief remarks on *personnalité* influenced the above-mentioned German writers in their views on the ethical significance of *In-
dividualität* and *Persönlichkeit* and their emphasis on *Totalität*.
Such ideas had been adumbrated in works much earlier and more
easily accessible than Hemsterhuis' writings. Shaftesbury's ideal of
the *virtuoso*, Leibniz' monadology, Kant's transcendental apperception, establishing the unity of all experience, pointed all in the same
direction as the principle of *personnalité* in *Alexis*. All we can say is
that Hemsterhuis expressed views on personality and ethics that
coincided partly with those entertained by some of his most prominent readers.

Returning to *Alexis*, we find that Diocles' friend likewise feels the
need to go back to the main theme of the dialogue, namely, the
golden age. Humans and animals, Alexis and his mentor agree, are
striving to attain the objects of their desires and through them happiness or enjoyment. While this attainment constitutes the perfect
golden age for animals, man also finds happiness when he sees his
fellows happy (II, 164). Without mentioning the term, Diocles-
Hemsterhuis alludes here to the *organe moral*. Alexis' remark that
Diocles' description of the golden age seems so far only concerned
with pastoral simplicity is taken up by Alexis' older friend, who
enters now upon a lengthy account of a conversation between
Pythagoras and a priest, named Hypsicles, who had instructed the
philosopher in astronomy. Pythagoras belabors the Arcadians for
claiming that their ancestors go back to a time when the moon did
not yet exist. Hypsicles, however, vindicates this tradition, claiming

that men actually lived on earth before the moon appeared. During that pre-lunar epoch the axis of the earth was perpendicular to its orbital plane, night and day were always of equal length everywhere on the globe, there were no seasons, nor differences in climates or tides. Vegetarian food abounded in all places at all times. Man knew neither property nor commerce or war. His language was absolutely perfect, consisting of gestures or words that were direct expressions of his emotions and in perfect agreement with the objects designated. Abstract and figurative expressions were unknown. A single sigh, word, or gesture sufficed to manifest the condition of the soul, "swimming in a sea of voluptuousness" (II, 175). Man felt vividly the divine omnipresence, lived without knowledge of evil. To be good required no effort, and death came to men without fear, like the fruit after the flower.

Hemsterhuis, here using Hypsicles as his mouthpiece, describes the golden age with an attention to imaginative detail that might seem to be inspired by his enthusiasm for this topic. We find, however, the same lively description also in the subsequent depiction of the cosmic catastrophe that terminated the golden age. It is the imaginative presentation of what Hemsterhuis believed actually to have happened rather than enthusiasm that characterizes these parts of *Alexis*.

What Hypsicles says about human language during the golden age reflects the author's interest in the *Ursprache*, the primordial stage of language, a concern he shared with Diderot, Condillac, Rousseau, Hamann, Herder, and others. Although Hemsterhuis avoids the much debated question of how human language arose, we can be sure that he probably would have agreed with Condillac and Herder that language was neither deliberately invented nor bestowed on man by God but rather sprang from man's nature. In view of this, it is rather surprising to see Hemsterhuis assert an absolute perfection of language during the golden age, a thesis that discounts evolution and that would fit better with the theories of invention or direct divine inspiration, especially with the latter. As a matter of fact, the perfect *Ursprache* before the cosmic catastrophe occurred reminds us of speculations about the language of prelapsarian Adam by the German mystic Jakob Böhme. Though Hemsterhuis emphasizes the role of gestures and inarticulate sighs as well as the absence of abstractions in the *Ursprache*, he denies the existence of figurative expressions, whereas Rousseau in his *Essai sur l'origine des langues*, unpublished during his lifetime, Hamann in his *Aesthetica in nuce* (1762), and Herder in his *Abhandlung über den Ursprung der Sprache* (1772) had insisted on the metaphoric, "poetic" character of the *Ursprache* and praised it for just this reason. Hemsterhuis, closer in this as also in other matters to Enlightenment thought, claimed that the perfection of language consists in the exclusion of figurative expressions, in what he calls the perfect agreement (II, 174) between the sign and the object signified. While d'Alembert demanded a purely denotative, logically consistent language of signs, independent of any metaphysical assumptions about the adequacy of signs and objects denoted by them, Hemsterhuis assumed that man was capable of a perfect, archetypal knowledge of essences which can be expressed in a language whose signs represent essences with perfect adequacy. Such perfect knowledge and language, he claimed, man had possessed during the golden age. Hypsicles marvels at the luminous knowledge man enjoyed then (II, 174). Since that time, Diocles surmises, mankind must have lost some senses or organs that allowed a more complete grasp of truth than is now given to most humans. These speculations about a perfect existence and knowledge from which man has fallen away are in line with Neoplatonism and indicate a fundamental difference between Hemsterhuis and the philosophers of Enlightenment, for whom the *Ursprache* was an inarticulate, imperfect language of savages.[14]

A cosmic catastrophe, described by Hypsicles in great detail, ended the pre-lunar state of bliss on earth. A comet came too close to our planet, was drawn into its gravitational field, and became its satellite, known as the moon. Henceforth, the axis of the earth was no longer perpendicular to the plane of its orbit. The evenly serene climate gave way to the inclemencies of weather as we know them now; enormous tides occurred, causing destruction. Man became a different creature. While he had formerly lived in undisturbed tranquillity, he now experienced misery, and embraced a religion of superstitious awe and the foolish notion of malevolent deities, of a cosmic struggle between good and evil powers. Death, previously experienced as a passing, voluptuous moment, not yet falsely embellished by hope ("espérance"; II, 177), assumed a new aspect of horror, of something forced on man ("un état forcé"; *ibid.*). After the traumatic experience of cataclysm, man vacillated for centuries between error and truth. Slowly, however, the wise among men adjusted to the world's shortcomings, finding beauty even in discord. The pre-lunar state and the catastrophe that ended it became a matter of a dim, distant past.

Hypsicles, the sacerdotal guardian of tradition and cosmic mysteries, introduced as authority to convince Alexis that the golden age actually existed, represents together with Diocles Hemsterhuis' ideas within the framework of an allegedly ancient dialogue. Such personae allow the author to speak indirectly and with modesty. Using Hypsicles as a mouthpiece, Hemsterhuis was able to avoid a direct assertion of unusual ideas, which were nevertheless his own. His letter to Princess Gallitzin of November 23, 1780, cited above, shows that he was convinced of the existence of a golden age. He was equally serious, as Brummel has pointed out,[15] about the cataclysm brought on by a comet that became our moon. Brummel lists a number of writers, among them the Swede Olaus Rudbeck, author of a book on the mythical continent of Atlantis, in whom Hemsterhuis found support for his speculations. A long note to *Alexis* (II, 169 ff.), accompanied by a diagram, attests to the seriousness of his astronomical speculations.

The hypothesis of a cosmic catastrophe involving the earth, recently revived by Immanuel Velikovsky in his book *Worlds in Collision* (1950), had many adherents in the eighteenth century.[16] As Frank E. Manuel has shown, a considerable number of writers endeavored to replace the account of creation in Genesis by what he calls "the rationalist myth of origins."[17] Nicolas-Antoine Boulanger, who was connected with the circle of materialist *philosophes* gathered around Holbach, ascribed in his book *L'Antiquité dévoilée*, published posthumously in 1766, the birth of a religion of superstitious fear to the "Trauma of the Flood" (Manuel). Far from indulging in creations of his own unbridled fantasy, Hemsterhuis presented views concerning the history of the earth that were widely current when he wrote *Alexis*. He tried to give what in his time could be considered a "scientific" account of the mythical golden age and its sudden termination by a cosmic catastrophe instead of the biblical "Fall." *Alexis*, supposedly an ancient dialogue, contains, of course, no reference to Hemsterhuis' contemporaries. But even in a detailed note (II, 169 ff.) neither Buffon nor Boulanger are cited, although the former was certainly known to Hemsterhuis. While Boulanger's dating of the Saturnian age after the Deluge differed from Hemsterhuis' chronology, both authors agreed that the "Trauma of the Flood" had brought on a change in religion. There is no evidence, as Gobbers points out,[18] for a repeatedly asserted influence of Rousseau's two Discourses on the depiction of the golden age in Alexis. Rousseau is never mentioned in Hemsterhuis' writings and only once, rather disparagingly, in his correspondence.[19]

Although Hemsterhuis was certainly familiar with the various expressions of the myth of the golden age in ancient literature as well as with the Judaeo-Christian notions about Paradise, the setting of Alexis confined him to Hesiod's description of the Saturnian age. The golden age became a literary topos with a long and varied tradition, which has recently been made the subject of an extensive survey by Hans-Joachim Mähl.[20] Alexis is an important link in the tradition of this topos. Its ubiquitousness makes it very difficult, however, to determine what writers Hemsterhuis consulted besides Hesiod.

Diocles concludes from Hypsicles' account that death, evil, vice are foreign to the nature of man, who has always felt that he is meant for greater happiness than that enjoyed at any present moment. The golden age gives an indication of what human existence could really be. Realizing the gaps in our present knowledge, we are led to assume that man most likely has lost some senses or organs together with corresponding "vehicles of action" (II, 178). These allowed man in some past age to perceive truth as a whole instead of the fragmentary knowledge he possesses now. A footnote, however, refers us to Sophyle, where it has been demonstrated that man can even in his present condition perceive the connection of truths. According to Hemsterhuis-Diocles, the very fact that we are conscious of the fragmentariness of our knowledge, far from warranting skepticism, furnishes proof that we must be capable of attaining perfect knowledge.

Alexis remains still unconvinced. According to him, Hesiod has described mere "shadows of things," existing in his imagination. Alexis is not even sure whether Hypsicles has not offered just another poetic fable. Diocles tries to dispel what he considers his friend's prejudice against "divine poetry," by pointing out that human knowledge rests upon three pillars, namely, history, philosophy, and poetry. History reports facts, philosophy establishes order among them, whereas poetry not only adorns but also enriches the findings of the former two (II, 182). Orpheus, Hesiod, Homer dwell in the Elysian fields with Thales, Pythagoras, Socrates, Plato. Our knowledge rests on first principles or truths which, as even geometry shows, are sometimes "felt" before they are proved ("des vérités senties . . . avant d'être prouvées"; II, 183). Poetry and rhetoric exhibit truths, beauties, sublime traits that were at first "felt" and only later analyzed by the intellect.

Correctly formed ideas, Diocles continues, reflect real objects or *rapports*. If the composition of such ideas exhibits beauty it must also exist in the composite formed by their objects. Consequently, poetry can convey truths. We have used our own wording to sum up Diocles' somewhat involved argumentation which actually seems to beg the question. To be sure, adequate ideas ("les idées ou les empreintes fidèles"; II, 184) or their composites constitute by definition a faithful rendering of objects or their *rapports*, but the real question is how we arrive at such ideas and whether poetry is based on them. Scientists and poets have made conflicting claims in this matter. To strengthen his argument, Diocles gives a definition of beauty in terms that are familiar from the *Lettre sur la sculpture*. Beauty is dependent upon—Diocles rather dubiously says "consists" in—the number of ideas and the shortness of time required to connect them or the ease with which the intellect grasps any whole (II, 185). We perceive most rapidly those *rapports* which are the easiest to grasp, i.e., those which constitute beauty. The works of genius evince an instantaneous insight into *rapports*. Genius, as Hemsterhuis writes in the *Réflexions sur la République des Provinces-Unies*, seizes and presents analogies between widely different, apparently disparate ideas where ordinary minds would sometimes need centuries of experience and reflection. To the ability to link a maximum of ideas in the most felicitous manner which gives rise to the beautiful and sublime, we owe also the insight into great truths.[21] Hemsterhuis uses in *Alexis* the term *intuition*, though qualified by the expression "so to speak" (II, 186), to designate an immediate *Anschauung*, in which truth is apprehended by philosophers and scientists as well as poets, independent and ahead of the slow process of exact ratiocination. The intellect works on the

data furnished by *intuition* and made available through the imagination, which is the more compact the more intuitively grasped
rapports it has at its disposal. *Intuition* establishes the link between
philosophy, science, and poetry as well as the cognitive value of the
latter.

Alexis, convinced that he understands now the role of poetry,
sums up what he has learned from Diocles. Through reasoning
alone, no matter how profound or exact, without the aid and
guidance of an "enthusiasm" (II, 188) that connects widely
different ideas, we could only rarely arrive at new truths. Following Diocles suggestions, Alexis emphasizes the role of "cet
enthousiasme actif," which seems to be due to inspiration by an
agent outside of us (II, 189). Alexis, who considers it very likely that
man may have lost some "véhicule de sensation" *(ibid.);* is now
ready to admit that Hypsicles' account of a past age of perfection is
highly probable. The prospect of some future perfection, in itself
perhaps too vague, finds corroboration in the assertion that man actually enjoyed a golden age.

Diocles-Hemsterhuis' remarks on "genius" and "enthusiasm"
were hardly startling within the context of then contemporary European criticism and so brief that they strike us as being somewhat
anemic. More characteristic of his own thought, and closely connected with his wish to prove that Hesiod's myth of the golden age
is not a figment of the poet's fantasy, is Diocles' vindication of
poetry. Convinced that knowledge consists of the combination of
ideas, the author of *Alexis* finds that poets, while aiming at beauty,
that is, at representing a maximum of ideas that can be grasped
with most ease in the shortest possible time, excel in connecting
widely different ideas. Hemsterhuis gives here a wider scope to his
definition of beauty. Originally referring to the sensory data of
sculpture and painting, it is now applied to the combination of
abstract ideas and thus connected with the theory of knowledge.
Relying on inspiration or enthusiasm, "qui rapproche les idées" (II,
188), and exercising the quick *intuition* that is called "tact" (II,
188 f.), the poets often anticipate truths later corroborated by the
findings of science or philosophy, which depend upon a slow
process of verification and ratiocination. New and great truths do
not result from rational analysis, but are "felt," intuitively grasped
before they can be proved.

While the notion of the poet as a *vates*, a seer and conveyor of truth, had a long literary tradition, Hemsterhuis vindicated the cognitive value of poetry as a philosopher, claiming that synthetic *intuition*, which leads to the discovery of new truths, is the special prerogative of poets, whereas scientists and philosophers rely mainly on analytic reasoning. Poetry was actually proclaimed superior, the poet declared to be free of the limitations of a mode of thinking that proceeds cautiously step by step.

Alexis admits that philosophy owes much to poetry, a rather unwarranted conclusion from an argument that has merely shown that intuitive insight, inspiration, enthusiasm, so essential for poets, also play a role in philosophy. But he has one more question: can the golden age, apart from the assertions of poets and historians about it, also be made the subject of philosophical contemplation? This question, as Diocles points out, amounts to asking whether it can be demonstrated, independent of inspiration or tradition, that man is potentially capable of leading a fuller and more noble life than he lives at present. The golden age, Diocles continues, is a "terme figuré" (II, 190), a figurative expression for a condition in which any being enjoys all the happiness it can attain in accordance with its essential nature. Animals reach a state of happiness proportionate to the limited nature of their desires, which do not aim beyond a momentary satisfaction. Man, in whom the principle of perfectibility is much stronger than in animals, rises above the instinctive level of existence. The fact that hope seems to be innate in man, a hope not concerned with a relative improvement of present conditions but with an absolute, though indeterminate, optimum, indicates that man's desires transcend the limitations of his present mode of existence. Man belongs apparently to another order of things ("un autre état"; II, 191), different from the one known to him on earth at present. When Diocles discriminates between the everyday kind of hope ("espérance journalière"; *ibid.*) and a hope concerned with the absolute best ("le meilleur absolu"; *ibid.*), he implies a distinction between *espoir* and *espérance*, although he uses only the latter term. Diocles-Hemsterhuis' argument reminds us of the role assigned to *espérance* in the philosophy of the twentieth-century French existentialist Gabriel Marcel.[22]

When Alexis asks whether man will attain the "other state" he hopes for, Diocles answers affirmatively. Just as most fledglings

have wings enabling them eventually to take to the air, man has
desires that will make him rise above the satisfactions that life on
earth can offer. Man is as little at home on earth as fish on dry
ground. Alexis' conclusion that only animals, then, are happy in this
world is confirmed by Diocles, who now proposes to consider once
more the moment when men and animals were almost equal and
both were happy inhabitants of the earth. This moment was of short
duration, since man's unlimited desires made him soon despise the
kind of animal happiness he had enjoyed. He came to suffer from
his indeterminate desires, which he sought in vain to satisfy by
restlessly turning from one object to another, in the false hope of
quenching his thirst for the true infinite by appropriating to himself
the spurious infinity of a limitless number of finite objects. Not content with his state of animal perfection (II, 193), man started to ex-
plore the heavens and seas, the interior of the earth, began wars,
conceived the notion of private property, formed governments, and
made laws. Man, who had been undivided in himself, became
"after his Fall" ("depuis sa chute"; *ibid.*) "amphibious," as Diocles
says, divided in nature, trying to hold on to the poles of his being
after he had lost some modes of perception that formerly established a unifying bond. Basically, however, he remained a being of
homogeneous nature ("un être d'une existence homogène"; *ibid.*).
His degeneration is only accidental, has not impaired his essential
nobility.

Urged by Alexis to be more explicit, Diocles asserts that during
the golden age described by Hesiod and Hypsicles man was as
perfect as his essential nature allowed him to be. Having survived
the cosmic catastrophe that terminated the golden age, he attained
by dint of his inherent principle of perfectibility to another golden,
or rather a silver, age (II, 194). This reference to a second golden
age comes as a surprise, since we have gotten the impression that
there had been only one Saturnian age in the past. It might have
been less confusing if Diocles-Hemsterhuis had clearly distinguished, as Hesiod did, between the golden and the silver age instead of calling the latter a second golden age. As Diocles points
out, man soon outgrew the relative perfection of the silver age and
became the unhappy creature described above until an "enlightened
philosophy" (II, 195) taught him to link the present with the
future and realize his basically undivided eternal nature, which the

"fall" had not really destroyed (*ibid.*).

"Enlightened philosophy" shows that man is capable of attaining yet another, third golden age, which will differ as much from the preceding two golden ages as these between themselves. The future golden age will come when man's knowledge has progressed as far as his present "organs" allow him to go. Perceiving the absurd disproportion between his desires and what he can enjoy on earth, man will then retrace his steps ("retourner sur ses pas"; II, 195) to find a salutary, just equilibrium between his desires and the objects actually at their reach. Having attained all the insights of which he is capable in this world, man will join these with the simplicity of the first golden age.

According to Diocles-Hemsterhuis, each individual will attain a golden age after his death, when all his enjoyments ("jouissances") will become more coherent, more inwardly felt ("plus intimes, plus cohérentes"; II, 195) and his knowledge will be fused into one luminous whole. Hemsterhuis thought perhaps, like Lessing in *Die Erziehung des Menschengeschlechts*, that a perfection which could be realized only in a distant future would deprive the preceding generations of the fruits of their striving for perfection. Lessing tried to overcome this dilemma by postulating a metempsychosis or palingenesis. Hemsterhuis' assumption of a golden age after death fulfills the same function.

Summing up the argument of the dialogue, Diocles claims that he has shown how much philosophy can assert concerning the different "ages of perfection" (II, 196). To know more of the "last age" (*ibid.*), we must turn to divine inspiration. *Alexis* concludes with Diocles' and his disciple's resolve to sacrifice to the God of Love on the following day. *Amour*, which meant so much in Hemsterhuis' life and thought, is the last word of the dialogue that affirms man's hope and that was to be the last of the works published during the philosopher's life.

II   *Two Letters on the Golden Age*

Hemsterhuis' two letters to Princess Gallitzin of November, 1780, to which we referred before, contain a sketch of the ideas that found expression in *Alexis*. The first one, dated November 23, gives an insight into the personal background of the philosopher's speculations about the golden age. Beset by somber thoughts, he finds no protection against them in the Stoics, whose vaunted impassibility conceals a pusillanimous fear of being human. Only the contemplation of man's future will shield him from his depressing thoughts. While rereading Hesiod's *Works and Days*, Hemsterhuis continues, he was struck more than ever before by the poet's description of the golden age, which he had formerly considered to be no more than a poetic fiction. Looking at the matter more closely, however, he claims, one will have to realize that the state of man described by Hesiod must have existed.

The remainder of the letter contains an outline of the argument presented subsequently in *Alexis*. Summing up his thoughts, Hemsterhuis offers three theses: (1) We can never return to Hesiod's golden age. (2) If man had been capable from the very beginning of the reflections outlined in the letter, he might have given a constant direction to the errant course of his perfection. (3) Man, after having realized the disproportion between his present imperfection and his inherent unlimited perfectibility, will turn back ("retourner en arrière"; III, 88), correct his absurd mistakes, and enter into a golden age infinitely superior to that described by the poets. Hemsterhuis asks his Diotima whether she detects any signs of this "return" ("marche rétrograde"; *ibid.*).

The second letter, dated November 30,[23] not November 20, as Meyboom has it (III, 89), indicates that Diotima had responded favorably to Hemsterhuis' ideas. He points out, however, that the "return" to a superior golden age, a matter of "pure speculation," will take place only in the very distant future. Man, who has made so much progress in physics, is still a child in the fields of metaphysics and psychology. Following the precept "Know thyself" and relying on feeling, even before the intellect can furnish proofs, man will anticipate or discover hitherto unknown truths. While the two letters contain an epitome of the author's views concerning the past and future golden age, *Alexis* includes, of course, a wealth of descriptive and narrative detail, references to persons and Greek mythology to which we have paid hardly any attention. These features, which enliven the abstract arguments of *Alexis* and Hemsterhuis' other dialogues, prompted August Wilhelm Schlegel to call them "intellectual poems".[24] Compared with the letters, *Alexis* shows also a number of important thematic changes. The former do not yet refer to the hypothesis of a cosmic catastrophe that furnished in *Alexis* what Hemsterhis considered a "scientific" explanation for the termination of the first golden age. In his earlier outline he explains, like Rousseau, man's imperfection as resulting from the dialectical nature of his capacity for limitless perfection. Adopting the hypothesis of cosmic catastrophe entailed for Hemsterhuis the assertion that man had passed through two golden ages, whereas the philosopher had at first referred to only one Saturnian reign. To convince his readers that a future golden age is within reach of man, the author of *Alexis* deemed it necessary to prove that such an age had existed in the past, although the expectation of a utopia does not need such a confirmation. Since the conditions of the pre-lunar epoch could not be repeated, Hemsterhuis had to show that man had attained another golden age even after the catastrophe, under circumstances still prevailing on earth. Only this second golden, or rather silver, age can be linked with its future return in one continuous process. Having asserted the existence of more than one "golden age," Hemsterhuis had to give a generic definition of it, since the term no longer referred to a singular historical event. Such a definition he proposed in *Alexis*, where we also find the surprising statement that the "golden age" is a "figurative term" (II, 190). We are here reminded of Rousseau's assertion in the preface to his *Discours sur l'inégalité* that the "state of nature" may never have existed and probably never will exist. Hemsterhuis, to be sure, saw in the golden age more than a mental construct, and tried to prove in *Alexis* that such an epoch had actually been experienced by man. But his letters to the Princess, especially the second one, which extols the role of introspection for the discovery of new truths, show clearly that the primary motive for his occupation with the golden age was an ideal of possible human perfection.

The straightforward argument of the letters was complicated and obscured in *Alexis* by the introduction of two past golden ages and by adducing two reasons for their termination: a hypothetical cosmic catastrophe on the one hand and man's unlimited perfectibility on the other. The former terminated the first golden age, the latter led man beyond the merely "animal perfection" (II, 194) of the silver age. While the hypothesis of a catastrophe was highly controversial, it was free of the paradox implied in the notion of a limitless perfectibility that results in imperfection. Hemsterhuis

solved the last-mentioned difficulty by asserting that the state of imperfection was only a temporary one, since the essential capacity for
unlimited perfection was left unimpaired, thus leaving hope for
man's future.

The ideal of a future golden age, shielding him from depressing
thoughts about the present condition of man, was from the very
beginning uppermost in Hemsterhuis' mind. His apparent preoccupation with man's past does not express a primitivistic longing to
return to a state of nature, nor a reactionary glorification of bygone
times. Like the Enlighteners, he looks forward, expecting his own
"enlightened" philosophy to be of help in preparing the advent of
the future golden age. He turned to former golden ages only to find
proof that perfection is possible, since it had actually existed. Even
when he speaks of retracing one's steps, of a "return" or a *marche
rétrograde*, he does not demand that we go back to a state of nature.
The possibility of a return to Hesiod's Saturnian age is explicitly
denied in the first letter. "Retracing one's steps" refers to a mental
procedure by which we find the moment when mankind embarked
on a wrong course.

III   *The Ideal of a Future Golden Age*

The ideal of a future golden age, which transcends the Greek setting of *Alexis*, belongs to the Judaeo-Christian view of history as
well as to its secularized form, the doctrine of progress, so prominent among the thinkers of Enlightenment.[25] While Hemsterhuis
shares with these the emphasis on man's unlimited perfectibility,
he, like Rousseau, stresses its problematic, dialectical nature and
does not accept the Enlighteners' concept of a rectilinear progress
from savagery to enlightened civilization. Jacobi would hardly have
been as enthused as he was about *Alexis* if he had seen in it a
description of the golden age envisioned by the *philosophes* of
Enlightenment. He likened their utopia without temples or altars,
where reason would rule supreme, to the states of ants or bees.[26]
Unlike the Enlighteners, Hemsterhuis believed in a golden age at
the beginning of man's life on earth, and maintained that mankind
had moved from this age of original perfection to a maximum of imperfection. Convinced that the one-sided cultivation of the intellect
had resulted in many ills, the author of *Alexis*, like Rousseau, urged
man to retrace his steps—a notion utterly foreign to the

Enlighteners—to advance to a condition that would be in keeping with his unlimited capacity for perfection. In Hemsterhuis' theory of history the three steps in which mankind moves from original perfection through imperfection to future perfection do not follow each other as stages in an unbroken line of progress. His theory differs from the ideas expressed by Lessing in his *Erziehung des Menschengeschlechts* and by the French philosopher Auguste Comte, who also distinguish three stages in mankind's advance to perfection, but adhere, in principle at least, to the notion of a rectilinear progress. Hemsterhuis' view of history seems to be closer to the traditional Judaeo-Christian triadic division of history with its stages of Paradise, "Paradise Lost" after the Fall, and "Paradise Regained," the Kingdom of Heaven on Earth or the messianic millennium. But his concept of history, especially of the future golden age, is thoroughly secular and humanistic. Unlike his German contemporary, the Swabian theosophist Friedrich Christoph Oetinger, who also tried to combine ancient philosophy with modern science and was convinced of the return of the golden age,[27] Hemsterhuis paid no attention to biblical tradition or to Christ. Although he spoke of man's "fall" ("sa chute"; II, 193), he did not see in it an irreparable event. While the conditions of the pre-lunar epoch could of course not be restored by human efforts, the principle of perfectibility had remained intact, as Hemsterhuis had already pointed out in *Simon* (II, 128). When he described the past golden age, it was not to contrast a paradise of absolute perfection with a subsequent fallen state out of which man could never extricate himself by his own power. Emphasizing that the perfection attained in the past was only of limited scope, the author of *Alexis* turned to it to kindle hopes for an even more perfect future.

The conviction that the ideal golden age lies ahead of us rather than in the past filled Hemsterhuis with an enthusiasm later also felt by Novalis and Friedrich Schlegel. Each found in the other, as Julius Petersen has pointed out,[28] the fervent belief that the return of a golden age was imminent and regarded the author of *Alexis* with special favor. Another favorite of theirs, Fichte, asserted in the fifth lecture of his discourses *Einige Vorlesungen über die Bestimmung des Gelehrten* (The Vocation of the Scholar), delivered in 1794, that the state of nature or the golden age, located in the past by Rousseau and some poets, lies really in the future.

What we are to attain in the future, Fichte continues, is often described as something we have enjoyed in the past and lost.[29] Convinced that Hesiod's Saturnian age had actually existed, Hemsterhuis differed on this point from Fichte.

Schiller, who characterized in his famous essay "Über naive und sentimentalische Dichtung" (On Naïve and Sentimentalic Poetry), published 1795—96, the idyll as the poetic description of innocence and happiness, of man living in harmony with himself and the world, maintained that such a life was not only enjoyed before civilization ("Kultur") but also constitutes the ultimate goal of civilized man. Rather than indulging in the sentiment of loss of an Arcadia to which man can never return, the poet ought to kindle the hope for Elysium, i.e., the future golden age. In a previous essay dealing with the beginnings of human society ("Etwas über die erste Menschengesellschaft," 1790), Schiller had demanded that man should restore his original innocence by dint of reason, return ("zurück kommen") to the point from which he had started as a plant ("Pflanze") or a creature of instinct, and advance from a paradise of ignorance and servitude to one of knowledge and freedom.[30]

Hölderlin's "Hymne an die Freiheit" (Hymn to Freedom), published in 1793, shows close affinities to ideas expressed in *Alexis*. In the preface to the "Thalia-Fragment" of his novel *Hyperion* (1794), Hölderlin states that the eccentric course ("die exzentrische Bahn") of the individual and of mankind is determined by two ideals of human existence. There is an initial state of highest simplicity, when the needs ("Bedürfnisse") and powers of man were in harmony by sheer organization of nature ("durch die blosse Organisation der Natur"), and there is a state of highest culture ("Zustand der höchsten Bildung"), in which the same harmony prevails over infinitely increased needs and powers by dint of an organization achieved by man himself.[31]

Fichte, Schiller, and Hölderlin agree with the author of *Alexis* that the ideal golden age lies ahead of us. They all maintain that the history of mankind proceeds in three stages: a state of original, relative perfection gives way to imperfection, which will be followed by a future state of ideal perfection. Fichte, to be sure, distinguishes in his lectures on Die *Grundzüge des gegenwärtigen Zeitalters* (1806), translated by William Smith as *The Char-*

acteristics of the Present Age (London, 1847), five stages. These, however, can be easily fitted into the triadic scheme if we single out the three most important stages: an age of innocence or reason as instinct ("Vernunftinstinkt"), of complete sinfulness ("Stand der vollendeten Sündhaftigkeit"), and of complete sanctification,[32] the last one involving a return to the beginning, though on a conscious level.

While Rousseau is expressly mentioned by Fichte and Schiller, we cannot be sure whether both knew Hemsterhuis. Oskar Walzel's claim in his introduction to Schiller's philosophical writings[33] that Fichte adopted literally ("wörtlich") Hemsterhuis' "formula" of the future golden age is, of course, exaggerated, and overlooks the important fact that the German philosopher emphasizes the role of restless activity in the formation of a future age, while the author of *Alexis* insists on the coincidence of *désir* and *jouissance*, on an ideal of passive enjoyment. The similarity between Hemsterhuis' views and those of Fichte and Schiller remains a puzzle, since neither of these two ever mentions the author of *Alexis*. To explain the parallels under discussion, however, we need not assume a direct influence of Hemsterhuis on Fichte or Schiller. There were on the one hand the religious notions about Paradise and the millennium, hardly relevant for the author of *Alexis*, who was inspired by Hesiod, but important for Schiller with his links to Swabian pietism and for Fichte, whose terminology ("Sündhaftigkeit", "Heiligung") definitely refers us to the Judaeo-Christian tradition. On the other hand, all three authors were surely familiar with Rousseau's ideas. His *Naturoptimismus* and *Kulturpessimismus*, combined with his belief in man's inherent perfectibility, could easily lead to a triadic conception of history, according to which mankind moved from original perfection via the imperfection of one-sided civilization to future perfection. To be sure, Rousseau did not explicitly speak of a future golden age. But his whole argument implied the possibility of advancing by retracing one's steps to the point where civilization went wrong.

After Rousseau the question arose of how civilized man could consciously regain the perfection and happiness he had formerly enjoyed instinctively. The question itself contained the answer. Having attained consciousness, man could not go back to a purely instinctual level of existence. He had to achieve consciously, by reason, the harmony that characterized his life when he was ruled by instinct alone. The old religious question of how to regain Paradise was now posed in a secular context. While the formulation of the problem and its solution varied from author to author, there was a general agreement that the future, third stage in the development of mankind, though in some respects involving a "return" to the first step, would be vastly superior to it. A true totality, now embracing instinct and intellect, would overcome the fragmentation, disharmony, alienation, and unhappiness engendered by the one-sided cultivation of the intellect.

Hemsterhuis' triadic conception of history implies a dialectical structure of thesis, antithesis, and synthesis, and combines the idea of a cyclic movement with that of progress and perfectibility, while at the same time taking into account Rousseau's negative attitude toward the ills engendered by civilization. Analogues to the view of history expounded in *Alexis*, which we detected in Fichte, Schiller, and Hölderlin, can also be found in Schelling's *System des transscendentalen [sic] Idealismus* (1800) and his *Vorlesungen über die Methode des akademischen Studiums* (1803),[34] in Heinrich von Kleist's essay on marionettes ("Über das Marionettentheater" [1810]), and much later still in Grillparzer's drama *Libussa* (published 1872), where King Primislaus sums up the poet's theory of history in the words "Im Anfang liegt das Ende" (Act IV), the beginning of history foreshadows its end. Even Karl Marx's view of history as a movement from primitive classless society via an epoch of class conflicts to a future classless society adheres to the triadic conception under discussion. None of these authors except Schelling ever mentioned Hemsterhuis. Independent of a belief in a past golden age, the future millennium may be conceived as the third age in accordance with a triadic theory of history that goes back to Joachim of Floris and differs from the one suggested by Hemsterhuis.

Hemsterhuis' assertion that man in the future golden age will unite the highest degree of knowledge or insight ("lumières") with the happy simplicity of the past golden age fits in with the triadic, dialectical formula of unity, manifoldness, totality ("Einheit, Vielheit, Totalität") favored by German thinkers after Kant. Maintaining that man will eventually achieve harmony in all his faculties after they have been developed to their highest degree and that science, philosophy, and poetry will be reunited in a future golden age, the author of *Alexis* enounced an ideal of *Totalität* that guided the thought of Novalis and Friedrich Schlegel, both familiar with *Alexis*, and of Wilhelm von Humboldt, who apparently never mentioned Hemsterhuis.

Peculiar to Hemsterhuis is the link he establishes in *Alexis* between the future golden age and life after death (II, 195). He expects from both a widening of insight and a coherence of knowledge denied to us in our earthly life. In an enraptured language, contrasting with the prevailing soberness, he expresses at the end of several of his writings the longing for a higher life after death, transcending the limits of individuation. The *Lettre sur l'homme* hints at an unfolding of the *organe moral* in the afterlife (I, 164). Death is necessary ("il faut la mort"), Hemsterhuis argues in *Aristée* (II, 74 f.), to shake off the crust of matter surrounding the soul, to embark on a flight leading to ever new developments. At the end of *Simon* (II, 138) the wish is uttered that the soul will get rid of the encrustations of matter to become "all organ" and thus perceive the universe in a godlike fashion. Death is the portal to new, higher activity in a universe where evil or even death are no absolutes and everything tends to organization and enhancement. In all the above-cited passages, excerpted by Novalis after his beloved Sophie von Kühn had died,[35] Hemsterhuis speaks of the soul as unfolding its hitherto nymphal wings to embark on a flight beyond the confines of present life on earth. These Neoplatonic notions are fused in *Alexis* with the idea of a future golden age.

IV   *Echoes of* Alexis *in the Writings of the Schlegels and Novalis*

Shortly after he had met Novalis, Friedrich Schlegel wrote to his brother in January, 1792, that his new friend, who favored Plato and Hemsterhuis above all other authors, had presented with "wild fervor" ("mit wildem Feuer") his conviction that there is no evil in the world and that everything points to a return of the golden age.[36] On the basis of his knowledge of unpublished manuscripts, Ernst Behler states that Friedrich Schlegel read Hemsterhuis as early as 1790; we may assume, however, that the friendship with Novalis gave new impetus to Schlegel's interest, now centered around the watchword "goldenes Zeitalter," as Julius Petersen emphasizes.[37]

From 1792 to 1794 there are numerous references to the philosopher in Friedrich's letters to his brother, especially to the German edition of Hemsterhuis' *Vermischte Schriften*. Schlegel claims to know all of the philosopher's writings contained in the first two volumes of that edition, except the eulogy for Fagel.[38] But it is only in December, 1797, after *Alexis* had appeared in the third volume, that Friedrich mentions this dialogue, which he wants to review.[39] Whether he knew *Alexis* before that at first hand or only through Novalis remains a moot question. Since Schlegel's review was never written, we must content ourselves with pointing out that some of his thoughts may have been stimulated or corroborated by Hemsterhuis.

Friedrich's often voiced demand to attain *Totalität* was perhaps influenced by the writings of the Batavian Plato. In the essay "Über die Philosophie: An Dorothea" (1799), where Schlegel refers to him as having pleased his beloved Dorothea,[40] he emphasizes that the true essence of human life consists in the totality ("Ganzheit"), completeness ("Vollständigkeit"), and free activity of all faculties.[41] While parallels to these thoughts occur in several of Hemsterhuis' writings, the reference to the beginning and end of human history reminds us of *Alexis*. Two other favorite ideas of Friedrich, the unification of all branches of knowledge and the fusion of philosophy and poetry find likewise their parallels in *Alexis*.[42] In Friedrich's notebooks, decoded and published by Hans Eichner, we find a number of entries dealing with the demand to unite "Poesie und Wissenschaft."[43]

The future golden age is explicitly spoken of in that part of the "Gespräch über die Poesie" (Dialogue on Poetry) which deals with mythology.[44] Mankind, it is asserted, must either perish or be rejuvenated. Anyone who is able to detect in the present epoch a process of universal rejuvenation will also understand the two poles between which mankind moves, its beginnings as well as the nature of the golden age to come ("den Charakter der goldnen Zeit, die noch kommen wird"). Poetry, it is said later on in the dialogue, once ruled supreme and will be dominant again in a future ideal state of mankind. Some of Schlegel's notes also refer to the golden age. Entry No. 1967 in the *Literary Notebooks* alludes to it in connection with the mythology of future mankind, while a note jotted down in 1799 speaks of the golden age as forever present in poetry.[45] An entry made in 1798[46] refers apparently to a plan to write a treatise on esthetics. Mankind, beauty, art form the center of esthetics and the golden age is "the center of this center." The concluding words of this entry, "die Sokratische Philosophie und der Optimismus," could be interpreted as an allusion to Hemsterhuis, who is explicitly mentioned in another note[47] as having applied the concept of the beautiful to Socratic philosophy and the golden age.

August Wilhelm Schlegel speaks in his review of Schiller's poem "Die Künstler" (The Artists) of the golden age conjured up by the poet's perfect sense for beauty and then refers specifically to Hemsterhuis' description of the first golden age.[48] Eight years later (1798), in "Athenäum-Fragment" No. 243, Schlegel called the notion of a past Saturnian age a phantom ("Trugbild"), one of the greatest obstacles to the golden age still to come. A truly golden past cannot have existed, since gold does not tarnish. August Wilhelm's sober remarks show none of his brother's enthusiasm.

August Ludwig Hülsen, a friend of the Schlegels, contributed to the *Athenäum*[49] an essay on the natural equality of men ("Über die natürliche Gleichheit der Menschen"), in which he alluded, significantly enough, to the myth of an original golden age of innocence and harmony as well as to the hope for a future when · heavenly peace would dwell again among men. The belief in a past age of innocent concord, though perhaps a mere dream, preserves a treasure of truth, of confident hope, while the ideal of a future golden age presents a challenge to the present epoch.

Recalling what Friedrich Schlegel wrote to his brother about Novalis' fervent belief in a future golden age, we should expect that the excerpts from *Alexis* in Friedrich von Hardenberg's "Hemsterhuis-Studien" would refer above all to this topic. Actually, these notes deal with all kinds of other issues, the reason being, as Mähl points out in his exemplary edition of the "Studien," that when these were jotted down in 1797 during a renewed study of the philosopher's writings, the central theme of *Alexis* was so familiar to Novalis that he no longer bothered to comment on it.[50] Friedrich Schlegel's letter shows that by the time it was written in January, 1792, Novalis had read Hemsterhuis, most likely in the German translation of 1782. *Alexis*, however, to which the letter apparently alludes, was accessible only in the French original or Jacobi's rendering, both of which had appeared in 1787. The poet himself did not

mention the Dutch philosopher before 1797. As Mähl has convincingly shown,[51] the "Hemsterhuis-Studien" of that year are based
on Jansen's edition of 1792, which Novalis borrowed from A.W.
Schlegel.[52]

We cannot be sure about the reasons for Novalis' renewed study
of Hemsterhuis, which coincided with Friedrich Schlegel's interest
in *Alexis*. The death of his fiancée, Sophie von Kühn, in the same
year, affected Novalis deeply and very likely made him return to
the Batavian Plato. The poet, who wanted to join his fiancée in
death, realized now that Fichte's philosophy lacked the "infinite
idea of love" which pervaded Hemsterhuis' writings together with
the conviction that death is a portal to a higher life. The
"Hemsterhuis-Studien" contain notes from the *Lettre sur l'homme*
dealing with the perfection of the moral organ after death.[53] An excerpt from *Aristée* (II, 75) refers to the accelerated flight of the soul
after life on earth.[54] Another entry[55] asserts that some of our desires
are so incongruous with our present condition that they seem to be
"wings" carrying us to a superior state. This is, as Mähl shows,[56] a
creative adaptation of a passage from *Alexis* (II, 191 f.). Entry No.
35, concerned with the same dialogue, speaks of death as a genuinely philosophic act.[57]

Surprisingly enough, Novalis did not take note of the link
Hemsterhuis established in *Alexis* between the golden age and
afterlife (II, 195). On the other hand, the poet gave much attention
to a related idea, the unlimited perfectibility of the *organe moral*.
Entries No. 27 and 29 of the "Hemsterhuis-Studien," referring to
the *Lettre sur l'homme*, deal with this leitmotiv of Hemsterhuisian
thought. Novalis excerpted a passage from *Simon* (II, 138) in which
the philosopher expressed the conviction that the soul will eventually become *one* perfect organ, no longer limited by the five senses.[58]
According to Novalis, Hemsterhuis' expectations concerning the
moral organ are of a truly prophetic nature.[59] In a collection of
notes known as the "Allgemeine Brouillon" (1798–99), the poet
mentions the philosopher's conjectures concerning the perfectibility
of the *organe moral* and the infinite possibilities accruing from its
activity.[60] The poet expected much for his project of a "magic
science" ("die magischen Wissenschaften") from the application of
the Hemsterhuisian moral sense to the other senses.[61] In a letter to
Friedrich Schlegel, dated July 20, 1798, he endorsed the "idea of a

moral astronomy" expounded by Hemsterhuis, who divined the
sacred way that leads to physics, as Novalis wrote to Karoline
Schlegel on January 20, 1799.[62]

While most of the immediately preceding quotes have no explicit
bearing on *Alexis*, they indicate the main interests guiding Novalis'
"Hemsterhuis-Studien" and apply also to the dialogue just mentioned insofar as it furnishes an example of "moral astronomy" and
is of a prophetic, divinatory character. Novalis' ideas concerning the
relation of poetry to philosophy and the sciences, on the other hand,
even if developed independently of Hemsterhuis, could find ample
support in *Alexis*. A part of entry 32 and all of entry 33 in the
"Studien"[63] refer to what is said about poetry in this dialogue. Entry 33 consists mainly of the poet's own translations from the text,
dealing with the power of the imagination to produce the beautiful
and sublime by condensing our perceptions (II, 185), with the
effects of genius and inspiration, with Hemsterhuis' definition of
"tact" (II, 188 f.), and the passage in which the spirit of poetry is
compared with the light of Aurora, making Memnon's statue
resound (II, 186). In entry 32 Novalis develops thoughts of his own
in connection with Hemsterhuis' distinctions between history,
philosophy, and poetry (II, 182). The latter, Novalis writes, raises
the insights gained by the former two to a higher level and realizes
the goal of philosophy. This part of entry 32 appears with slight
changes—poetry is now called the key to philosophy—in another
collection of aphorisms.[64] Out of Hemsterhuis' conception of poetry
grew, as Mähl points out,[65] the plan of a "poetic" treatment of all
knowledge. Combining suggestions from the *Lettre sur l'homme*,
where Hemsterhuis emphasizes that "ideas of rapport" alone constitute knowledge, and from *Alexis*, where poetry is shown to be
superior to ratiocination in establishing rapports, Novalis conceives
the ideal of a "poetization" of all "Wissenschaften" and a
philosophical poetry. As some notes in the "Allgemeine Brouillon"
show,[66] Hemsterhuis influenced, besides d'Alembert, also the poet's
project of an "Encyclopaedistik" and "Totalwissenschaft," an en-
cyclopedic unity of all branches of knowledge.

Of the entries in the "Hemsterhuis-Studien" concerned with
Alexis,[67] Nos. 33 and 34 have been taken up before and No. 36
needs no discussion here. Entry No. 35 deals with the general
character of Hemsterhuis' philosophy, which insists on the spirit of

independent thinking and advances "Stosssätze," theses that elicit reflection or dialogue rather than teaching doctrines. This Philosopher, it is claimed, encourages "ächtes Gesammtphilosophiren" (sic), a genuine "sym-philosophizing," instead of trying to impose a system on his readers. Novalis saw in Hemsterhuis' dialogues, which insinuate and stimulate thoughts, a necessary antithesis to the domineering spirit of Fichte's philosophy.

The part of entry No. 32 which has not been considered yet contains excerpts from *Alexis* in Novalis' own translation, concerning Hemsterhuis' definition of perfect enjoyment, the role of instinct, the principle of *personnalité*, and the philosopher's views on prejudice. While his astronomical hypotheses are not mentioned at this time, Novalis alludes a little later, in the "Freiberger Studien" of 1798—99, to the changes which the earth may have undergone when the moon became its satellite, and refers explicitly to Hemsterhuis.[68]

For the following discussion of the idea of the golden age in Novalis' oeuvre we are greatly indebted to Mähl's book *Die Idee des goldenen Zeitalters im Werk des Novalis*. The absence of any references to the golden age in the "Hemsterhuis-Studien" is due, as pointed out above, to the fact that this idea was already familiar to Novalis, as Friedrich Schlegel's letter to his brother of January, 1792, and Hardenberg's "Fichte-Studien" of 1795—96 attest. The latter contain two contradictory views. One passage[69] asserts that although golden ages may occur, they will not signify an *eschaton*, an end of all things, since the cognitive activity of the Ego ("denkende Ich") will never come to rest in face of an infinite world. The golden age is not a legitimate goal for man's striving. Entry 19 of the "Hemsterhuis-Studien," referring to the *Lettre sur les désirs*, states that perfect enjoyment, in which the soul becomes *one* with its desired object, is unattainable. In this, Novalis follows Fichte as well as Herder, whose essay "Liebe und Selbstheit," critical of some of Hemsterhuis' views, was known to the poet.[70] A contradictory conviction concerning the golden age is expressed at the end of the "Fichte-Studien,"[71] where the principle of perfectibility is asserted. Mankind would not be truly itself if a millennium ("ein tausendjähriges Reich") did not have to come ("kommen müsste").

As empirical, scientifically trained thinker that the poet also was,

Novalis thought of the golden age as a mere fiction, necessary perhaps to urge man on to perfection. Under the impact of his fiancée's death, however, he became more than ever convinced that the spatio-temporal world was not ultimate reality. A poet could enter the realm of the eternal at any time in any place. In accordance with this conviction. Novalis no longer saw in the golden age, as Hemsterhuis had done, an actual event that had occurred or would take place at a definite point of time. The poet was therefore little interested in Hemsterhuis' supposedly scientific proofs for the existence of a past pre-lunar golden age. The "goldnes Zeitalter" was now for Novalis neither a fiction, a Kantian regulative idea, nor a mere historical fact, but a spiritual reality. Mähl correctly emphasizes[72] that the poet's ideas are indebted to Hemsterhuis as well as Fichte, to the former's longing for a higher life, "un autre état," to be realized after death, and to Fichte's "Unendlich-keitsziel," a goal that can never be actually attained. Hemsterhuis, incidentally, had also maintained that perfection can only be approximated asymptotically, a fact not sufficiently stressed by Mähl. While the author of *Alexis* tended to regard the golden age as a state of passive enjoyment and happiness, Novalis saw it more in the light of a Fichtean demand ("Forderung") to be realized by the poet as redeemer. Being a Post-Kantian, Hardenberg was no longer convinced, as Hemsterhuis was, that harmony pertains to the structure of the universe. It should also be noted that Novalis' use of the term "tausendjähriges Reich" for a future golden age indicates his indebtedness to a pietistic background entirely absent in the Dutch philosopher.

Novalis espoused a triadic view of history similar to that assumed by Hemsterhuis and, as we have seen, widely current in Germany at that time, so that it is difficult to determine exactly what he owed to the Dutch philosopher. Fichte's ideas on history, in any case, were not published during the poet's lifetime. Eventually, Novalis writes in the "Allgemeine Brouillon," man will return to instinct with which he began in Paradise. History will turn back to the point from which it started ("d [ie] Gesch [ichte] wird wieder, wie sie anfing"); the future world will be in everything like the former and yet entirely different, because it will be "das Vernünftige Chaos," initial "chaos" plus reason.[73] To use our own words, the "return" to the beginning will take place on a higher level. Instinct will be wedded to knowledge. Harmony, distinct from primitive monotony, will be achieved after separation and disharmony. This large-scale historical process is mirrored in the lives of the hero of Novalis' unfinished novel *Heinrich von Ofterdingen* and of Hyacinth in a fairy tale that forms part of *Die Lehrlinge zu Sais*. The idea of a return to the beginnings, also expressed in *Alexis*, is coupled in Novalis with an intense, nostalgic longing to return "home" (*Heimweh*, *Heimkehr*) that is lacking in Hemsterhuis.

Hardenberg turns from a present epoch of alienation to a golden age of concord, either past or future, in nostalgia or hope, always found together in the poet's works. His notion of the "goldnes Zeitalter" manifests his yearning for a "home" beyond time ("ewige Heimat") that is everywhere and nowhere. The Orient, "Atlantis," ancient Greece furnish the settings for the past golden age. Loving and childlike souls, we read in the fragment of the novel *Die Lehrlinge zu Sais*, come close to realizing the golden age, while the poets try in their songs to transplant love, the seed of such an age ("Keim des goldnen Alters") to other times and zones.[74] In the "Allgemeines Brouillon,"[75] Novalis speaks of the power of raising ("Erhebung") any age to the golden age. To be sure, the poet did not entirely abandon his triadic view of history. But his belief in the power of "Erhebung," in the ability to make present ("Repraesentation") what is not present by the magic of "fiction" ("Wunderkraft der Fiction")[76] made Novalis escape into the delusion that a golden age was imminent or already present. This is apparent in "Glauben und Liebe" (1798), a collection of aphorisms concerned with the King and Queen of Prussia (see especially No. 41) and in the essay "Die Christenheit oder Europa" (Christianity or Europe [1799]). Novalis, who dreamed of inaugurating together with Friedrich Schlegel a new religion or at least religious age, detects in his time signs of a new mankind and Messias, of an imminent "neue goldne Zeit," a "prophetic" time of reconciliation, which will work miracles and cure wounds.[77] In "Glauben und Liebe" as well as "Die Christenheit oder Europa," the poet goes beyond Hemsterhuis, who neither believed in the imminence of a coming golden age nor in a Christian millennium in the guise of an ideal monarchy or quasi-"totalitarian" theocracy.

It is characteristic of Hardenberg's free, poetic conception of the golden age that the fifth of his "Hymnen an die Nacht" (Hymns to

Night)[78] presents pagan antiquity in a way that reminds us of Hemsterhuis' description of the past golden age, when Venus Urania ruled *(Simon)* and death was not yet experienced as the enemy of life *(Alexis).* We follow here Mähl's interpretation,[79] although the text of the hymn leaves room for questions.

Die Lehrlinge zu Sais offers another "paradigm" (Mähl) of the golden age, this time realized in communion with nature in a mythical past, nostalgically recalled. Men were then visited by the children of heaven and the generations of man followed each other in never-ending play. This description of the past "goldne Zeit,'" of man's naïve, complete unity with nature and of his unquestioned acceptance of death, which made him immortal, as it were, is certainly indebted to *Alexis,* as Bulle, Brummel, and Mähl have pointed out.[80] What Novalis says about the holy language ("heilige Sprache"), which the travelers set out to recover, may have been influenced by the speculations about the *Ursprache* in *Alexis.* For the termination of the age of friendly communion with nature, the poet adduces, like Hemsterhuis, two reasons: a cosmic catastrophe and man's urge to perfection or, as Novalis says, his desire to become like God. Man must exercise his moral sense ("sittlichen Sinn")[81] to regain the golden age, already present in children, lovers, and poets. In this assumption as well as in the emphasis on the active role that man is to play as an educator and a Messias of nature,[82] Novalis differs from Hemsterhuis.

The following brief remarks on *Heinrich von Ofterdingen* are largely indebted to Mähl's findings.[83] Throughout the novel we find explicit or implicit allusions to the golden age, past or future, and to the ever present possibility of its being realized. Heinrich von Ofterdingen's whole career is an initiation into poetry, entailing an increasing preoccupation with the golden age, which is present, however, only in remembrance or in anticipation. Mähl's observation[84] that none of Novalis' works has a Saturnian age as its actual setting applies also to *Heinrich von Ofterdingen,* often wrongly interpreted as depicting the realization of the golden age during the Middle Ages.

In the course of the novel the emphasis is shifted more and more to a future age of universal harmony. Klingsohr's *Märchen* at the end of the first part of *Heinrich von Ofterdingen,* entitled "Die Erwartung," expresses the expectation of a future golden age when peace, love, and poetry will rule; it is also manifest in the song of Astralis at the beginning of the unfinished second part, "Die Erfüllung," planned as the fulfillment of Heinrich's desires and hopes. The whole novel was to end with the inauguration of a new golden age prophesied by Astralis, of a marvelously strange future when the whole world would become a dream and the dream the whole world.[85] The paralipomena to *Heinrich von Ofterdingen*, in which Novalis jotted down his ideas about the continuation of the novel, refer to a "goldne Zeit am Ende" and the "neue goldne Zeit" when all mankind will finally become "poetic."[86] After a battle with the powers of prosaic intellect, described already in Klingsohr's *Märchen*, poetry would rule supreme. Heinrich would help to complete the poetization of the world.

We have seen that the "Hemsterhuis-Studien" of 1797 contain excerpts from *Alexis* in Novalis' own translation as well as thoughts stimulated by certain passages of this dialogue. Besides a number of notes that have no bearing on Hardenberg's poetic production, there are others referring to Hemsterhuis' views on *personnalité*, genius, inspiration, and the quick "apperception" — Hemsterhuis says "intuition" — called "tact." These views and above all what the author of *Alexis* had to say about the incongruity of our desires with our present condition, about the relation of poetry to philosophy, were close to Novalis' own convictions. He found in *Alexis* a vindication of the cognitive value of poetry, of intuition and inspiration over the claim that knowledge can be obtained only through the slow process of observation and ratiocination. Although the idea of the golden age plays an important role in Novalis' works, his "Hemsterhuis-Studien" do not refer to the philosopher's views concerning the golden age. There can hardly be any doubt, however, that the poet was impressed by Hemsterhuis' expectation of a future state of harmony following an epoch of alienation as well as by his ideal of a harmonious totality of all knowledge and all faculties of the human soul. While the triadic concept of history espoused by Novalis was basically similar to that advanced by Hemsterhuis, the poet developed views concerning the golden age that differed considerably from those of the author of *Alexis*. Novalis fused the secular notion of a future golden age with a pietistic eschatology of a millennium and, what is much more important, poetized the idea of a golden age, so that its realization

depends upon the poet's activity, the poetization of the world. The
golden age, past or future, is no longer, as for Hemsterhuis, fact or
reasonable extrapolation, located within the framework of empirical
history, but becomes a *Märchen*, independent of the phenomenal
world of time and space, which will be annihilated altogether in the
future golden age envisioned by Novalis. Even so, he and
Hemsterhuis shared a longing for a state of harmony beyond the
confines of the present world.

V *Summary*

There are several reasons for having devoted so much space to
Alexis. This dialogue was the only work of the philosopher to be
published in its French original and a German translation, both
managed by Jacobi, in faraway Riga, a fact which shows that
Hemsterhuis' fame had spread and that his thought had entered the
mainstream of German intellectual life. It was *Alexis* above all that
conveyed ideas then widely debated in Germany, the only country
where its author found real recognition among the leading intellectual circles. As Mähl points out,[87] *Alexis* influenced more than any
other work the ideas the early German romantics entertained concerning the golden age. Especially the assertion that the true golden
age was still to come attracted the attention of Novalis and the
brothers Schlegel, all of whom had read *Alexis*. While it is a matter
of conjecture whether Hölderlin was familiar with this dialogue, or
Schiller and Fichte with any of Hemsterhuis' works, the much more
important fact remains that the triadic view of history, the ideals of
totality and personality, the notion of the golden age as they were
set forth in *Alexis* found their analogues among these and other
German writers. Obviously, this dialogue expounded thoughts that
were then current in Germany. *Alexis*, less concerned with
philosophical problems in the more restricted sense than most of
Hemsterhuis' writings since the *Lettre sur la sculpture*, made, as far
as we can see, no impression on Herder, who had shown earlier a
vivid interest in the *Lettre sur les désirs* and the *Lettre sur l'homme*.
Novalis, to be sure, commented on philosophical problems raised in
Hemsterhuis' writings, but except for the philosopher's views on the
organe moral and the afterlife his Pre-Kantian *Weltanschauung* did
not influence the poet to the same degree as the ideas presented in
Alexis. It is through this work rather than as a systematic

philosopher that Hemsterhuis found wider attention and recognition. His speculations on the course of human history are certainly outdated, but his conviction that man is perfectible and the true golden age is still to come makes him a critic of the world as it is and a spokesman for what the contemporary German philosopher Ernst Bloch calls "the principle of hope," "das Prinzip Hoffnung."

Notes and References

Chapter One

1. See *Oeuvres philosophiques de François Hemsterhuis*, ed. L. S. P. Meyboom, III (Leuwarde, 1850), p. 110. References to this edition, indicating volume by Roman and page by Arabic numerals, in the footnotes usually preceded by Meyboom, will henceforth appear in the text. Some authors, notably Brummel, prefer the Dutch form of Hemsterhuis' first name, Frans. The philosopher spelled his last name "Hemsterhuis." Older sources often contain the spelling "Hemsterhuys."

2. Jan Gerard Gerretzen, *Schola Hemsterhusiana. De herleving der Grieksche Studiën aan de Nederlansche Universiteiten in de achttiende eeuw van Perizonius tot en met Valckenaer*, Studia Graeca Noviomagensia, Fasc. I (Nijmegen and Utrecht, 1940). Tiberius is discussed on pp. 77–156, François on pp. 291 ff.

3. Letter of September 4, 1780, cited by Leendert Brummel, *Frans Hemsterhuis: Een Philosofenleven* (Haarlem, 1925), p. 28. Henceforth cited as Brummel.

4. Meyboom, III, p. 128 f., gives an extract from Hemsterhuis' commission on December 23, 1755.

5. See Waltraud Loos, "Hemsterhuis' Briefe an Amalia von Gallitzin in den Jahren 1786–1790," *Duitse Kroniek* 22 (1970), 129 f. (henceforth cited as *DK*, 22). The October, 1970, issue of the *DK* contains (pp. 49–133) the printed versions of lectures given at a "Symposion over Frans Hemsterhuis" that took place near Utrecht in September, 1969.

6. Marie Muller, "Mindestens Europa. 1785. Ein Brief des Philosophen Hemsterhuis an die Fürstin Gallitzin," in *Fürstenberg, Fürstin Gallitzin und ihr Kreis. Quellen und Forschungen*, ed. Erich Trunz (Münster, 1955), pp. 37–41.

7. Waltraud Loos, "Der Briefwechsel des Philosophen Hemsterhuis mit Fürstin Gallitzin. Mit einem Schlüssel zu seiner Geheimschrift," *Westfalen*, 39 (1961), 11–127, especially p. 124; also Brummel, pp. 46f, 185.

8. Two minor writings, published posthumously, evince a serious interest in politics and political science: a draft of recommendations to the State Council, a piece of writing closely connected with Hemsterhuis' official position, and the unfinished reflections on the Republic of the Netherlands. Both works were reprinted in J. H. Halbertsma, *Letterkundige Naoogst* (Deventer, 1840–45), pp. XI–XXIV and 564–588, respec-

182

FRANÇOIS HEMSTERHUIS

tively. This book, consisting of two parts with continuous pagination, will be cited as Halbertsma.

9. On the Princess, see Diderot, *Oeuvres complètes*, ed. J. Assézat and M. Tourneux, XIX (Paris, 1876), pp. 342, 350 (letters to Mlle Volland); on Hemsterhuis, a passage in the *Voyage de Hollande*, *ibid.*, XVII, pp. 444 f.

10. Brummel, p. 140.

11. François Hemsterhuis, *Lettre sur l'homme et ses rapports, avec le commentaire inédit de Diderot. Texte établi, présenté et annoté par Georges May*, Yale Romanic Studies, 2nd Series, 12 (New Haven, Yale University Press, 1964). Henceforth cited as May.

12. Brummel, p. 63.

13. See Annie N. Zadoks-Josephus Jitta, *La collection Hemsterhuis au Cabinet Royal des Médailles à La Haye* (La Haye, 1952) and her article "Hemsterhuis als gemmenverzamelaar," *DK*, 22, 75—80. Both publications contain illustrations.

14. Brummel, p. 78, n. 4.

15. On the Princess: Theodor Katerkamp, *Denkwürdigkeiten aus dem Leben der Fürstin Amalia von Gallitzin . . .* (Münster, 1828); Joseph Galland, *Die Fürstin Amalie von Gallitzin und ihre Freunde* (Köln, 1880). See also the short biography in *Goethe und der Kreis von Münster. Zeitgenössische Briefe und Aufzeichnungen*, ed. by Erich Trunz in collaboration with Waltraud Loos, Veröffentlichungen der Historischen Kommission Westfalens, XIX, Westfälische Briefwechsel und Denkwürdigkeiten, Band VI, Münster in Westfalen: Aschendorffsche Verlagsbuchhandlung, 1971, pp. 119—204. Furthermore: Siegfried Sudhof, *Von der Aufklärung zur Romantik. Die Geschichte des "Kreises von Münster,"* Berlin: Erich Schmidt Verlag, 1973.

16. See Brummel, p. 140.

17. Quoted from a letter to J. C. van der Hoop of December, 1782 (Brummel, p. 138).

18. On this subject: Paul Kluckhohn, *Die Auffassung der Liebe in der Literatur des 18. Jahrhunderts und in der deutschen Romantik*, 2nd ed. (Halle, 1931).

19. See Diotima's letter to Hemsterhuis of April 27, 1777, reprinted in German translation by Christoph Bernhard Schlüter, *Briefwechsel und Tagebücher der Fürstin Amalie von Galitzin*, III (Münster, 1876), p. 20. The first volume appeared in 1874. The volumes of this collection have varying subtitles. We refer to it simply as Schlüter.

20. See Schlüter, II, pp. 79 f. and Brummel, pp. 144 f.

21. Diotima to Hemsterhuis, November, 1779 (Brummel, p. 179).

22. Diotima to Hemsterhuis, June 19, 1777, and July 29, 1778 (Schlüter, II, pp. 25 ff. and 41 f.).

23. Letters of April and June 1777 (Schlüter, III, 17, 34).

24. Brummel, p. 57.

25. Jakob Elias Poritzky, *Franz Hemsterhuis. Seine Philosophie und ihr Einfluss auf die deutschen Romantiker. Eine Monographie*, Philosophische Reihe, 81. Band (Berlin and Leipzig, 1926), pp. 15, 33.

26. Brummel, p. 157.

27. *Ibid.*, p. 158.

28. *Ibid.*, pp. 171 ff.

29. See Pierre Brachin, *Le Cercle de Münster (1779—1806) et la pensée de F. L. Stolberg*, Bibliothèque de la Société des Études Germaniques, Vol. V (Lyon and Paris, 1951), and his "Hemsterhuis' Beziehungen zum Gallitzinkreis," in *Pariser Universitätswoche an der Ludwig-Maximilians-Universität zu München vom 14. bis 19. Februar 1955* (München, 1955), pp. 203—216. See also the works by Trunz and Sudhof cited in note 15 of this chapter.

30. Erich Trunz, "Hemsterhuis' Reise nach Weimar 1785 und die Klauersche Hemsterhuis-Büste," *DK*, 22, 81—111.

31. See Schlüter, III, p. 150.

32. See the *Weimarer Ausgabe* (henceforth: *WA*) of Goethe's works, Series IV, Vol. 7, pp. 109 f.

33. Caroline Herder's comment is quoted in Brummel, p. 214; for Herder's opinion, communicated to Hamann, October, 1785, see C. H. Gildemeister, *Johann Georg Hamann's des Magus im Norden, Leben und Schriften*, III, 2nd edition (Gotha, 1875), p. 123. This work will be cited as Gildemeister.

34. Trunz, in his above-mentioned article in the *DK*, quotes from the Dutch original of the letter (pp. 83 ff.). The entire letter with a facing German translation is now reprinted by Trunz on pp. 168—175 in the work cited in note 15 of this chapter. On Ploos van Amstel, see Brummel, pp. 21, 75 f., 258 ff.

35. Brummel, p. 199.

36. *Vermischte philosophische Schriften des H. Hemsterhuis*, 2 vols. (Leipzig, 1782); a third volume apeared in 1797.

37. Brummel, p. 204.

38. For this and what immediately follows, see Brummel, pp. 207 f.

39. *Ibid.*, p. 208. Jacobi wrote to Hamann on February 1, 1785, that Hemsterhuis found the Bible unbearable. See *J. G. Hamann's Briefwechsel mit F. H. Jacobi*, ed. Friedrich Roth, in *Friedrich Heinrich Jacobi's Werke*, IV.3 (Leipzig, 1819), p. 23. This edition will be cited as Jacobi, *Werke*.

40. See *Mittheilungen aus dem Tagebuch und Briefwechsel der Fürstin Adelheid Amalia von Gallitzin nebst Fragmenten und einem Anhange* (Stuttgart: S. G. Liesching, 1868), p. 31.

41. See Brachin, *Le Cercle* . . . , note 2 to page 162.
42. Brummel., p. 224.

Chapter Two

1. Both the undated letter from 1777 and the later one of December 23, 1788, are cited by Loos, *Westfalen*, 39, 120 f., n. 5.
2. Letter of December 16, 1775, quoted by Loos, *Westfalen*, 39, 121, n. 7.
3. Brummel, p. 58.
4. Loos, *Westfalen*, 39, 121, n. 7.
5. Meyboom, III, pp. 217 ff.; Galland, *op. cit.*, pp. 53, 88.
6. *Campagn in Frankreich* (*WA*, I, vol. 33, p. 194).
7. Brummel, pp. 32 f.
8. *DK*, 22, 121—124; see also Klaus Hammacher, *Unmittelbarkeit und Kritik bei Hemsterhuis* (München: Wilhelm Fink Verlag, 1971), pp. 34 f. Subsequently cited as Hammacher.
9. Brummel, p. 94.
10. Hammacher, pp. 26 ff.
11. *De l'Allemagne*, ed. Comtesse Jean de Pange, IV (Paris, 1959), p. 159 f. (Troisième Partie, Chap. VII).
12. Poritzky, pp. 32 f.; Trunz, *DK*, 22, 108, n. 24. The opinions of Heinse and the Schlegels will be documented elsewhere in this book.
13. Poritzky, pp. 30 ff.
14. See Ferdinand Bulle, *Franziskus Hemsterhuis und der deutsche Irrationalismus des 18. Jahrhunderts*, Diss. Jena, 1910 (Leipzig, 1911), henceforth cited as Bulle. A concise evaluation of Hemsterhuis is given in Brummel's article "Frans Hemsterhuis (1721—1790)," *Algemeen Nederlands Tijdschrift voor Wijsbegeerte en Psychologie*, 34 (1940), 17—26. Henceforth: Brummel, *Tijdschrift*.

Chapter Three

1. When Hemsterhuis speaks of "imiter la nature" and "renchérir sur la nature" (I, 14), he follows a well-established tradition. See Albert Funder, *Die Ästhetik des Frans Hemsterhuis und ihre historischen Beziehungen*, Renaissance und Philosophie: Beiträge zur Geschichte der Philosophie, 9. Heft (Bonn, 1913), pp. 94 f. This study, subsequently cited as Funder, is valuable for its discussion of Hemsterhuis' views within the context of the history of esthetic doctrines. Funder is less convincing in the assertion of "influences," which were also the subject of his Bonn 1912 dissertation *Frans Hemsterhuis und die Ästhetik der Engländer und Franzosen im 18. Jahrhundert* (Bonn, 1912).
2. Funder, pp. 99 and 103 f.; on Harris, also William Guild Howard in

his introduction to *Laokoon: Lessing Herder Goethe* (New York: Henry Holt, 1910), pp. XCI ff.

3. His words are: ". . . le plus grand nombre d'idées possible, dans le plus petit espace de temps possible" (I, 29).

4. See Montesquieu, *Oeuvres complètes*, ed. Édouard Laboulaye, VII (Paris: Garnier Frères, 1879), pp. 123 f. and 130. Émile Boulan in his *François Hemsterhuis: Le Socrate hollandais. Suivi de Alexis ou Du militaire* (Groningen and Paris, 1924), p. 66 and Brummel (pp. 105 f.) consider it very likely that Hemsterhuis knew Montesquieu's *Essai*, which agrees in several other points with the *Lettre sur la sculpture*.

5. I, 21, and a long note (pp. 21—24) by Hemsterhuis.

6. In an article entitled "Beau" in Volume II of the *Encyclopédie* (1752), Diderot considers beauty and esthetic pleasure grounded in the perception of *rapports*, a term applied to the relations obtaining between the parts of a work of art as well as to the associations evoked by it in the perceiving subject. The article has been reprinted by Paul Vernière in his edition of Diderot's *Oeuvres Esthétiques* (Paris: Éditions Garnier Frères, 1965) under the title *Recherches philosophiques sur l'origine et la nature du beau*, a title also given to it in the above-cited *Oeuvres complètes* (Vol. X, Paris 1876). Diderot speaks of a "cortège d'idées accidentelles," an "association d'idées" (*Oeuvres Esthétiques*, p. 434) as a factor influencing esthetic experience, though mostly in a negative way. Funder (p. 2) believes that Hemsterhuis knew this article and became acquainted through it with the doctrines of Hutcheson and others.

7. Funder, pp. 104 f. On Abbé Dubos' *Réflexions critiques sur la poésie et sur la peinture* (1719) and Harris' *Three Treatises . . .* (1744), see W. G. Howard's introduction to *Laokoon*, pp. LXII ff. (especially LXV f.) and XCII f. All the authors mentioned in the text, except Hemsterhuis, are discussed in René Wellek, *A History of Modern Criticism: 1750—1950*, Volume I, *The Later Eighteenth Century* (New Haven: Yale University Press, 1955).

8. Émile Grucker, *François Hemsterhuis: Sa vie et ses oeuvres* (Paris, 1866), pp. 197 f. Henceforth cited as Grucker.

9. *Oeuvres Esthétiques* (ed. Vernière), p. 418.

10. I, 45: ". . . que proprement le repos at la majesté lui conviennent."

11. *Vorlesungen über dramatische Kunst und Literatur*, ed. Giovanni Vittorio Amoretti (Bonn and Leipzig, 1923), I, p. 8.

12. See Lessing's *Laokoon*, chapters III and XXV.

13. Poritzky, p. 43.

14. Eliza Marian Butler, *The Tyranny of Greece over Germany* (Cambridge [England]: Cambridge University Press, 1935); Henry Hatfield, *Aesthetic Paganism in German Literature. From Winckelmann to the*

Death of Goethe (Cambridge [Mass.]: Harvard University Press, 1964). Neither author mentions Hemsterhuis.

15. Brummel, p. 99.

16. *Ibid.*, pp. 102 ff. Hemsterhuis corresponded with Caylus (*ibid.*, p. 61).

17. See Jacobi's *Über die Lehre des Spinoza, Werke*, IV.1 (Leipzig, 1819), p. 81.

18. *Moses Mendelssohn's gesammelte Schriften*, ed. G. B. Mendelssohn, IV.1 (Leipzig, 1844), pp. 120 f.

19. See Eberhard Reichmann, *Die Herrschaft der Zahl. Quantitatives Denken in der deutschen Aufklärung*, Dichtung und Erkenntnis, No. 6 (Stuttgart, 1968), especially Chapter IV, "Geist der Zahl und Theorie des Schönen." Mendelssohn's argument against Hemsterhuis is quoted, pp. 59 f. and n. 25. After this chapter had been written, we found that J. H. Merck, who will be mentioned later in this book, gave a highly critical account of Hemsterhuis' definition of beauty in a letter to the novelist Sophie von La Roche. See Johann Heinrich Merck, *Briefe*, ed. Herbert Kraft (Frankfurt, 1968), Letter No. 43 of December 31, 1771 (pp. 60 ff.). Merck, whose arguments are too involved to find place in a footnote, insists on succession as a precondition for esthetic enjoyment.

20. M. Christian Gotthilf Herrmann, *Kant und Hemsterhuis in Rücksicht ihrer Definitionen der Schönheit, nebst einigen Einwürfen gegen Letzteren* (Erfurt, 1791).

21. *Vorschule.* I. Programm, paragraph 4.

22. A. W. *Schlegels Vorlesungen über schöne Litteratur und Kunst. Erster Teil (1801—1802). Die Kunstlehre*, ed. Jakob Minor, Deutsche Litteraturdenkmale des 18. und 19. Jahrhunderts, No. 17 (Heilbronn, 1884), pp. 13, 125, 142, 156.

23. For Goethe's remarks, see *WA*, I, vol. 33, pp. 234 f.

24. "Joannis-Henrici-Nicolai Defooz Commentatio Litteraria . . . ," *Annales Academiae Leodinensis 1824—1825* (Leodii, 1827), pp. 55—101. The question was: "Postulatur commentatio, definitionem pulchri a clar. Hemsterhuis datam cum reliquorum philosophorum definitionibus comparans atque dijudicans."

25. We refer for the foregoing to Robert Zimmermann, *Geschichte der Aesthetik als philosophischer Wissenschaft* (designated as *Aesthetik: Erster, historisch-kritischer Theil*), I (Wien, 1858), pp. 302—309; Max Schasler, *Kritische Geschichte der Ästhetik* (Berlin, 1872), pp. 328—333; William Knight, *The Philosophy of the Beautiful: Being the Outlines of the History of Aesthetics* (New York: Charles Scribner's Sons, 1906), p. 153 (the original British edition had appeared in London, 1895); Benedetto Croce, *Aesthetic as Science of Expression and General Linguistic*, trans. Douglas Ainslie

(New York: The Noonday Press, 1955), p. 262 (the original Italian edition was published 1902); Katharine Everett Gilbert and Helmut Kuhn, *A History of Esthetics* (New York: The Macmillan Company, 1939), p. 297; Karl Heinrich von Stein, *Die Entstehung der neueren Ästhetik* (Stuttgart, 1886), pp. 113 f.

Chapter Four

1. Brummel, p. 78.
2. *Ibid.*
3. Funder, pp. 79, 88.
4. *Ibid.*, p. 87, and Zimmermann, *op. cit.*, p. 303. See also Heinrich Ritter, *Geschichte der Philosophie*, XII (Hamburg, 1853), pp. 595 ff.
5. See A. E. Taylor, *Plato: The Man and his Work* (New York: The Dial Press, 1936), p. 223.
6. I, 68: "C'est une force étrangère qui a décomposé l'unité totale en individus; et cette force est Dieu."
7. Rudolf Haym, *Herder nach seinem Leben und seinen Werken*, I (Berlin, 1880), pp. 688 f.
8. "Über das Verlangen. Von Herrn Hemsterhuis," *Der Teutsche Merkur* (henceforth: *TM*), Windmond, 1781, pp. 97—122. It is interesting to note, as Trunz has emphasized (*DK*, 22, 89), that Herder used in his translation the singular form *das Verlangen* for the plural *les désirs*. Max Morris, *Goethes und Herders Anteil an dem Jahrgang 1772 der Frankfurter Gelehrten Anzeigen* (Stuttgart and Berlin, 1909), pp. 128—132, reprinted a review of the *Lettre sur les désirs* in the *FGA* and ascribed it to Herder. In the third edition of his book (1915), Morris designated Merck as the author, a finding with which Brummel, who cites also the literature on this question (pp. 295 f.), agrees. Hermann Bräuning-Oktavio, in his *Herausgeber und Mitarbeiter der Frankfurter Gelehrten Anzeigen 1772*, Freies Deutsches Hochstift: Reihe der Schriften, Band 20 (Tübingen: Max Niemeyer Verlag, 1966), pp. 73 ff., 101, 162 f., has come to the conclusion that this "review" and one of the *Lettre sur l'homme* in the *FGA*, actually excerpts edited by Merck, were most likely written by Louis von Schrautenbach (Ludwig Carl von Weitolshausen).
9. For the foregoing, see *Herders Sämmtliche Werke*, ed. Bernhard Suphan, XV (Berlin, 1888), pp. 55 f. This edition will subsequently be cited as Suphan.
10. "Liebe und Selbstheit. Ein Nachtrag zum Briefe des Herrn Hemsterhuis," *TM*, Wintermond, 1781, pp. 221—235; Suphan, XV, pp. 304—326.
11. See Herder's letter to Hartknoch of August 10, 1773, in *Von und an Herder: Ungedruckte Briefe aus Herders Nachlass*, ed. Heinrich Düntzer

and Ferdinand Gottfried von Herder, II (Leipzig, 1861), p. 43.

12. *Johann Georg Hamann: Briefwechsel,* ed. Walther Ziesemer and Arthur Henkel; IV, ed. A. Henkel (Wiesbaden, 1959), 373 f. This edition will be cited as Hamann, *Briefwechsel.*

13. Lessing's views were reported by Jacobi in his *Über die Lehre des Spinoza (Werke,* IV.1, pp. 84 f.). Jacobi refers to two letters, one of August, the other of December 4, 1780.

14. "Einige Gedanken, veranlasst durch das Lesen der Bekenntnisse einer schönen Seele . . . ," *Philosophisches Journal,* IV. Band, 3. Heft (Neu-Strelitz, 1796), 185—204 (especially 187 f., 191). Another article, entitled "Die Liebe, betrachtet nach Pope, Wieland, Fielding und Hemsterhuis," appeared in the *Berlinisches Archiv der Zeit und ihres Geschmacks,* Jahrgang, 1796, II. Band, Julius bis December, pp. 136—157.

15. See *Novalis: Schriften,* ed. Paul Kluckhohn and Richard Samuel, 2nd ed., Vol. II (Stuttgart: W. Kohlhammer Verlag, 1965), pp. 360—378. In this volume, subtitled *Das philosophische Werk,* sections II and III, containing the "Fichte-Studien" of 1795—96 and the "Hemsterhuis-und Kant-Studien" of 1797, are edited by Mähl. This edition will subsequently be cited as *KS,* followed by number of volume, page, and sometimes of entry.

16. *KS,* II, pp. 361 f.

17. Brummel, p. 97.

Chapter Five

1. Letter to Diotima of April 14, 1786 (Brummel, p. 63). In Jansen's and Meyboom's editions we find a dedication to Fagel ("À M. F. F.") lacking in a copy of the first edition of the *Letter on Man* in the University of Pennsylvania Library. This copy (12°, 242 pp.) agrees with the facsimile reprint edited by Georges May. A title page with a motto from Lucretius is followed by the "Avertissement" on pp. 3—6; on page 7 we find the title once more and before the text begins one line consisting of the address "Monsieur," which is left out by Jansen and Meyboom.

2. *Journal Encyclopédique,* September, 1772, p. 360.

3. See Brummel, p. 19.

4. On this and the following, Brummel, "Eenig nieuws omtrent Hemsterhuis" *Het Boek,* 18 (1929), pp. 310 ff. Henceforth: Brummel, *Het Boek.*

5. Boulan, pp. 14 ff.

6. Meyboom, I, 74—78; May, pp. 35 ff. Another outline is given by J. G. Ottema, "Commentatio," pp. 30 ff. Ottema's work, written in answer to a question proposed by the Academy at Louvain, is entitled: "Joannis Gerardi Ottema Commentatio ad quaestionem propositam ab ordine philosophorum in Academia Lovaniensis: Exponatur quaenam fuerint in

tractanda philosophia Francisci Hemsterhusii merita," *Annales Academiae Lovaniensis*, IX, 1825–26 (Lovanii, 1827).

7. May, p. 61.

8. See May, pp. 61, 71, 77 where Diderot denies the coexistence of *rapports* in the mind.

9. With regard to animals the "faculté intuitive" is always the faculty of beholding; in man, it may also be reason (I, 84). See Brummel, pp. 116 f.; Brummel, *Tijdschrift*, pp. 19 f.; Th. C. van Stockum, "De philosophie van François Hemsterhuis," *Tijdschrift*, 16 (1922), 196.

10. May, pp. 89 ff.

11. *Ibid.*, p. 127.

12. *Ibid.*, pp. 65, 103.

13. *Ibid.*, pp. 157, 159.

14. *Ibid.*, p. 163.

15. *Ibid.*, p. 175.

16. See above, Chapter 4.

17. May, p. 235.

18. See Halbertsma, pp. 580 ff.

19. Grucker, p. 115. The protagonist of Jacobi's novel *Woldemar* (1779) quotes from the Letter the passage referring to Brutus. Henriette, Woldemar's friend, tells him that this time she cannot agree with Hemsterhuis (*Werke*, V [Leipzig, 1820], pp. 112 f.).

20. Meyboom, I, 126, n. 1, and 129, n. 1. Ottema (pp. 138 ff.) reprints a review of the *Vermischte Schriften* (1782) in the *Allgemeine deutsche Bibliothek*, 54, 1. Stück, 199 ff., in which the assumption of a specific moral organ is declared superfluous, since the faculty of judgment ("Urteilskraft") and the laws of association suffice to explain our reaction to phenomena that have moral significance (Ottema, pp. 142 f.).

21. May, p. 227, 229, 261.

22. *Ibid.*, pp. 239, 241, 247.

23. *Ibid.*, pp. 297, 311.

24. *Ibid.*, pp. 241, 323, 327.

25. See on this also Fritz Mauthner, *Wörterbuch der Philosophie: Neue Beiträge zur Kritik der Sprache*, I. (München and Leipzig, 1910), p. 508, in the entry "Hemsterhuis' 'Organe Moral' " (pp. 503–509).

26. Herder, *Briefe, das Studium der Theologie betreffend*, Vierter Theil (1781), Suphan, XI (Berlin, 1879), p. 126; Jacobi, *Etwas, das Lessing gesagt hat* . . . , in *Werke*, II (Leipzig, 1815), p. 357. See also Novalis, *KS*, II, p. 367.

27. Suphan, V (Berlin, 1891). This review appeared in the *Frankfurter Gelehrte Anzeigen*, XCI (November 13, 1772), 721–726. See Chapter 4, note 8.

28. Suphan, XI, pp. 126 f.
29. See Brummel, p. 125.
30. May, p. 485.
31. Suphan, XI, pp. 125 f.
32. Letter to Herder of June 3, 1781 (*Briefwechsel*, IV, p. 304).
33. *KS*, II, pp. 368 f.
34. Katerkamp, *op. cit.*, p. 201. This illustration for the notion of palingenesis was widely used in the eighteenth century.
35. Leibniz had hinted at the possible existence of still unknown "senses" in paragraph 25 of his *Monadology*.
36. May, p. 323.
37. Bulle, p. 38, n. 3.
38. May, p. 117.
39. *Ibid.*, pp. 441 ff.
40. *Ibid.*, pp. 307, 289.
41. *Ibid.*, p. 513.
42. Parts of the letter, written on December 20, 1784, are quoted by Jean de Booy, "Quelques renseignements inédits sur un manuscrit du *Rêve de D'Alembert*," *Neophilologus*, 40 (1956), 83 f., while other parts are adduced by Henri L. Brugmans, "Diderot, le voyage de Hollande," in *Connaissance de l'étranger. Mélanges offerts à la mémoire de Jean-Marie Carré* (Paris: Didier, 1964).
43. Letter of February 12, 1784, cited by Brugmans, p. 157.
44. *KS*, II, p. 365. The notes to the Letter on Man comprise pp. 362–369 of this volume.
45. Letter of July 26, 1777. See Brugmans, p. 160, n. 3.

Chapter Six

1. Brummel, p. 219.
2. *Ibid.*, pp. 222 f.
3. Preface to the second edition of *Über die Lehre des Spinoza*.
4. *Paul Vernière, Spinoza et la pensée française avant la Révolution*, II (Paris, 1954), pp. 668 ff. For Hemsterhuis' treatment of Spinoza in the Letter and his Diotima's reaction, see letters Nos. 170, 171, 172 (all written March, 1789), printed by Trunz in *Goethe und der Kreis von Münster*. Letters Nos. 127, 178, 179, 180, 181, dealing with Herder's *Gott. Einige Gespräche* (1787) are also of interest in this connection.
5. *KS*, II, pp. 376 f.
6. See above, Chapter 1, note 8.
7. Halbertsma, p. 569.
8. *Ibid.*, p. 572.
9. *Ibid.*, pp. 572, 573, 576.
10. Letter to C. J. Kraus of June 1 and 2, printed in *Hamann's Schriften*,

ed. Friedrich Roth, VII (Leipzig, 1825), p. 428.

11. The letter is discussed by Marie Muller in an article cited above, Chapter 1, note 6.

12. Hamann's letter is quoted in Gildemeister, V, *Johann Georg Hamann's Briefwechsel mit Friedrich Heinrich Jacobi* (Gotha, 1868), pp. 655 f. On May 14, he had written that he had studied *Alexis II* for the second time *(ibid.* p. 648). Hamann referred to the *Lettre sur l'homme as a* corpus delicti and quoted from it the observation that so-called philosophy is often no more than the dregs left by the effervescence of the imagination, obviously applying this dictum to Hemsterhuis' philosophy.

Chapter Seven

1. Letter of September 23, 1779 (Brummel, p. 158.).

2. Brummel, pp. 158, 258 ff., and also Meyboom, III, 164. According to Brummel (pp. 158, 260), a fragment of a manuscript of *Sophyle* bore originally the title "Aristée ou de la philosophie."

3. Boulan, p. 16; Brummel, *Het Boek*, pp. 111, 113.

4. Brummel (p. 227) emphasizes that this statement is corroborated by the correspondence between Hemsterhuis and the Princess.

5. Brummel, p. 234.

Chapter Eight

1. See above, beginning of Chapter 7.

2. Grucker, p. 201; Jan and Annie Romein's chapter on Hemsterhuis, in *Erflaters van onze Beschaving: Nederlandse gestalten uit zes eeuwen,* 7th ed. (Amsterdam, 1956), III, p. 82.

3. Boulan, p. 84. This author praises also the style of the dialogue.

4. Vernière, *Spinoza,* p. 670.

5. *Sämmtliche Werke,* ed. Schüddekopf; Bd. VIII, 2. Abteilung, ed. Albert Leitzmann (Leipzig, 1925), p. 164.

6. As Diocles says, order arises among things "par les qualités qu'elles ont en commun pour former ensemble un tout déterminé." Order is "la disposition des parties qui forment un tout déterminé quelconque" (II, 20).

7. See Jacobi's *Über die Lehre des Spinoza in Briefen an den Herrn Moses Mendelssohn* (henceforth cited in the text as *Spinoza-Briefe), Werke,* IV.1, pp. 81 f.

8. See Schlüter, III, p. 20, for the letter, written in 1777, and *ibid.,* II, pp. 79 f., for the entry in the diary (February, 1787).

9. See Kluckhohn in his above-cited *Die Auffassung der Liebe . . . ,* p. 237. The author discusses Hemsterhuis on pp. 230 ff.

10. See Jacobi, *Werke,* V, pp. 222, 226, 228, 230, 282.

11. See Chapter 4, note 13.

12. *Sämmtliche Werke,* VIII.2, pp. 162 f.

13. See Chapter 4, note 14.

14. *Werke*, IV.2, p. 260. Jacobi's *Wider Mendelssohns Beschuldigungen* . . . (1786) was an answer to Mendelssohn's equally polemic tractate *Moses Mendelssohn an die Freunde Lessings* (1786).

15. "Dans l'homme bien constitué, un seul soupir de l'ame *[sic]*, qui se manifeste de temps en temps vers le meilleur, le futur et le parfait, est une démonstration plus que géométrique de la nature de la divinité" (II, 64).

16. *Werke*, IV.1, p. 159. Another reference occurs in Jacobi's *Wider Mendelssohns Beschuldigungen* (*Werke*, IV.2, p. 260), with the characteristic difference that the "seul soupir" is now translated as "einziges heisses Verlangen" ("single ardent desire"), implying an enthusiastic ardor of which there is no indication in Hemsterhuis.

17. Galland, *op. cit.*, p. 53, cites Hemsterhuis' dictum with approval, but does not adduce any statement by the Princess.

18. Pierre Brachin, "Hemsterhuis' Beziehungen zum Gallitzinkreis," p. 214.

19. II, 65: " . . . la conviction purement sentimentale naît dans l'essence et ne sauroit être communiquée."

20. *Werke*, IV.1, p. 160 *(Spinoza-Briefe)*.

21. Quoted by Jacobi, *Werke*, IV.1, pp. 82 f. *(Spinoza-Briefe)*.

22. See the preceding footnote.

23. *Werke*, IV.1, pp. 123–162.

24. *Ibid.*, IV.2, pp. 260 ff.

25. Hamann's letters are printed in Jacobi, *Werke*, IV.3, p. 80 (September 28), p. 94 (November 3).

26. *Sämmtliche Werke*, VIII.2, pp. 134–136, 158–165.

27. See Brachin, *Le Cercle de Münster*, p. 137, who quotes from a letter by Diotima to Hemsterhuis of September 26, 1779.

28. For Novalis' notes from *Aristée*, see *KS*, II, pp. 369–372.

29. *Franz von Baader's Sämmtliche Werke*, ed. Franz Hoffmann et al., XI (Leipzig, 1850), pp. 171 ff. The entries are from December 4 and 6, 1788.

30. *Werke*, IV. 1, p. 83.

31. *Ibid.*, 123 ff.

32. Heinse, *Sämmtliche Werke*, VIII.2, pp. 160, 163 f.

33. Vernière, *Spinoza*, II, p. 668; on *Aristée*, pp. 669, 670. Leopold Flam, "Hemsterhuis, Proclus en Hegel," *DK*, 22, 51–74, also emphasizes Hemsterhuis' affinity with Spinoza.

34. Vernière, *Spinoza*, p. 668.

Chapter Nine

1. In a letter to Princess Gallitzin of July 15, 1780, Jacobi told her that

he had lent Lessing everything he possessed of Hemsterhuis' writings except "the manuscript." On March 16, 1781, Jacobi identified the manuscript he had shown to von Knebel in Weimar as *Simon*. See Siegfried Sudhof, ed., *Der Kreis von Münster: Briefe und Aufzeichnungen Fürstenbergs, der Fürstin Gallitzin und ihrer Freunde* (Veröffentlichungen der Historischen Kommission Westfalens, XIX), 1. Teil (1769–1788); 1. Hälfte: Texte (Münster, 1962), letters Nos. 88, 118, and the footnotes to them in the same work; 2. Hälfte: Anmerkungen (Münster, 1964).

2. See pp. XIV f. of Jansen's "Avertissement de la première édition" in Vol. I of the 1809 edition.

3. For Jacobi's letter, see this chapter, note 1; Herder's letter: Hamann, *Briefwechsel*, IV, p. 275.

4. Letter No. 1113, *WA*, IV, vol. 5, p. 47.

5. Wieland's letter is cited by Julius Petersen in a note to letter No. 557 (No. 1113 in the *WA*) in his edition of *Goethes Briefe an Charlotte von Stein*, 1. Band, 2. Teil (Leipzig, 1923), pp. 618 f. For Merck, see the above-cited edition of his *Briefe*, letters Nos. 180 (to Duke Karl August von Weimar, February 28, 1781), 221, 223; in the last two letters of November, 1782, Merck asks for the return of a Hemsterhuisian manuscript sent two years before.

6. For Jacobi's letter, see *Der Kreis von Münster*, I.1 (No. 167); Merck, *Briefe*, No. 180.

7. See Hamann's letters to Jacobi of May 17, and to J. G. Scheffner of May 12, 1785, in *Briefwechsel*, V (Frankfurt, 1965), pp. 441, 434.

8. Letter of May, 1781, in Hamann, *Briefwechsel*, IV, p. 275.

9. *Friedrich Schlegel: 1794–1802. Seine prosaischen Jugendschriften*, ed. Jakob Minor, I (Wien, 1882), 47 ("Über die Diotima") and 104 ("Über das Studium der griechischen Poesie"). This edition will be cited as Minor.

10. Ernst Müller, *Hölderlin: Studien zur Geschichte seines Geistes* (Stuttgart, 1944), p. 83. Chr. Th. Schwab stated in his early edition of Hölderlin's works that Hemsterhuis was one of the poet's favorite authors (quoted by Bulle, p. 45). An undated letter by Hölderlin to his stepbrother shows that he had sent him Part One of Hemsterhuis' writings. Since they had pleased his correspondent, the poet promised to send him Part Two soon. See Friedrich Hölderlin, *Sämtliche Werke und Briefe*, ed. Franz Zinkernagel, V (Leipzig, 1926), p. 387. Wilhelm Böhm, *Hölderlin*, I (Halle, 1928), p. 84, gives 1793 as date of the letter.

11. Letter No. 2003, *WA*, IV, vol. 6, p. 386.

12. Letter of November 9, 1779 (Schlüter, III, pp. 73 f).

13. See René Wellek, *A History of Modern Criticism: 1750–1950*, I, p. 164 f.

14. See the works cited above in Chapter 3, note 14.

15. Grucker, p. 168.

16. Vol. II, pp. 292—314, in the 1809 edition of Hemsterhuis' *Oeuvres*.

17. Brummel, p. 248, n. 3.

18. See W. G. Howard's introduction to his above-cited edition of *Laokoon*, p. XXV.

19. Brummel, p. 249.

20. See Marie Muller, "Le Baron métaphysicien. Eine Charak-terschilderung des Freiherrn Franz von Fürstenberg aus dem Jahre 1778," *Westfalen*, 39 (1961), 50—52.

21. See Brummel, pp. 228 ff.

22. For Novalis' notes from *Simon*, see *KS*, II, pp. 374—377; other references occur *ibid.*, p. 379 (No. 41), and *KS*, III, p. 276 (No. 203).

Chapter Ten

1. Gildemeister, III, pp. 332 f.

2. Brummel, p. 204 and nn. 3, 4.

3. *Ibid.*, p. 206.

4. See letter No. 167, in *Der Kreis von Münster*, I.1, p. 146, and the commentary on it (I.2, p. 114).

5. Brummel, 206 and n. 2.

6. Jacobi to Princess Gallitzin on June 5, 1787; letter No. 418, in *Der Kreis von Münster*, I.1, pp. 360 f.

7. Letter No. 2047, in *WA*, IV, vol. 7, p. 7.

8. See *Der Kreis von Münster*, I.2, pp. 223 f. (note to letter No. 423), and Brummel, p. 267.

9. Brummel, pp. 266 f.

10. See page VI of Roth's introduction to Jacobi, *Werke*, VI (Leipzig, 1825). *Alexis* is reprinted *ibid.*, pp. 465—552.

11. Bulle, pp. 60 f., Brummel, p. 244.

12. Eduard Spranger in his *Wilhelm von Humboldt und die Humanitäts-idee*, 2nd ed. (Berlin, 1928), mentions Hemsterhuis frequently, but does not adduce, as far as we can see, any passage from Humboldt himself that refers to the philosopher.

13. *KS*, II, p. 372.

14. The discussion of language in the *Réflexions* (Halbertsma, pp. 580 f.) contains no reference to a perfect *Ursprache* and advances the notion of rectilinear progress espoused by Enlightenment thinkers.

15. Brummel, p. 203.

16. See John C. Greene, *The Death of Adam: Evolution and its Impact on Western Thought* (Ames: Iowa State University Press, 1959), Chapter 2.

17. Frank E. Manuel, *The Eighteenth Century Confronts the Gods* (Cambridge [Mass.]: Harvard University Press, 1959), Chapter 4, especially

section I, "The Rationalist Myth of Origins," pp. 132 ff., and section V, "Nicolas-Antoine Boulanger: The Trauma of the Flood," pp. 210 ff.

18. Walter Gobbers, *Jean-Jaques Rousseau in Holland*, Koninkiijke Vlaamse Academie voor Taal- en Letterkunde, VIe Reeks, No. 91 (Gent, 1943), pp. 197, 202. On Rousseau's ideas concerning the golden age, see also the work by Mähl (pp. 170 ff.) cited below in note 20. Brummel (p. 255) detects in Diocles' description of the golden age "the spirit" of Rousseau.

19. Brummel, p. 82.

20. Hans-Joachim Mähl, *Die Idee des goldenen Zeitalters im Werk des Novalis: Studien zur Wesensbestimmung der frühromantischen Utopie und zu ihren ideengeschichtlichen Voraussetzungen*, Probleme der Dichtung, Band 7 (Heidelberg, 1965). Henceforth cited as *Idee*.

21. Halbertsma, p. 578.

22. See Gabriel Marcel, "Sketch of a Phenomenology and a Metaphysic of Hope," in *Homo Viator: Introduction to a Metaphysic of Hope*, trans. Emma Craufurd (Chicago: Henry Regnery Company, 1951).

23. Brummel, p. 202, n. 3.

24. "Athenäum-Fragment," No. 142.

25. These and other theories of history are discussed by Karl Löwith, *Meaning in History* (Chicago: The University of Chicago Press, 1949).

26. Jacobi, *Werke*, II, pp. 277 ff. This passage occurs in *David Hume über den Glauben . . . .*, published in the same year as Jacobi's edition and translation of *Alexis*.

27. See Mähl, *Idee*, pp. 236 ff.

28. See Julius Petersen, "Das goldene Zeitalter bei den deutschen Romantikern," in *Die Ernte. Abhandlungen zur Literaturwissenschaft. Franz Muncker zu seinem 70. Geburtstage* (Halle, 1926), pp. 117—175, especially p. 119.

29. *Johann Gottlieb Fichte's sämmtliche* [sic] *Werke*, ed. I. H. Fichte, VI (Berlin, 1845), pp. 342, 343. A translation by William Smith (London, 1847) bears the English title mentioned in the text.

30. *Schillers Sämtliche Werke*, Säkular-Ausgabe, ed. Eduard von der Hellen (Stuttgart and Berlin, n.d.), XII, pp. 221—228 ("Über naive und sentimentalische Dichtung"), and XIII, p. 25 ("Etwas über . . ."). This edition will be cited as *Säkular-Ausgabe*. See also the epigram "Das Höchste," *Säkular-Ausgabe*, II, p. 89.

31. Hölderlin, *Sämtliche Werke*, Kleine Stuttgarter Ausgabe, ed. Friedrich Beissner, III (Stuttgart, 1965), p. 169 (preface to "Thalia-Fragment").

32. *Fichte's sämmtliche Werke*, VII, p. 11 (first lecture); pp. 9 f. in Smith's translation; see also *Werke*, VII, pp. 133 f. (ninth lecture) and

Smith, pp. 137 f.

33. *Säkular-Ausgabe*, XI, p. LXIII.

34. Schelling wrote in his *Magisterdissertation* of 1792 that man had forfeited Paradise by losing his instincts and that reason would lead him to a new paradise. In the *System*, he asserted that history began with the termination of the golden age and will end with the instauration of the *Vernunftreich*. *Alexis* was mentioned in "Fernere Darstellungen aus dem System der Philosophie" (*Sämmtliche Werke*, Erste Abtheilung, Band 4 [1859], pp. 490 f.), where Schelling indicated agreement with Hemsterhuis' hypothesis concerning the moon.

35. Mähl, *Idee*, p. 269.

36. See Max Preitz, *Friedrich Schlegel und Novalis: Biographie einer Romantikerfreundschaft in ihren Briefen* (Darmstadt, 1957), p. 9. The same letter had been printed as undated in *Friedrich Schlegels Briefe an seinen Bruder August Wilhelm*, ed. Oskar F. Walzel (Berlin, 1890), p. 34 (letter No. 8). References to Walzel's edition will henceforth appear as *Briefe*, followed by the numbers of the letters cited.

37. Ernst Behler, *Friedrich Schlegel in Selbstzeugnissen und Bilddokumenten*, Rowohlts Monographien (Reinbek bei Hamburg: Rowohlt, 1966), p. 22; Petersen, *Die Ernte*, p. 119.

38. *Briefe*, Nos. 13, 26, 28, 59, 70; 30, 32, 33, 35.

39. *Ibid.*, Nos. 96, 99.

40. Minor, II, p. 317. We also follow this edition in the numbering of the "Fragmente" from various collections.

41. Minor, II, p. 326.

42. "Georg Forster," Minor, II, p. 139, "Lyceum-Fragment," No. 115; "Athenäum-Fragment," Nos. 302, 304, 451; "Ideen," No. 108.

43. Friedrich Schlegel, *Literary Notebooks: 1797–1801*, ed. Hans Eichner (University of Toronto Press, 1957), entries Nos. 92, 99, 312, 330. See also *Kritische Friedrich-Schlegel-Ausgabe*, XVIII, ed. Ernst Behler (München-Paderborn-Wien, 1963), entry No. 965, p. 275. Since the entries from Schlegel's notebooks in this volume, henceforth cited as *KA*, XVIII, are not numbered consecutively, page numbers will also be indicated.

44. *Athenäum*, III.1 (1800): "Rede über die Mythologie" (Minor, II, pp. 357–363).

45. *KA*, XVIII, p. 339, No. 202.

46. *Ibid.*, p. 197, No. 8.

47. *Ibid.*, p. 207, No. 124.

48. "Über die Künstler, ein Gedicht von Schiller," *August Wilhelm von Schlegel's sämmtliche Werke* [sic], ed. Eduard Böcking, VII (Leipzig, 1846), pp. 20 f.

49. II.1 (1799), 152–180.

50. See Mähl, in his introduction to the "Studien," *KS*, II, p. 310.

51. *KS*, II, pp. 321 ff.

52. See Novalis' letters to A. W. Schlegel of November 30 (No. 146) and December 25, 1797 (No. 148) in Vol. IV of the first edition of *Novalis: Schriften* by Kluckhohn and Samuel (Leipzig: Bibliographisches Institut, 1929). Letters Nos. 30, 32, 33, 35 (August to December, 1793) in Walzel's above-cited edition of *Friedrich Schlegels Briefe* indicate that August Wilhelm owned Jansen's edition.

53. *KS*, II, p. 369, No. 29.

54. *Ibid.*, p. 372, No. 31.

55. No. 34; *KS*, II; p. 373.

56. *Ibid.*, pp. 326—328.

57. *Ibid.*, p. 374.

58. *Ibid.*, p. 377, No. 38.

59. *Ibid.*, p. 562, No. 179.

60. *KS*, III (Stuttgart: W. Kohlhammer Verlag, 1968), p. 420, No. 782.

61. *Ibid.*, p. 275, No. 197.

62. Letters Nos. 156 and 176, in Vol. IV of *Novalis: Schriften*, cited in note 52. The passage from the last letter appears also in entry No. 1096, *KS*, III, p. 469.

63. *KS*, II, pp. 372 f.

64. *Ibid.*, p. 533, No. 31.

65. *Ibid.*, pp. 315 f.

66. *KS*, III, p. 275, Nos. 197—199.

67. Nos. 32—36; *KS*, II, pp. 372—374.

68. *KS*, III, p. 64.

69. *KS*, II, p. 269, No. 565.

70. Mähl, *Idee*, p. 269; *KS*, II, p. 360, No. 16.

71. *KS*, II, p. 291, No. 631.

72. Mähl, *Idee*, p. 286.

73. *KS*, III, p. 301, No. 340, and p. 281, No. 234.

74. *KS*, I (Stuttgart: W. Kohlhammer Verlag, 1960), pp. 103 f.

75. *KS*, III, p. 440, No. 894.

76. *Ibid.*, p. 421, No. 782.

77. *Ibid.*, p. 519.

78. *Athenäum*, III.2 (1800).

79. Mähl, *Idee*, pp. 387 ff.

80. Bulle, p. 75; Brummel, pp. 323 ff.; Mähl, *Idee*, pp. 354 ff.

81. *KS*, I, p. 90.

82. *KS*, III, p. 252, No. 73; p. 248, No. 52.

83. Mähl, *Idee*, pp. 397 ff.

84. *Ibid.*, p. 360, n. 8.

85. *KS*, I, pp. 318 f.
86. *Ibid.*, p. 345, and p. 347.
87. Mähl, *Idee*, p. 158, n. 183.

Selected Bibliography

PRIMARY SOURCES

A. Collected Works

There exists as yet no definitive, critical edition of Hemsterhuis' works. Several manuscripts remain still unpublished. Of the vast number of the author's letters only a very small fraction has appeared in print in widely scattered publications and even then in mere excerpts or, worse yet, in German translation. The original editions of individual works are rather rare and will not be noted below. Concerning most of these, bibliographical information can be found in the *Catalogue Général des livres imprimés de la Bibliothèque Nationale: Auteurs*, Tome XX (Paris: Imprimerie Nationale, 1919), columns 389–391.

Oeuvres philosophiques de M. F. Hemsterhuis. Ed. Hendrik J. Jansen. Paris: De l'imprimerie de H. J. Jansen, 1792. 2 vols.

Oeuvres philosophiques de F. Hemsterhuis: Nouvelle édition, revue et augmentée. Ed. H. J. Jansen. Paris: L. Haussmann, Imprimeur-Libraire, 1809. 2 vols. In this edition the *Lettre sur une pierre antique* was added.

Oeuvres philosophiques de François Hemsterhuis: Nouvelle édition augmentée de plusieurs pièces inédites, de notes et d'une étude sur l'auteur et sa philosophie. Ed. L[ouis] S[usan] P[edro] Meyboom. Leuwarde: W. Eekhoff, 1846 and 1850. 3 vols. (I and II: 1846; III: 1850). Contains valuable biographical information and an evaluation of Hemsterhuis' thought. Still the standard edition.

A publication of one of Hemsterhuis' dialogues deserves special mention:

Lettre sur l'homme et ses rapports avec le commentaire inédit de Diderot. Texte établi, présenté et annoté par Georges May. Yale Romanic Studies, 2nd Series, No. 12. New Haven: Yale University Press, and Paris: Presses Universitaires de France, 1964. A facsimile edition of a copy of the *Lettre* with Diderot's marginalia.

B. Works containing source material not published by Jansen or Meyboom.

HALBERTSMA, J[OOST] H[IDDES]. *Letterkundige Naoogst.* Deventer: J. de Lange, 1840 and 1845. The first part (1840), not designated as such, contains on pp. XI—XXIV the *Ebauché [sic] d'un avis du conseil d'état par F. H.*; the *Réflexions sur la République des Provinces-Unies* . . ., are printed on pp. 564—588 of the second part ("Tweede Stuk"), published 1845.

BOULAN, Émile. *François Hemsterhuis, le Socrate hollandais; suivi de: Alexis; ou Du militaire (dialogue inédit).* Groningue: P. Noordhoff, and Paris: L. Arnette, 1924. (The title appears as it is given in the LC Catalogue). Contains on pp. 103 ff. the fragment of a dialogue usually designated as *Alexis II.*

Goethe und der Kreis von Münster: Zeitgenössische Briefe und Aufzeichnungen. Ed. by Erich Trunz in collaboration with Waltraud Loos (Veröffentlichungen der Historischen Kommission Westfalens, 19: Westfälische Briefwechsel und Denkwürdigkeiten, Band VI. Münster: Aschendorffsche Verlagsbuchhandlung, 1971). This important publication, which reached us after completion of our manuscript, contains excerpts from letters by Hemsterhuis, his letter to Ploos van Amstel on the journey to Germany (1785) in the Dutch original and a German translation (pp. 166—175), the unpublished essay "De la divisibilité à l'infini" (pp. 186—190), and and excellent résumé òf the philosopher's life and thought (pp. 204—211).

C. *Translations*

Vermischte philosophische Schriften des H. Hemsterhuis. Leipzig: Weidmann, 1782 and 1797. 3 vols. (I and II: 1782; III: 1797). Contains in Vol. III an analysis of Hemsterhuis' works (pp. 201—241) and "Einige Bemerkungen zum Vergleich der Hemsterhuisischen Philosophie mit der kritischen" (pp. 242—260).

Philosophische Schriften. Trans. Julius Hilss. Karlsruhe and Leipzig: Dreililien Verlag, 1912. 2 vols. Does not include the *Letre sur une pierre antique* and the eulogy on Fagel.

SECONDARY SOURCES

BAUMGARDT, DAVID. *Der Kampf um den Lebenssinn unter den Vorläufern der modernen Ethik.* Leipzig: Felix Meiner Verlag, 1933. Contains on pp. 256—283 a chapter entitled "Frans Hemsterhuis," an important critical assessment, especially of Hemsterhuisian ethics.

BOULAN, ÉMILE. *Op. cit.* A stimulating, witty essay, intended to introduce French readers to Hemsterhuis.

BRACHIN, PIERRE. "Hemsterhuis' Beziehungen zum Gallitzinkreis." In *Pariser Universitätswoche an der Ludwig-Maximilians-Universität zu*

München vom 14. bis 19. Februar 1955 (München, 1955), pp. 203—216.

BRINK, R. C. BAKHUIZEN VAN DEN. "Franciscus Hemsterhuis." In *Studiën en Schetsen over vaterlandsche Geschiedenis en Lettern*, He Deel, pp. 87—158. Ed. E. J. Potgieter. 'S Gravenhage: Mart. Nijhoff, 1870. This important article, emphasizing Hemsterhuis' indebtedness to the Lockean tradition of empiricism, was first published in 1834 in the journal *De Muzen*.

BRUMMEL, LEENDERT. *Frans Hemsterhuis: Een Philosofenleven*. Haarlem: H. D. Tjeenk Willink & Zoon, 1925. In thoroughness and scope an unsurpassed achievement of Hemsterhuis' scholarship, this monograph is indispensable for any study of the philosopher.

———. "Eenig nieuws omtrent Hemsterhuis." *Het Boek*, 18 (1929), 305—314.

———. "Frans Hemsterhuis (1721—1790)." *Algemeen Nederlands Tijdschrift voor Wijsbegeerte en Psychologie*, 34 (1940), 17—26.

BULLE, FERDINAND. *Franziskus Hemsterhuis und der deutsche Irrationalismus des 18. Jahrhunderts*. Diss. Jena 1910. Leipzig: Spamersche Buchdruckerei, 1911. An important dissertation, dealing with the contribution of Hemsterhuis' philosophy to the current of irrationalism in Germany during the last decade of the eighteenth century. Bulle's assumptions of "influences" on German writers are not always supported by sufficient evidence.

FUNDER, ALBERT. *Die Ästhetik des Frans Hemsterhuis und ihre historischen Beziehungen*. Renaissance und Philosophie: Beiträge zur Geschichte der Philosophie, ed. Adolf Dyroff, 9. Heft. Bonn: P. Hanstein, 1913. A comprehensive account of Hemsterhuis' esthetics in relation to other esthetic doctrines. The assumption of "influences" on and by Hemsterhuis is sometimes rather hypothetical. Contains an appendix by Dyroff on "Hemsterhuis in Deutschland."

GRUCKER, ÉMILE. *François Hemsterhuis: Sa vie et ses oeuvres*. Paris: Durand, 1866. The most comprehensive treatment of the philosopher before Brummel's monograph. Superseded in biographical details, but still important.

HAMMACHER, KLAUS. *Unmittelbarkeit und Kritik bei Hemsterhuis*. München: Wilhelm Fink Verlag, 1971. A discussion of Hemsterhuis' philosophy from a systematic viewpoint, based partly on unpublished material not used before. Because of its technical, often rather involved language definitely not an introduction to the philosopher for the general reader.

HARTMANN, NICOLAI. *Die Philosophie des deutschen Idealismus. I. Teil: Fichte, Schelling und die Romantik*. Berlin and Leipzig: Walter de Gruyter & Co., 1923. Contains on pp. 190—198 a section on Hemsterhuis as the precursor of German Romanticism ("der Vorläufer der Romantik").

HERRMANN, M. CHRISTIAN GOTTHILF. *Kant und Hemsterhuis in Rücksicht auf ihre Definitionen der Schönheit, nebst einigen Einwürfen gegen Letzteren.* Erfurt: Keyser, 1791. The first systematic treatment of Hemsterhuisian esthetics.

LOOS, WALTRAUD. "Der Briefwechsel des Philosphen Hemsterhuis mit Fürstin Gallitzin: Mit einem Schlüssel zu seiner Geheimschrift." *Westfalen,* 39 (1961), 119—127.

————. "Hemsterhuis' Briefe an Amalia von Gallitzin in den Jahren 1786—1790." *Duitse Kroniek,* 22 (1970), 112—133.

PORITZKY, J[AKOB] E[LIAS]. *Franz Hemsterhuis: Seine Philosphie und ihr Einfluss auf die deutschen Romantiker, Eine Monographie.* Philosophische Reihe, 81. Band. Berlin and Leipzig: Gebrüder Paetel, 1926. An introduction for the generally interested reader.· Poritzky's essayistic study evinces strong opinions, but is not always reliable in details.

RITTER, HEINRICH. *Geschichte der Philosophie,* XII (Hamburg: Friedrich Perthes, 1853), pp. 585—597.

ROMEIN, JAN AND ANNIE. "Frans Hemsterhuis: De filosoof van de ziel." In *Erflaters van onze Beschaving: Nederlandse gestalten uit zes eeuwen,* III (Amsterdam: Em. Querido, 1939), pp. 68—97.

STOCKUM, TH. C. VAN. "De philosophie van François Hemsterhuis." *Tijdschrift voor Wijsbegeerte,* 16 (1922), 190—208; reprinted in his *Ideologische Zwerftochten* (Groningen and Djakarta: J. B. Wolters, 1957), pp. 278—291.

TRUNZ, ERICH. "Hemsterhuis' Reise nach Weimar und die Klauersche Hemsterhuis-Büste." *Duitse Kroniek,* 22 (1970), 81—111.

WALZEL, OSKAR. *Romantisches.* Mnemosyne: Arbeiten zur Erforschung von Sprache und Dichtung, Heft 18. Bonn: Ludwig Röhrscheid Verlag, 1934. Deals on pp. 93—110 with Hemsterhuis (Section VI of "Frühe Kunstschau Friedrich Schlegels").

Index

Note: François Hemsterhuis and, to a lesser degree, Princess Gallitzin are mentioned too often to be included in the Index. Historical persons appearing as participants in the dialogues are not listed.